The Magus of
Freemasonry

Also by Tobias Churton

Why I Am Still an Anglican
The Gnostics
Miraval—A Quest
The Fear of Vision
Elias Ashmole—A Mighty Good Man
The Golden Builders
Gnostic Philosophy

The Magus of
Freemasonry

The Mysterious Life of
Elias Ashmole—Scientist,
Alchemist, and Founder
of the Royal Society

Tobias Churton

Inner Traditions
Rochester, Vermont

Inner Traditions
One Park Street
Rochester, Vermont 05767
www.InnerTraditions.com

Library of Congress Cataloging-in-Publication Data

Churton, Tobias, 1960–
  [Magus]
  The magus of freemasonry : the mysterious life of Elias Ashmole, scientist, alchemist, and founder of the Royal Society / Tobias Churton.
    p. cm.
  Originally published as: Magus.
  Includes bibliographical references and index.
  ISBN-13: 978-1-59477-122-4 (pbk.)
  ISBN-10: 1-59477-122-7 (pbk.)
  1. Ashmole, Elias, 1617-1692. 2. Great Britain—Officials and employees—Biography. 3. Antiquarians—Great Britain—Biography. 4. Alchemists—Great Britain—Biography. 5. Freemasons—Great Britain—Biography.   I. Title.
  CT788.A762C48 2006
  920.041—dc22

                                                              2006013045

Printed and bound in the United States by Lake Book Manufacturing

10   9   8   7   6   5   4   3   2   1

Text design and layout by Priscilla Baker
This book was typeset in Sabon, with Book Antiqua and Avenir used as display typefaces

To send correspondence to the author of this book, mail a first-class letter to the author c/o Inner Traditions • Bear & Company, One Park Street, Rochester, VT 05767, and we will forward the communication.

Contents

Acknowledgments

I should like to thank the following for their encouragement in producing this biography. Dr. Christopher McIntosh was the first to suggest in print that Ashmole deserved a wider appreciation and a new biography, and that Tobias Churton could do worse than attempt it.

Friends and colleagues who have helped me on the way include the publisher Philip Wilkinson, Adam McClean, Columba Powell, the late and much missed Peter Maxwell Jones, Michael Embleton, and my agent, Tuvia Fogel.

I should like to thank Mr. and Mrs. Williamson and their daughter, Sue Steer, for their kindness in showing me the remains of Colonel Henry Mainwaring's Hall at Kermincham, Cheshire—one of the most magical memories in my treasured box of Ashmole "accidents." Warm thanks are also due to the Principal and Fellows of Brasenose College, Oxford, for permission to photograph the Library and old Quad of my (and Ashmole's) old college.

Interest in the project over the years has been stimulated by lively and frequent dialogue with Masonic historian Matthew Scanlan; he deserves the credit for showing the world of scholarship the signal importance of the early records of "acceptions" in the accounts of the London Masons Company. Freemasonry is not an invention of the eighteenth century; there was never such a thing as "speculative Freemasonry" in the seventeenth century. The Master Mason of freestone in that period knew more about the Craft in symbol, allegory, theory, and practice than Freemasons do today; he judges us, not we him.

The resources provided by J. R. Ritman's Bibliotheca Philosophica Hermetica, Amsterdam, have been invaluable to all serious researchers into Hermetic and Rosicrucian ideas and history, not least to this one.

My feeling for Ashmole's life and sensibility was enhanced considerably following an invitation from Sir William and Lady Dugdale to photograph Blyth Hall, Warwickshire, for this book. Ashmole was a regular visitor to Blyth Hall over several decades and I am not entirely sure that something of the warm friendship he shared with a past Sir William Dugdale has altogether vanished.

I should like to thank the current owner of Penketh Hall near Warrington for allowing us to photograph his property and for explaining something of its checkered history. Tom Baker of Smallwood also elicits gratitude for granting permission to investigate the site of Peter Mainwaring's now long-since demolished manor house in Cheshire. Seventeenth-century England is much more difficult to find than one might imagine. This is a great shame, for much of it was exceedingly beautiful. If only contemporary architects would take up where the Jacobean masters left off!

The book has benefited greatly as a result of the kindness of the staff at a number of other significant places. The staff of Ansons Solicitors in Breadmarket Street, Lichfield (Ashmole's birthplace), have never been anything less than helpful and friendly. The kindly gentlemen who work at the St. Mary's Heritage Centre, Lichfield, deserve special thanks for permitting Ashmole's Loving Cup a brief, touching parole from behind exhibition glass. The caretaker at Swallowfield Park who left her lunch to help us find our way around the property also warrants a warm "thank you"—as do the enthusiastic and helpful staff at the Museum of Gardening History, St. Mary's, Lambeth. I am sure they would have moved their offices from above Ashmole's tomb had it been physically possible.

Enormous thanks are due to the painstaking professionalism exhibited daily by staff of the Lichfield Record Office, Stafford Record Office, and the Bodleian Library, Oxford, for their goodly assistance in this search for the real Ashmole and his fascinating world. Ashmole himself was one of history's great preservers and would doubtless have been cheered by the care now attendant upon the nation's written treasures.

This book has been greatly enhanced by the use of photographs. For these, I have to thank Philip Wilkinson, Joanna Edwards, and Mark Reynolds for their time and care.

The goodness, patience, and encouragement of my wife, Joanna, have gone beyond the call of duty. She has seen what the world has not. Now the world can see what she saw long ago.

This book is dedicated to all who seek the Stone of the Philosophers. "Whosoever shall fall upon that stone shall be crushed; but on whomsoever it shall fall, he shall be winnowed" (Luke 20:18).

INTRODUCTION

Ex Uno Omnia

Twelve years ago, I was standing at Birmingham Airport waiting for a connection to Göteborg. Thanks to the encouragement of Jan Arvid Hellström, the late bishop of Växjö, I was about to begin training for the priesthood in the Church of Sweden. This connection was expected to mark a turning point in my life. Indeed, it did. I found myself hailing a taxi to take me back home to the city of Lichfield, Staffordshire. As the driver released the hand brake, the gate to a possible future slammed shut.

Within a week I found myself in the Lichfield Record Office, strangely motivated and poring over anything I could find on the life of Lichfield-born Elias Ashmole (1617–92). I had long been aware of the little stone memorial set into the wall above Ansons Solicitors in Breadmarket Street. However, while knowing something of Ashmole's place in the story of the seventeenth-century Rosicrucian movement, what I had known meant curiously little to me. I say "curiously" because I had been seriously engaged in studying the history of that extraordinary movement since the mid-1980s. The Rosicrucians were part of Gnostic history, which has been my chief intellectual and spiritual interest since the late 1970s. Somehow, I had passed by the works of Ashmole as casually and unthinkingly as the many shoppers who today pass his memorial stone on the way to Lichfield's thrice-weekly market.

1

Within a few quick steps of the birthplace of Elias Ashmole, those shoppers and tourists can hardly miss the birthplace of another of Lichfield's luminaries, Dr. Samuel Johnson. The tireless author of the *Dictionary of the English Language* has garnered all the attention. Johnson's birthplace, unlike Ashmole's, is itself a museum and Lichfield has gained national notice as the provincial home of the great wit who informed us that the man who is tired of London is tired of life. But as Johnson also informed Boswell in 1776, "Sir, we [of Lichfield] are a city of philosophers; we work with our heads, and make the boobies of Birmingham work for us with their hands." He had not tired of Lichfield but Lichfield had, it seems, tired of him. The city has been trying to make up for this appalling lack of judgment for the last two centuries.

Something must have been stirring subconsciously to explain the sudden turnabout in my life. I had been back in Lichfield for four years. Lichfield has been considered by some to be the true spiritual center of England. And, as freemasons should know, "At the center of the circle, a master mason cannot err."

Right at the center of that circle was Elias Ashmole, the privileged blend that is Renaissance Man, the British Hermetic philosopher *par excellence,* the self-styled *Mercuriophilus Anglicus* and "mighty good man." And if Elias, the "expected one," the harbinger of new arts and revealed knowledge, was indeed at the center, then Elias Ashmole was everything and everywhere. For as Nicholas of Cusa reminds us, "God is an infinite sphere whose center is everywhere and circumference nowhere." For twentieth-century English mage Edward Alexander (Aleister) Crowley, Ashmole was a saint of the Gnostic Church. And I had somehow missed him. You cannot be everywhere at once, can you?

Elias had remained hidden not only from me, but also from mainstream history. I needed to know why.

Ashmole was a magus. He inhabited a world where science and magick were still handmaidens to religion and philosophy. He was one of the last men of learning to enjoy that world before the family broke up. All too soon, science would leave home to plow her own furrow independently and at times in contempt of her troubled parents. Nevertheless, Ashmole was a founding member of the Royal Society—a harbinger of that fateful parting—and was himself unconcerned with theological disputes. The philosophy he espoused stood above them; and so did he.

THE GREAT MAN

Ashmole's contemporaries saw him as a great man. In their eyes, his greatness was discerned in several attributes topped by one crowning glory.

First, his fame rested on being a man of enormous knowledge. He was not only a forward-looking collector of antiquities and botanical lore but a veritable Fort Knox of civilizing facts; he appeared to know—and care about—every aspect of British history. By no means confined in his interests to Britain, he was nonetheless a kind of national curator, for one should recall that there was neither a British Museum nor a British Library in Ashmole's day. It was Ashmole who founded the first purpose-built public museum in the world, and it was Ashmole who in himself embodied the nation's library. An example: Ashmole had personally collected the seal of every English monarch since the Conquest. His incredible coin collection went back to Roman times and he had thoroughly researched its background.

Second, he seems to have ignited the pleasure and admiration of a great many people from all classes. King Charles II regarded Ashmole as a depository not only of occult insight but also of good old red-blooded, look-you-straight-in-the-eye *honesty;* women trusted him too. Antiquary John Aubrey called his friend a "mighty good man," echoing a phrase used by Dr. Thomas Browne about Elias Ashmole's towering hero, polymath and magus Dr. John Dee.

Ashmole's character and attainments were great. He lived life with consideration, energy, flair, discretion—and effectiveness. Larger than life, Ashmole triumphed over countless setbacks. He was powerfully creative, driven along on a paradox. The late biographer of Ashmole, C. H. Josten, thought his greatness probably lay in a dynamic tension between the man of the world and the Hermetic soul of a spiritual mystic, indifferent to the judgments of the worldly. Garnering sufficient for himself, he was remarkably generous and charitable.

Ashmole had another trick up his capacious velvet sleeve—and the reference to John Dee encapsulates it. Ashmole was a Renaissance man in an era that was slipping away from the limitless ambition of the Renaissance philosophy of human dignity. Ashmole's era was beginning to focus sharply on the earthly virtues of patient experiment and worldly profit.

The works of Dame Frances Yates have spotlighted the ideal Renaissance type—so apparently distant from his post-Cartesian successor. It was the figure of the *Magus* who dwelled at the center and summit of Renaissance intellectual, spiritual, and scientific life. The Magus activated within himself an expanded humanity, allowing him to operate between the powers of earth and the active symbols of heaven.

In spite of all the dangers, the image of the Magus still held enormous appeal to the educated and uneducated alike in Ashmole's lifetime. Two contrasting classic literary examples of the image and of its power lie in Shakespeare's Prospero (*The Tempest*) and Marlowe's Dr. Faustus.

For those unfamiliar with the word *magus,* let us examine its meaning.

THE MAGUS

The word comes from the class of Magi, the priests who at various times provided the governing counsel to ancient Persia. The Greek historian Herodotus wrote about their widespread power and influence in his histories (c. 450 B.C.). The Magi were philosophers who cultivated knowledge of nature: a nature, that is, held to be magickal. Magick was the art of the Magi. Every person who has seen a Christmas crèche has seen a Magus.

The image of the Magus, a master of Magick (I prefer the old spelling), went through many changes from pre-Christian times to the stirring of Western civilization. A magus could be a fraudulent purveyor of cheap tricks or the exalted bridge between earth and stars. He could be a kind of arch-priest evoking demons and invoking angels. He could be a profound philosopher, an astrologer, an alchemist, a maker of charms, and a foreteller of the future, or even, as in the case of the legendary Merlin, a not-quite-human caretaker of the vicissitudes of earthbound but heaven-destined imperial British history—King Arthur's true friend (if only he'd listened).

THE HERMETIC MAGUS

In 1460, a group of manuscripts landed in the intellectual ferment of Florence to set a fire raging in the hearts of men groping for clear, accurate, liberating knowledge of the infinite. *Where do we come from? Who are we? What is our destiny?*

Renaissance philosophers such as Pico della Mirandola, Joannes Reuchlin, Giordano Bruno, Marsilio Ficino, and Lodovico Lazzarelli were alerted to the ancient manuscript tradition named after their supposed author, Hermes Trismegistus—Thrice Greatest Hermes, ancient mystagogue and incarnation of Thoth-Hermes, the Greco-Egyptian god of writing, magick, and communication. The documents were collectively called the *Corpus Hermeticicum* or, simply, the Hermetica.

The enthusiasts of this material were called Hermetic philosophers or Hermetists. They believed they were reanimating an ancient brotherhood of knowledge. We know there had been Hermetists in ancient Alexandria around the time of Christ, and recent scholars (such as Roelof van den Broek) have suggested that by at least the second century they met collectively for prayer and inspiration at Hermetic "lodges."

This tradition was ancient, linked to Egypt, and these two facts alone ensured that in the fifteenth and sixteenth centuries, the Hermetica would gain enormous respect as "pristine," pure, untarnished knowledge. Hermetic knowledge encompassed philosophical knowledge and primal wisdom: the original, clear knowledge inscribed for the future of humankind before "it all went wrong" and knowledge and language became divided against themselves, generating confusion, conflict, and a profound sense of loss. Such a state represented the Hermetic Fall of Man, and the aim of the Hermetic Magus was to restore the original unity of man and God.

Such a restoration would constitute a second birth, the opening of the spiritual eye, and the uncovering of a *new being*.

The key to the Hermetic rebirth resided in attainment of *gnosis*, spiritual knowledge to free the mind from the bonds of material perception. Before the Great Deluge—identified symbolically with the biblical Flood—Hermes had tasted the cool, creamy milk of divinity and had breathed the fresh Olympian oxygen of divine inspiration. His opened mind had risen to a clear blue clarity as perfect as the first sky ever seen, when blue was new and the earth and cosmos smiled and sang a silvery song of cosmic harmony and golden hope. Hermetic knowledge was, and still is, intoxicating.

ALCHEMY

Elias Ashmole began calling himself the *Mercuriophilus Anglicus* (the English Mercury Lover) during the 1650s, after the illegal execution of King Charles I and the beginning of Oliver Cromwell's decade of power. *Mercurius* was the Latin form of the Greek Hermes. As the divine Mercurius, Hermes, the *pater philosophorum* (father of philosophy), was crowned as the lord of the ancient art of alchemy. Alchemy was the subject of Ashmole's first three books. Mercurius is also a staple element of alchemical processes. In simple words, there could be no alchemical transformations without the implicit principle of transformation, mercurius. Hermes was the *psychopomp* (psychic lord) of the Art.

Alchemical mercury is not to be understood as the chemical element alone. According to the alchemist physician Paracelsus, "There are as many mercuries as there are things." Alchemical mercury suffuses all things. It was thought to be the secret or hidden principle that is the creative essence of the cosmic *Pan* (All) in all things. While mercurius is the principle manifest in the strange properties of chemical mercury, the word nonetheless represents a deeper reality: the principle of change itself.

In his thirties, Ashmole had set himself up as the English Mercury Lover—and the world took him at his word. The secret principle embodied in his life and work undoubtedly added or crowned the luster of Ashmole's greatness. It is impossible to imagine such a combination of talent engrossing the attention of our current intellectual classes, but that is surely no surprise. Contemporary enthusiasms have all the permanence of Tupperware.

We have no way of knowing whether the public or even Ashmole's own intimate circles were aware that in 1653 Ashmole was entrusted with the secret of the philosopher's stone by his spiritual master or "father," William Backhouse of Swallowfield Park, Berkshire. The stone is to alchemy what plutonium is to the nuclear technician.

The phenomenon of initiation into secrets rare and potent would characterize the inner pulse of Ashmole's life; he had found a secret purpose.

LICHFIELD

Ashmole was not all "esoteric." He enjoyed a basic respect for the emotions and obligations both of family and of place. Born and bred in Lichfield, Elias Ashmole never forgot the power of his native place in granting him the first lights of life and education. He would give money to Lichfield's poor on an annual basis; he was instrumental in the restoration of Lichfield's great cathedral following the vandalism of parliamentarian occupation. He also actively encouraged the independent spirit of Lichfield's local government, the City & Corporation.

Ashmole returned from London to Lichfield frequently. He helped to preserve Lichfield's antiquities and twice very nearly became Member of Parliament for the City & County of Lichfield by popular approbation. Lichfield loved Ashmole; it should still. Lichfield, Staffordshire, was in his blood and seldom far from the marrow of his mind.

It seems most fitting that the radiating power of Ashmole's birthplace should have struck deep chords with other visitors and friends of the ancient city. To some esoteric observers Lichfield is the *omphalos,* the creative navel of England, the hidden fountain of invisible spiritual power. This mystical identity transcends the city's current moves to become a classy-ish dormitory town for the aspiring ranks of pleasure-seeking, safety-conscious New Britons.

I think I can guess what Ashmole would think of "political correctness." Having experienced a decade of people who have banned Christmas, theaters, and Maypoles, I think he would suggest that people consider that Nature is Nature and eats herself for breakfast. Any attempt to contravene her laws with "good intentions," to make her conform to abstract political or moral ideals, merely invites an inevitable reaction akin to a Deluge, to wash away yet another folly of foolish humankind. Ashmole's motto *Ex Uno Omnia,* "From the One, All," enjoins us all to be inspired more by source than by derivation. Magick means working *with* Nature.

Ashmole was a seeker after the stone: the cornerstone where the material meets the spiritual; the firestone whose spark generates light; the foundation stone that is an alien in the world; the philosopher's stone that transforms lead into gold.

The alien stone that fell from heaven into terrestrial exile is the friend of humankind who gives his blood for all. And what is humankind? Is it not the blind fool who squats lamely with a begging bowl by the side of the road that leads to life?

Ashmole felt himself close to the chosen few who could stand and say, "Arise; walk! Within you is a Stone that fell from a Star. Seek it—and you will uncover the Miracle."

C. H. JOSTEN

This new biography is indebted to the magisterial study of Conrad Hermann Hubertus Maria Apollinaris (Kurt) Josten (1912–94). C. H. Josten's five-volume compilation of Ashmole's diaries and autobiographical and related notes, published by the Oxford University Press in 1966, will forever stand as the masterwork of Ashmole studies.

In 1949, Josten solved Ashmole's cipher, as a result of which new light on Ashmole's public and private activities was shed. That light guided Dr. Josten through a tenure as curator of the Museum of the History of Modern Science that began in 1950 and ended only when his wife's illness led him to retire in 1964. That museum occupied the "Old Ashmolean Building," the original Musaeum Ashmoleanum in Broad Street, Oxford.

Josten grew deeply attached to the place; it was said that he spoke of "Mr. Ashmole" as if they inhabited the same staircase. Josten is the only figure of whom I have any knowledge who seems to have been drawn to Ashmole with an intensity akin to that which I have experienced.

Josten was a remarkable man and his life, by the standards of today, was extraordinary. Studying at the universities of Geneva, Freiburg, and Bonn, Josten gave up a legal career in Germany in 1935 "because law no longer existed." In 1934 he had joined a clandestine opposition to Hitler and his cult. On June 30 of that year he himself witnessed the Night of the Long Knives, when Hitler's Vice Chancellor Franz von Papen was arrested as most of his staff were butchered at their desks by the SS.

Lucky to escape, he hid until the purges passed. Going into hiding again in 1943, he then fled to Paris before returning to Franconia prior to the war's end. His life—like Ashmole's—would make an interesting and exciting film.

Josten chaired the de-Nazification tribunal at his hometown of Neuss after the war and then, in 1948, he went to Oxford, where he began studying the Ashmole manuscripts in the Bodleian Library. Two years later he became curator of the Museum of the History of Science and in 1951 was made a member of Brasenose College—a privilege also enjoyed by Elias Ashmole and the author of this book.

Josten became a Fellow of the Society of Antiquaries in 1961 and was awarded the Oxford DLitt in 1968, receiving the honorary title *Curator Emeritus*. Dr. Josten was, according to *The Times*'s obituary of July 16, 1994, "of mystical inclination; sharing some of Ashmole's beliefs, or perhaps truer to say, sharing a renaissance image of his place in an orderly but partly paranormal universe."

Needless to say, to follow in the footsteps of such a man gives the new biographer pause for thought. I can only take refuge in the assumption that Ashmole himself was the sole cause and magnet of our interest while, in my case, the neglect of Ashmole provided sufficient motivation to embark on this biography. This work follows twelve years of Ashmole-related projects, from a short biographical study to a dramatic reconstruction of Ashmole's masonic initiation and a documentary about his life (*A Mighty Good Man, Elias Ashmole and the Initiation*, Dragon Films, 2002).

The first volume of Josten's study comprises its author's very thorough biography of Ashmole, based on the vast body of material that Josten put into chronological order with detailed notes in the succeeding four volumes. Josten's sober treatment of Ashmole's life was devoid of speculation (though there are some subtle hints) and certainly of the sensationalism that some of Ashmole's activities might engender in the pen of a less careful man. Dr. Josten was not attempting a popular biography of his subject.

I hope that in my own treatment of Ashmole's life I have been true not only to the source of my own inspiration and interest but also to Josten's high standards of scholarship, gravity, and decency. My task has been to make Ashmole known to a wider, nonacademic public, while at the same time making a small contribution to the scholarly debates around the subject.

This ambition itself incurs a risk of falling between ever more divergent stools. The culture available to the "educated layperson" of today seems less broad than was the case forty years ago. Conversely, there probably has not existed such a wide interest in history as obtains today; interest in the paranormal is probably a constant.

Antiquarian subjects garner significant audiences on national television, albeit frequently treated with a brush broad enough to make an academic blush. Nevertheless, the link must be built, lest the span between popular knowledge and serious study become unbridgeable. Such a state of affairs—while already taken for granted by many publishing executives—would be a tragic waste of the communication possibilities of our era. Ashmole himself chose to make his Oxford Museum a *public* museum, over 300 years before "access to higher education" became a political football.

In the years since the publication of Dr. Josten's work on Ashmole, research on the related topics of Rosicrucianism, Gnosis, and Freemasonry has blossomed beyond the expectations of many older authorities. Subjects that forty years ago seemed to have been lost to rational study have come under the purview of serious scholars determined to remove the cobwebs and mystification from the confines of esoteric studies. It has been the author's privilege to bring the latest researches to bear on the life of Elias Ashmole and his place in the total history of British and Continental Hermetism.

As British studies of the period (with some notable exceptions) have until very recently seriously lagged behind German, Dutch, Italian, and French studies of the Hermetic movement, so also Continental studies have tended to overlook some of the riches available in Britain. I hope this biography will further alert Continental scholars to the significance of Elias Ashmole.

Furthermore, studying in Lichfield, Ashmole's birthplace, has also provided fresh manuscript material concerning the reconstruction of the city after the Restoration of King Charles II in 1660, a process that greatly occupied Ashmole's mind. Living in Lichfield over a sixteen-year period has also familiarized the author with many of the details of Ashmole's sense of place and family relationships. I have walked in his footsteps, though not in his shoes. This familiarity is reflected in the novel form of this biography.

This is a photo-biography of a type that I hope may become more common in the future. Many a biography suffers from very limited illustrative possibilities, often a result of publishing costs. Modern technology enables a more exciting marriage of text and image. If every picture tells a story, then the reader has the opportunity to enjoy double the value of the research and share in a portion of the author's pleasure in following the trail of his subject: a process of visual archaeology. I am sure that Ashmole himself, who was fond of drawing the monuments and places he studied, would more than approve of this method. Possibilities for increasing the dramatic documentary approach to bookmaking seem to me practically endless.

These are my only excuses for daring a new biography of Ashmole—save for one. It has become fashionable in some circles—perhaps since Josten's death in 1994—to denigrate and demean Ashmole's contribution to the history of British learning (a development that Josten would not have tolerated). There are several reasons that might account for this development.

Perhaps the most significant is the tendency within the history of science to dismiss the occult and magickal studies that attended the genesis of "modern science" in the seventeenth century. Ashmole gets in the way of a neat classification of eras of knowledge. He is a Renaissance magus-type, yet still a rational mathematician and founding member of the Royal Society. He is historically inconvenient. However, his esoteric interests give hostile scholars the opportunity to quietly airbrush him out of the picture. That is to say, according to the demands of the current history of science, Ashmole could have advanced modern materialist science but chose to stay in the world of Hermetism; he somehow "missed the boat." Besides, was he not really a "player"; was he not an innovative scientific lawmaker, as Newton was?

This inadequate picture is explored in this biography with a question: Would not the development of scientific knowledge have gained something important if the Hermetic concepts had been fully understood?

The contemporary concern for spiritual understanding seems to bear out the value of the question.

Meanwhile, some historians of science simply wave a less than magic wand and cry "Superstition!" at the New Age regiments. The rationalist professor of biology Lewis Wolpert once made "the sign of the cross" at me at a Jean Gimpel salon in London in mock self-defense from spiritual influences. One wonders if he would wear garlic at a lodge of Freemasons! The new Inquisition does not require sticks and fire, only sneers and silence.

I trust this biography will serve as a timely reminder of the significance and (with hindsight) power of Ashmole's surprising life. I also hope that Conrad Josten would have found value in these efforts, which owe so much to his own quest for decency and meaning in a spiritually empty society.

ONE

The Coming One

In March 1604 the astronomer Kepler observed new stars in the constellations of Serpentarius and Cygnus. In the days when astronomy and astrology were inextricably linked, Kepler, like many a Continental astro-prophet, saw this epiphany of stellar magic as an intelligible sign from the Architect of the Universe.

Kepler himself predicted the onset of great political changes and the possible appearance of a new religious sect. Other men predicted nothing less than the inauguration of a New Age, even a golden age. It was, after all, widely believed that such an age would precede the final rolling up of the scroll of time and space. A final outpouring of divine and natural knowledge would be set before the intellectually hungry and the spiritually inquisitive. Men's minds were moved to contemplate the end of the world—and the beginning of a new one.

As the leading minds of Europe pondered the significance of the stars, a letter was dispatched to Lichfield, Staffordshire, by senior courtiers of Queen Elizabeth I, now fast approaching her final year on earth.

The surviving superscription to the letter reads thus: "This letter was delivered to Mr Bayliffe Ashmole by John Swynfen, gent., att Tamworthe on Saturday the xiiii daye of October."[1]

Mr. Ashmole, Lichfield's mayor, was unlikely to have been pleased with the letter's contents. Senior members of the Queen's court saw fit to petition the Corporation of Lichfield to surrender the lease to the ancient City's Lordship and Manor to the thirteen-year-old son of the late Earl of Essex. The late Earl, once the Queen's amorous and ambitious favorite, had pushed his suit too far, rebelled against her, and, in the end, lost his head completely.

In happier days, seven years before his appointment with the executioner's ax, the Earl of Essex had received a gift from the Queen.

In 1548, Bishop Sampson of Lichfield had conveyed the manorial rights of Lichfield to the new City and Corporation; the lease, however, went to the Crown. In 1597, Queen Elizabeth granted this lease to Essex and his son for the duration of their lives. The lease entitled them to rents and services. Those rents and dues had been falling into the coffers of the Corporation. Bailiff Ashmole had no choice but to surrender the lease to provide income for the earl's son.

This assignation of cash went against the grain; Lichfield had struggled long and hard for its partial independence from ecclesiastical control. For over half a century, the City had enjoyed county status, with its own sheriff and a Corporation of two bailiffs and twenty-four proud brethren. The Queen's will, however, was the source of all liberties, and there was no brooking it.

By a strange weave of circumstance, the lives of the late Earl of Essex and his son would come to have peculiar reverberations on the lives of the Ashmoles of Women's Cheaping, the little street beneath the tower of St. Mary's in the town's center.

THE ASHMOLES

Thomas Ashmole, the City's senior bailiff and mayor, had two sons. Thomas Ashmole the younger was encouraged to follow in his father's civic-minded footsteps. That left his brother Simon (born in 1589) to find a life for himself, a difficulty encountered by many second sons. In fact, Simon Ashmole had something in common with the late Earl of Essex, excepting of course the privilege of nobility that granted the earl the blade rather than the noose at his last breath.

The Ashmoles were of yeoman stock, the backbone of England. Nevertheless, like the earl, Simon was given to intemperate passions, sustained a profligate attitude to money, was foolishly optimistic (when not deeply depressed), and succumbed to the lure of overseas military campaigns in vain quests for personal advantage. Simon seems to have been one of those fatalistic men who always want to begin again but who never finish what they have started. He served under Essex's command in the latter's ill-fated expeditions to Ireland and the Low Countries.

Military campaigns of the ill-fated kind begin with promises and end in excuses. Essex's military failures cast an immovable wedge between himself and the Queen he had claimed to adore.

In his twenty-eighth year, the twelfth year of the reign of Elizabeth's successor James Stuart, Simon Ashmole fathered a son. His wife, Ann Ashmole (née Bowyer), would not experience motherhood again. May 23, 1617, would be a special day in her personal calendar of memories.

The baby's christening took place at the church of St. Mary the Virgin, a few steps across Women's Cheaping from the Ashmole family home. At the christening, something remarkable occurred. When the rector inquired as to what was to be the boy's name, the baby's godfather, Thomas Ottey (sacrist of the cathedral), received an instantaneous revelation. "Elias!" Ottey declared, would be the baby's name. All present were taken aback. The boy was surely to be named after his father or grandfather; this was the long established custom for first sons.

Left: Ashmole's birthplace, Breadmarket Street, Lichfield, formerly Women's Cheaping.

Below: Plaque above Ashmole's birthplace.

Rear of Ashmole's birthplace.

There is something almost biblical about this account of Elias Ashmole's first appearance on the great stage of the world. The name of the
child upstaged the local family tradition; his identity-to-be came from
"on high." That the name issued from the lips of a clergyman surely
added weight to the unexpected cry. No one demurred. Elias would be
the boy's Christian name.

One wonders whether Elias's father was present at the baptism. Was
this a little silent triumph for the long-suffering mother? At least now
she would only have to cope with *one* Simon Ashmole. And who could
say? Perhaps her little son might be a spiritual prize to render the pains
worthwhile.

"Elias" was not simply another name that would smell as sweet. Elias,
better known to the scripture-read of today as Elijah, held a fascination
for the religious thinkers of Ashmole's time. Elijah had been a star of
apocalyptic narratives and prophecies for at least 1,600 years. Elias was
the "expected" or coming one.

Prophecies circulated throughout Europe to the effect that "Elias
Artista" would return to earth to inaugurate a pre-messianic age of natural revelation. New arts and sciences would achieve their perfection
under the aegis of the one who had last departed the world in a fiery

chariot. Returning in glory, he would initiate a fresh blazing of cosmic light. This new spiritual fire would inspire the faithful of earth before the final consummation of terrestrial history.

When Christ himself asked his disciples who people thought he really was, they answered: "Some say *Elias*" (Mark 8:28).

Such a weight of expectation is a great deal to place upon the tender, if broad, shoulders of a baby boy. Godfather Ottey's utterance came as no less a surprise to him as it did to the baptismal assembly; Ashmole later described the phenomenon as "a more than ordinary impulse of the Spirit." If Thomas Ottey was unaware as to why he should be the sponsor of the boy child's new name, Elias himself would come to understand the import of his name very well. C. H. Josten writes of Elias Artista as "a great alchemist who would reform and renew the world by his art."[2] Such knowledge, however, Ashmole kept to himself. From the very start, Elias Ashmole's extraordinary life would grow about a mystery.

FORMATIVE INFLUENCES

Ashmole's correspondent Anthony Wood (1632–95), writing about the alumni of Oxford after Elias's death, declared Ashmole to be "the greatest virtuoso and curioso that ever was known or read of in England before his time. *Uxor Solis* took up its habitation in his breast, and in his bosom the great God did abundantly store up the treasures of all sorts of wisdom and knowledge."[3] "Uxor Solis" refers to Luna, or Minerva: the goddess presiding over the arts and sciences. *She,* Wood declared, was within him.

Was Simon Ashmole, son of the forceful and outspoken pillar of Lichfield governance, a wife-beater, an abuser of those in his care? We cannot be sure. Elias Ashmole's friend the astrologer William Lilly (1602–81) would leave to posterity an interesting account—all too brief—of Elias's parents.

Simon Ashmole was "very melancholy," a man "not of many words, or not much uxorious." He was, according to Lilly, "of a strong temper, apt to be angry or malcontented, passionate and violent." Lilly adds that Simon was "subject unto many misfortunes during his life."[4]

Elias Ashmole's own account of his father makes a telling complement

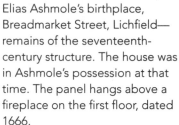

Elias Ashmole's birthplace, Breadmarket Street, Lichfield—remains of the seventeenth-century structure. The house was in Ashmole's possession at that time. The panel hangs above a fireplace on the first floor, dated 1666.

to Lilly's account (which itself must have been based on his friend's recollections). His father, he admits, was "an honest faire conditioned man, and kind to others; yet through ill husbandry became a great enemy to himself and poor family."[5]

The description suggests a troubled man with the body of a bruiser. A picture emerges of what we would now call a "damaged" child who had craved a father's love and approval. But does it portray Elias or his father?

Simon Ashmole's brother inherited the civic responsibilities that the successful Thomas Senior had garnered from the Corporation. The two Thomases held the office of bailiff "no less than seven times," as Howard Clayton informs us in his book on Lichfield in the Civil War, *Loyal and Ancient City*. Clayton also provides a glimpse of the outspoken character of the Ashmole family, of yeoman stock but now established in the city as saddlers (only the well-off rode horses). The leather trade was important to the Lichfield economy, the Saddlers' Company claimed to have been founded in the reign of Edward I.

By the time Elias was six, his grandfather Thomas Ashmole had been sheriff, junior bailiff, and twice senior bailiff (mayor). He was what one might today call a "Big Noise" in the little city. He was also a member of the Company of Corvisors (shoemakers) of Lichfield, and their surviving records reveal how on May 8, 1626 (Elias was eight at the time), Thomas Ashmole was fined a shilling by John Warde, probably the company master, apparently for failure to attend meetings. Thomas did not take this forfeiture lying down. Rather, the record informs us, he "did abuse the said John Warde at the Hall done in the open street, and called him a Cobbling Clown." For this outburst Ashmole was fined a further three shillings and four pence.

Whether the possessor of this fiery temperament was Elias's grandfather or uncle is impossible to ascertain. It could probably have been either of them; one receives a vivid picture of a proud and independent-spirited family.

While the two Ashmoles were influential in local politics, it does not seem difficult to understand why Elias's father spent so much time away with English armies. Presumably there was only so much room for fighting in Lichfield. Was Simon Ashmole seeking his own heroic scenario? Perhaps he was tired of boxing with his brother's shadow. One cannot tell whether he joined the troops "to forget" or to be remembered with glory. A melancholic temperament such as his doubtless entertained both possibilities. One certainly senses the frustrated destiny of the unfulfilled life, the son who might have wondered what use he was to any but himself.

As the great Swiss psychologist Carl Jung wrote in 1929 when considering the life of Ashmole's alchemical predecessor Paracelsus (1493–1541),

Views of the cellar, the attic, and a window in Ashmole's birthplace.

"Nothing exerts a stronger psychic effect upon the human environment and especially upon children, than the life which its parents have not lived."[6]

It is to be suspected that Elias, painfully aware of his father's deep-seated miseries, would come first to recognize the importance of a secure social setting for ambition, and second to fire up his own ambition to justify the unexplored potential hidden within the father's melancholy. He may have been unconsciously driven to "put right" his father's failure. Does not the Son usually have to justify the doubted Father?

Ashmole was aware that his father was "kind to others" but immediately states that "ill husbandry" led him to be a great enemy not only to himself but also to his "poor family." How many nights of tears lay behind this summary statement? A *great* enemy . . .

Add to this Lilly's account of the "violent and passionate man" who made poor and probably hasty judgments, and it seems reasonable to assume that young Elias would have suffered eruptions from silence manifested perhaps in beatings and harsh and regrettable—if not regretted—words.

Ashmole, the sensitive, artistic child, born of a mother of noble ancestry, must have wondered about the depths of the human personality and the hidden springs of motivation. His interest in such matters was lifelong and was reflected in his love of astrology, his unique dream records (according to Jung, who studied them), and his many sociable virtues.

Elias Ashmole was also deeply concerned with transcendence and the path to the gate of transcendence that is knowledge. He took his forward drive from his family's characteristics but prevented these strengths from becoming weaknesses by superimposing the balancing virtues of concentration, tolerance, discretion, good humor, and mindfulness.

From both parents came honesty and a directness that would serve him well. From the depths of himself, perhaps recovered through unspeakable, deep personal pain, came the light of *gnosis,* the desire for transcendence and the essence of mystical alchemy: the taking up of the dark matter and its transformation into light.

MOTHER

For all his faults, Simon Ashmole the bellicose, the sad adventurer, had married well. Ann Bowyer was, according to her son, a "discrete [*sic*], sober, provident woman [her husband being none of these], and with great patience endured many afflictions. Her parents had given her good breeding, and she was excellent at her needle; which (my father being improvident) stood her in good stead [Lichfield was home to dozens of tailors]. She was competently read in Divinity, History and Poetry, and was continually instilling into my Eares, such Religion and Moral Precepts as my younger yeares were capable of. Nor did she ever fail to correct my faults, alwaies adding sharp reproofs and good Lectures to boot."[7] Clearly, Ann Ashmole was determined that no one could later sigh, "Like father, like son."

Ann's married life must have been a continual struggle to offset the downward trajectory of her ill-destined husband. In this she was remarkably successful, instilling in her son the requirement of life that to get on in the world meant getting on with those who have made a profitable peace with the world, while at the same time keeping one's own counsel, being discreet and plain to oneself. One can hardly doubt that Elias's mother would have shielded the boy from his father's worst outbursts, inevitably aggravated by financial hardship combined with darker, deeper undertones.

"She was," said Elias after her death from plague in July 1646, "much esteemed by persons of Note with whom she was acquainted, she lived in much friendship among her Neighbours, and left a good name behind her. In fine, she was truly Religious and Virtuous."[8] Each line of this brief encomium is telling in some significant way of the tensions that manifest themselves in the dynamic thrust of Elias Ashmole's life.

Elias would make it his business to get on with the world as he found it, but almost always on his own terms. It took him a long time to find out precisely what those "terms" consisted of, but one feels in his development contrary thrusts deep in his being.

When that fascinating man C. H. Josten wrote the established biography of Ashmole for the Oxford University Press in 1966, he sought to express Elias Ashmole's greatness not in the terms of Ashmole's contemporary reputation (great attainments of knowledge and intellect) but otherwise.

Interior of Ashmole's birthplace. The panel dates from Ashmole's lifetime and is on the second floor of the building.

For Josten, Ashmole's greatness lay in the manner in which his life expressed, contained, and found strength from an essential inner duality: how he made himself lord and master of his own inner house. This was the sole authentic "heroic scenario" permissible to Josten's academic contemporaries in a post-Freudian world: "The quiet pleasures of contemplation and of lonely study, which were at no time foreign to his nature, became gradually the more powerful motive of his conduct. Thus, while gaining the secure position and the eminence for which he had longed in his youth, he did not rise as high in the world as he might have done had he been less an Hermetic philosopher and more a man of the earthly plane."[9]

Perhaps Ashmole had seen a little too much of the earthly plane in his childhood and youth. But Josten was fully aware of the power of Ashmole's ambition, even though that ambition had something mysteriously and distinctively unearthly about it. "The mystical urge," writes Josten, "was never strong enough to make him entirely abandon the bustle of the world. Thus he vacillated between the ideals of magus, savant, and man of the world, and if the tension produced by the sustained co-existence in one person of seemingly incompatible qualities and desires is the secret of a powerful personality, then we hold here probably the key to Ashmole's greatness among his contemporaries."[10]

Maybe this is the key, not to his contemporaries' appreciation of him, but to ours. Perhaps Ashmole's life and character now represent a vital model for our own times. Within his story may be discerned a demonstration of how to reconcile the miserable facts of the lower life (for which we now have an almost impenetrable wall of evidence) with the spiritual aspiration of the awakened human mind—that is, an indication of how to reconcile our need for reality and our need for the transcendence of that reality. Ashmole's life is in a sense a case of, and for, the alchemical, spiritual life.

But before Ashmole was a Hermetic philosopher dedicated to the raising of earth to heaven, he was already an antiquarian. In order to find the source of this urge we may look not only to his inner investigation of personal identity (inevitable given his father's distance from him), but also to Lichfield itself and, again, to his beloved, stern, and thoroughly sensible mother. Ann Ashmole was what the downstairs staff of Edwardian fictions would call "a Real Lady."

The Ann Bowyer, daughter of Anthony Bowyer, citizen, and draper of Coventry, who married Simon the saddler of Lichfield was a descendant of Richard the Forester, the Hunter, the Crooked Oak. According to the Domesday record of 1086, *Ricardus Forestarius, vel Venator, vel Chenelware* held Biddulph, Knypersley, and Biddulph Moor from the king. These estates were all to be found in the moorlands of Staffordshire, some thirty and more miles north of Lichfield. The wild moorlands bordering on Cheshire were home to the county's most powerful lords.

The Forester's son was Ormus (the Elm) le Guidon (the standard bearer), married to the daughter of the Norman sheriff of Stafford. Ormus was possibly a Templar knight. From the issue of his children—Robert, Edward, Thomasin, Alured, and Sir Thomas Bidulf—we can trace half a millennium of landed Staffordshire life. From their marriages were joined the genealogies of the de Audleys, the de Knypersleys, the de Verdons, the de Gresleys, the Mainwarings, the Bidulfs, the de Venables—and the Bowyers, who joined a line that stretched back to Ormus le Guidon's son Alured de Knypersley.

Ann Ashmole had no reason to be reticent about her family history where her son was concerned. All about the growing boy hung the ethos of the ancient, the hallowed, and the mysterious. For the rest of his life Ashmole would collect genealogies. Streams of history, both above and underground, fascinated him. He liked to trace phenomena to their source. His instincts were preservative, comprehensive, and particular; detail mattered. He cared about things that went missing, things hidden, things that were losing their temporal grip on posterity; he drew with great skill many hundreds of pictures of English monuments and preserved dozens of inscriptions that would otherwise be lost to us. Thanks to the preservation motive he did so much to encourage, these works are themselves preserved at the Bodleian Library and the Ashmolean Museum in Oxford.

Ashmole keenly felt the impact of history's march—and mankind's ignorance—that obliterated, or tried to obliterate, its inheritance. Has this country gained any more than Esau for bartering its soul for the "mess of pottage" that is short-term gain?

Perhaps it was the stories of ancient lineages told him by his clear-thinking mother that gave Elias the insight that we are all part of a tree, that "now" is no time at all: everything that is has already been. We are the passing faces of an unfolding; all is contained in the seed. Its working out is time itself: the effects of fate, chance, and providence. His motto was *Ex Uno Omnia*: from the One, All.

Ashmole would have borne an informed contempt for the "modern" or its twisted offspring, the "postmodern." Rather, we are all part of a living tree whose roots feed us vital sap from the past. That a thing was past did not mean that it had ceased to be; rather, the present and the future were utterly contingent upon the life that flowed through all time. The folly of man was to forget the reality that all that has been, *is*. "It" is in our eyes, our ears, our homes, our dreams, our aspirations, our blood. The memory required jerking from time to time—that was a task for the antiquarian. Nothing is dead unless it has been killed.

Ashmole would come to look at the Dissolution of the Monasteries (1534– c. 1540), for example, in the worst possible light. What had been hailed in its day as the clearing away of old and bad—and sometimes very bad—habits, a vital modernization of the state's relationship with religion, even the rationalization of care, was for Ashmole nothing less than "the Great Deluge."

Ruins of Croxden Abbey, Staffordshire moorlands.

View of Staffordshire–
Cheshire border
looking northwest from
the summit of Bosley
Cloud.

He referred to an event as terrific, mythic, and epoch-blasting as the Great Flood itself, the wiping away of all but what was preserved in the Ark. So was not Noah the first antiquarian, both ante- and post-diluvian? And was not the Ark that floated above the waves of change and catastrophe a kind of museum? And was not Elias Ashmole to be a new helmsman entrusted with the history of all that was noble, true, real, and of good repute?

Taking on this task was not simply a matter of philosophical principle. The monasteries had preserved the knowledge of the nation. It is estimated that the Dissolution led to the destruction of 98 percent of the books and manuscripts of England. Hitler himself never managed such a conflagration of knowledge. Ashmole's hero, the magus John Dee (1527–1608), had petitioned Queen Mary to establish a national library to preserve what was left; the request was ignored. A state of national burglary went hand in hand with the Reformation. Ashmole would distinguish himself as one who saved what he could.

How could Ashmole not look kindly upon the monasteries, with their deep, practical ties to the families of nobility and to the poor and humble, the hungry and haunted, whose brightest and benighted sons sought refuge there? Ashmole knew of the monasteries' connections with British alchemy, cosmology, medicine, botany, philosophy, art, and architecture. The monasteries were a vital conduit to the past.

Three great monasteries had once dominated the Staffordshire moorlands: Croxden, Hilton, and Dieulacres, their chartularies witnessed and guaranteed by the de Verdons, the de Audleys, and the Mainwarings, respectively. They preserved records, monuments, and reputations; there was no great need for "antiquarians" so long as they stood and breathed.

Between the demise of one set of institutions (the monasteries) and the birth of others (such as the Royal Society), there was work for ideological freelancers. Ashmole was one of them—and he would play his part in establishing new institutions to link the past with the present, to reunite the Many to the One. Ashmole was trying to show the way back to the way forward.

Young Elias did not need to travel to the moorlands to find his soul's mirror. All about him, in Lichfield, lay the keys to England's extraordinary heritage.

TWO

Lichfield—The Hidden Light of England

A t the time of Elias's birth, Lichfield, properly called the City and County of Lichfield, was home to some 3,000 people, dwelling in neat streets of timber-framed lath-and-plaster houses. The streets themselves were not paved with gold, but they *were* paved—with stone—thanks to the paternal hand of Bishop Walter de Langton (1296–1321).

During the Middle Ages, a powerful bishop needed a powerful king, though many a king might have preferred otherwise. Walter de Langton celebrated his patron Edward I's life with a grand series of frescoes that decorated the great hall of the palace he built, measuring one hundred feet in length and fifty-six feet wide. Visitors were looked down upon by images of Edward being crowned king (surrounded by noble bishops); Edward being married (bishops again); and Edward victorious in battle (bishops carrying swords). It was, after all, a bishop's palace, even a bishop's world.

The power of the king to bring victory, and the power of the bishops to confer righteous judgment, came from one source: God the Father (not the will of man) manifest on earth through the majestic incarnation of His Son. However, in the twelfth and thirteenth centuries, there was a growth in enthusiasm for what is today described as a "divine feminine principle." It may have been the case that there already existed an enthusiasm for a divine female figure (such as Brigid, the "Bride" and earth mother) and that the Church transmuted the principle.

In official or mainstream ecclesiastical circles, this spiritual need was met by the elevation of the Virgin. It had long been a feature of pagan belief to think of the Great Mother Goddess as both whore and virgin: ever fertile, ever willing, ever renewed in purity. The Church could Christianize the "Bride and Mother of the Church" by emphasizing the virginity while leaving the whore image to the Magdalene. The Virgin offers herself freely to the Holy Spirit and will of God, thereby demonstrating the very "wisdom" (*sophia*) that in more ancient times was the central characteristic of the Holy Sophia, virgin-whore, stellar goddess, and earth mother combined.

Given the unconscious associations of the Virgin, it is no surprise that she inspired the lives of men and women in a way that the frequently austere image of Christ the Judge could not. The Virgin was the patroness of the Knights Templar, capable of inspiring fanatical devotion. Bishop Walter made his own marvelous contribution to the movement by adding a massive Lady Chapel to the cathedral's east end. During the Civil War, those who regarded the elevated Mary as a pagan idol (while idolizing Parliament) gutted the Lady Chapel, while Bishop Walter's Great Hall with its frescoes disappeared forever.

Lichfield Cathedral as seen from Aldershaw to the south.

As we shall see, there is reason to think that the Great Mother had been worshipped at the site of the cathedral before the Christians came to preach the message of her Son.

Bishop Walter was a good patron of the masons and freemasons (master masons of freestone). He enhanced the building work of his twelfth-century predecessor Roger de Clinton. Under de Clinton (1129–48), the Cathedral Close had been transformed into a fortified mini-state, a sandstone holy island of power and miracle, rising above the waters below like the unbreakable will of God triumphing over chaos. Power temporal and power spiritual were concentrated there. Great walls and turrets, great gates and towers protected the cathedral's mysteries from the wayward, hell-bound world beyond.

At the center of the mystery lay the holy bones, the relics of St. Chad, patron saint of madmen. In his life he had lived with awe-inspiring simplicity, forgoing the horse that was the sign of power, walking everywhere, spending timeless hours in concentrated prayer. In death, his remains occupied the center of a great multicolored cake of tiered stone and stained glass that thrust upward as a sinuous stone forest to the Father of Lights. Medieval artists had perceived the incalculable glory of Chad's spirituality and they represented this exemplary mystery and image of Christlike life in the manner they knew best: with every ounce of their intelligence, technology, artistry, geometrical sophistication, and proportional ingenuity.

For the builders, no contradiction marred the contrast between the gold of spiritual purity and the lesser gold that adorned the images and inscriptions of the church. It was *because* they recognized the spiritual glory of Chad's sainthood that they wanted to draw attention to the eternal within by the seemingly infinite material without. Rude rock was to be transfigured into squared and righteous stone. The stable of Christ's birth, the simple cell of the saintly hermit, would become an image of that heavenly City and Temple beyond this world. The cathedral was clothing, dress for the infinite transcendent principle held within.

The body, with its sense of sin and spiritual illegitimacy, was to be overwhelmed with massive, overarching beauty so that the spirit would be awakened and the contrite soul would shake off its own gaudiness and come to humble recognition of the will of God. Here man's bread became God's flesh. Within the transformations, miracles were possible. Man might hope with hope purified.

So, at least, ran the theological theory. As a result of this magical marriage of theology, art, and science, Lichfield became one of the world's great pilgrimage centers. By the grace of God, and by the intercession of Virgin and Saint, there were cures to be had. That is to say, cures were sometimes offered to those who themselves made offering: some sacrifice, a sign of penitence. Heaven was watching; the eyes and the stars looked down. *Dig deep, penitent, into thy purse.* The cause is worthy: the glory of the Church and its sacred charge, the healing of your degenerate flesh, the salvation of your delinquent soul.

ST. CHAD AND THE ORIGINS OF LICHFIELD

As has been said, there is every reason to think that Lichfield had been a spiritual center even before Chad's arrival there in 669. Since his arrival from York came with the cooperation of the pagan king Wulfhere of Mercia, based at nearby Tamworth, it might be that the link with the past came from the king's mind.

Since Chad came to plant—or replant—the Christian tree in Mercia,

The Bridestones: site of a neolithic temple, below Bosley Cloud, Staffordshire moorlands.

it would make logical and, from the point of view of evangelical custom, consistent sense to plant that tree in a locus where religion was already seen as its focal purpose. Chad aimed to show the pagan Saxons of his diocese a higher path out of their established traditions. Furthermore, both legend and archaeology attest to a significant Christian presence in Lichfield before the Saxons themselves settled in the valley; Lichfield was already spiritually significant. Why else, one might ask, would a man as holy, respected, and, in Celtic ecclesiastical terms, powerful come to Lichfield from the monasteries of Lindisfarne and Lastingham, pulse centers of Celtic Christianity in the north?

What was there at Lichfield in those days but a marshland dampening a shallow valley, a series of pools and streams, and much untamed forest? According to the *Victoria County History of Lichfield,* Lichfield may mean, prosaically, a field or *feld* (Saxon) "by the gray wood" (from the old Welsh, *luitcoit*), while local traditions since the thirteenth century have preferred the etymologically unsound interpretation, "the field of the dead."

The earliest manuscripts of the eighth-century Saxon historian Bede call the place Lyccidfelth, which might derive from the Old English *lic,* meaning a corpse. Unfortunately, there is no way of being sure whether the name for the area assigned by King Wulfhere to Chad was of predominantly Celtic or Saxon origin, though Celtic seems the more likely.

St. Chad's Well at
Stowe.

Whether one prefers one interpretation or the other, the single consistent element that has shone through the murk is that the place is somehow associated with death. In an early Welsh poem there is a reference to a bloody battle that took place when *Caer Lwydgoed* was raided in the seventh century. That place, wherever it may actually have been, has been identified with the Celtic word "Letocaiton," and with the Romano-British settlement at Wall (the Latin "Lectocetum") a little to the south of the city.

Meanwhile, Matthew Paris (d. 1259) of St. Alban's Abbey linked the idea of a field of corpses with the martyrdom of 999 Christians who had escaped north after the execution of the Romano-British saint Alban during the reign of Diocletian (A.D. 284–305). This interpretation was accepted in Ashmole's day. In a letter of thanks sent to Ashmole by Lichfield's bailiffs in 1666, reference is made to "three knights martyred," "as ancient as the days of Diocletian."[1] This story has been discredited by scholars but has proved nonetheless popular, and when the City and Corporation designed its coat of arms, it included some corpses for good measure.

Also for good measure, I should add that *laec, lecce,* and *lic* are Old English words for "stream" or "bog," but it is still unlikely that the Saxons had been in "Lyccidfelth" long enough to give the place or area their own name.

There may be something in the "field of the dead" idea that has lingered in the subconscious minds of local people. Could Lichfield once have been a place where the sick were brought to be healed, or the dead to be buried—or the guilty to be sacrificed? Healing, death, sacrifice, burial, and religion go together and, as far as we know, always have.

We know that pools and lakes held a special, even profound fascination for Celts and pagan Saxons alike. Expensive votive objects—and human bodies—were cast into them at sundry times: a practice going back into the mists of time. Danu the water goddess (after whom the Danube was named) was worshipped in ancient Staffordshire, as the river Dane in the Staffordshire moorlands testifies. In the last century, I have been informed, it was customary in the Marchington Woodland and in the Ridwares (after the Saxon for "reed-folk") for the few retainers of the old traditions to cast corn dollies into flowing streams at pro-

Greenhill, topped by the spire of St. Michael's.

pitious times of year. The winding stream and the old hill still evoke in us strange and powerful feelings of belonging and spiritual beauty, even of "Englishness," a divine love of homeland transcending politics: the feet of ancient time walking on the "mountains green."

If today you go to Greenhill, Lichfield's high point, you may see a sign next to St. Michael's Church informing passersby that Greenhill is "one of the five oldest Christian sites in the country." Matthew Paris may not have been the sole author of the legend of Christians making their way up the Watling Street to Lichfield (Etocetum) for refuge after the martyrdom of St. Alban at Verulamium. This legendary story even seems to have subconsciously inspired the founder of the Quaker movement, George Fox, to an act of unconscious folly.

In the winter of 1651, catching sight of Lichfield from a distance, Fox ran barefoot across the damp and frosty fields into the freezing streets of the city. Oblivious to the reality about him, he shouted for all he was worth, "Woe unto the bloody City of Lichfield!" to the surprise and annoyance of the already hard-pressed populace.

Unaware of a legend he later reckoned to have been "behind" this strange experience, he had, at the time (or out of it) undergone a vision of the city flowing with blood. The implication in Fox's mind seems to have been that Lichfield was in some manner complicit in the blood spilling and would have to pay for it. Perhaps Lichfield has buried itself.

While it is recorded that four Northumbrian missionaries were brought to Mercia by Peada, Wulhere's brother, in 658, eleven years before Chad's arrival to take up the new bishopric, it is also quite possible that Romano-British Christianity had survived in pockets in the Midlands into Saxon times. Stories survive of a cell near Warwick nourished by visits from monks from Christian churches in Wales.

The fact that the church atop Greenhill is dedicated to the archangel St. Michael is significant. St. Michael "slew the dragon" of the ancient "earth religion" with its tendrils of mystery rising from the depths. Michael's spear, aimed at the dragon's mouth, "plugged up," as it were, the earth magic of pagan times, leaving it "in hell," its denizens damned as demons unredeemed and deadly. Hell has always held a fascination that fear itself generates, a thirst for which is currently slaked by horror movies, "Gothic" computer games, and sword and sorcery play of every kind. A cinematic recreation of J. R. R. Tolkien's Catholic *Lord of the Rings* stories is currently enjoying tremendous success. Tolkien appears to have found the models for his "hobbits" in the villages around Cannock Chase.

There is topographical evidence that Greenhill was once the site of an ancient fortification, reached by a causeway over the marshes of central Lichfield, part of whose path may still be seen at the cut sandstone ridge by Wissage Lane. Greenhill was very likely a religious sanctuary as well as a site of refuge. Old churches were usually built on venerated pagan centers. (Perhaps this goes some way to explain the somewhat forlorn character of so many relatively new urban and suburban churches—as well as so many modern estates themselves; they have no true center and one experiences in their midst a sense of soul-loss and energy depletion. The "kids" are *not* all right.)

Below Greenhill to the northeast lay the ancient hamlet of Stowe beyond the City boundary, the marshy place that Chad made his personal spiritual retreat after his arrival in Lichfield in 669. There beneath a wooden canopy is St. Chad's Well. Covered today, it was used—and venerated—in Ashmole's day. A sign recently uprooted by vandals used to tell the pilgrim that the site of the well "is Holy Ground." Legends of Chad's life tell of how he would leave his simple cell at dawn and stand naked by the well to say prayers or sing a hymn to his Creator at the

St. Chad's church at Stowe, Lichfield, traditionally held to be the site of the saint's private retreat.

rising of the Sun (the practice may derive from Hermetic circles in Egypt via Ireland).

It is reported in Bede's *Ecclesiastical History* that Chad believed that every natural phenomenon—especially severe winds, storms, and climatic changes—contained a message from God. During one terrific storm, for example, Chad could not cease from profound praying in his chapel. As the rain and tempest lashed all about him and his frightened inner circle who tried to restrain him, Chad prayed fervently that mankind be spared harsh and final judgment.

For Chad, as for the Hermetist, the cosmos was a cryptogram, a palimpsest; beneath the obvious image were a sign and message hidden from the "blind"—those who refused to see. Mastery of the body was a path to keep the spiritual eyes clear and in focus so that God's will could be "read." God sends his seers for the guidance of mankind; this was also Elias Ashmole's belief.

The universe reflected the divine will mediated through nature as through a symbol. Ashmole shared much of Chad's Orient-derived spiritual-magical vision of the divine cosmos; it gave Ashmole great stability and not a little insight. He could see the timeless principle operating behind the panoply of change, the light behind the passing, flickering celluloid of life.

After Chad's death in 672, his bones were moved half a mile from Stowe to a sandstone shelf overlooking the northern banks of what is now Lichfield's Minster Pool. This area had probably been the site of Chad's chapel. A Saxon cathedral was built around the saint's remains.

Lichfield grew to be not only the largest diocese in the country but also from 788, an archdiocese of England, until 802, when Pope Leo III restored Canterbury's rights. From Lichfield's center, the Christian message was taken to the greater part of the nation's body. It is still a light in the darkness, though light has become very expensive and the dean and chapter of today might well wish for those extensive resources formerly garnered from the gilded hopes of pilgrims.

GAIA

The site of the cathedral may already have held spiritual significance. To the northeast of that site today runs the ancient way called Gaia Lane. The name Gaia first appears in extant Lichfield records in the late 1200s as a name for the area to the northeast of the cathedral where the clergy grew their crops. The two half plots of land may be supposed to have extended upward to what is now called Prince Rupert's Mount. Gaia was of course a name for the Greek earth goddess and many today will be familiar with Lovelock's "Gaia Principle"—that the earth is a living, self-regulating, even spiritual being, involving some kind of self-consciousness.

The appearance of the word Gaia as a place-name is certainly puzzling. Gaia (whose name seems to derive from an ancient Greek word for earth), wife of Uranus, the god of the heavens, was mother of the Titans. Her role in Greek mythology suggests a *hieros gamos* or sacred marriage idea somewhat reminiscent of the Ishtar-Tammuz myths of Syria and Babylonia.

Gaia was the Earth Mother or Great Mother. If Mary had been renamed by the ancient Greeks, she would have been called Gaia. The Motherhood of the Earth was strongly emphasized. The name was passed over to the culture of the Romans, who were wont to call the bridegroom and bride at weddings Gaius and Gaia for the special day. A higher or holier marriage was thus invoked; the marriage had a sacred dimension. Gaia then could be the word for Bride.

The Celtic earth goddess worshipped in ancient Staffordshire was Brigid, or Bride (hence the word we know). Uranus comes from the Greek *ouranos,* meaning heaven. Gaia is the Bride of Heaven: earth and heaven locked in sacred union. *Ex Uno Omnia.* To *unite* is to make One.

Greek and Phoenician traders came to Britain in ancient times. Is it possible that pre-Christian Lichfield was the locus of a Greek-founded religious cult? If it was, then Walter de Langton's Lady Chapel was certainly built at the right place.

Hills have long been associated with divine presence. One thinks of the seven hills of Rome or Mount Moriah in Jerusalem. Men have indeed looked to the hills for their salvation for many thousands of years. To the northwest of the city, the observant eye cannot fail to notice a series of three well-rounded hills, rising like distant, serpentine waves in a line to the south around Swinfen. In the foreground we see three more hills.

Borrowcop Hill, just outside the city's old southern boundary, has its own place in Lichfield's mythology. It was almost certainly the site of an ancient fortification, close to the Mercian royal family's burial mound at Offlow. There is a legend of three kings being buried at Borrowcop. To the northeast of Borrowcop stands the aforementioned Greenhill, and to the northeast of Greenhill, the mount that rises above the fields of Gaia. These hills were once partially "moated" by streams that flowed into Lichfield from the west. When Ashmole was a boy, these streams supported four water mills, at Leomansley, Dam Street (just outside of the Cathedral Close's southern gatehouse), Stowe, and Ponesfield.

The waters from springs at Aldershaw in the southwest were piped to conduits in the City. Ashmole's family would have obtained their water from one of these (provided by the Conduit Lands Trust, founded in 1545). References to Conduit Street in the town center exist from the twelfth century, though it is not clear where the water for such a conduit would have come from before the Franciscan friary activated its own conduit from the springs at Aldershaw in 1301.

The confluence of hills and water, springs and pools within a "contained" environment was irresistible to the imagination of our ancient ancestors. Their priests recognized the signs of a transcendent pattern; the universe was bound by patterns, and man was caught in the weave. On the principle of "As above, so below," the earthscape reflected patterns derived from the heavenly realms. Where such a pattern was seen to concentrate, spiritual associations and images flowed from the human soul, or as Jung would put it, archetypes buried in the unconscious would be "constellated" by analogous phenomena in the natural world.

This is what the visionary artist William Blake (1757–1827) meant by saying that Albion, his archetypal Ancient Man or giant (representing England as a spiritual being), *contained within himself the earth and the stars* in a primal harmony. Blake was an enthusiastic reader of Ashmole's friend John Aubrey's book on the religious landscape of Wiltshire.

Spiritual vision, or what Blake called "Jesus the Imagination," was the key to seeing this landscape: heaven in a wildflower, eternity in an hour. Ashmole seems to have enjoyed something of this gift. However, according to Jung (who analyzed Ashmole's dreams), he was inclined to suppress it, favoring the path of the more "masculine" rational intellect. Nevertheless, Ashmole was deeply moved by the spiritual universe. His belief in magick saved him from becoming another harbinger of the Age of (rational) Enlightenment. The enlightenment Ashmole sought was deeper and more elusive.

Jung's principle regarding the mind's tendency to "see" archetypes projected as images when confronted by particular patterns in life and nature may explain the phenomenon of today's spiritual seekers finding "earth energy" lines, magnetic or "leylines" radiating from the center of Lichfield. Such observations have concluded that the place is a radix of subtle spiritual power capable of drawing in souls and nourishing departing ones, like moons drawn to the orbits of powerful planets. As above, so below, indeed.

Modern Lichfield is in dire and perhaps irreversible danger of burying its magnetism and its meaning beneath so much modern builders' tat, selling its soul for a mess of council-tax pottage. *Not in my backyard!* saith the Lord. Those with ears to hear, let them hear.

CHILDHOOD

When Elias Ashmole wandered about his home city as a lad, he would have found an atmosphere quite different from that which is now pervasive. Indeed, Providence could hardly have chosen a finer birthplace for one who would distinguish himself in, among other things, antiquarian studies and alchemy, the Royal Art, the *black* art. For that ancient phrase "As above, so below" derives from the first lines of the gospel of alchemy, the *Emerald Table* of Hermes Trismegistus, patron saint or (to use Jung's phrase) "psychopomp" of alchemy. Alchemy, Ashmole was at pains to point out in *Theatrum Chemicum Britannicum,* his brilliant study of English alchemists (1652), was an art once practiced in the religious houses of pre-Reformation Britain.

The boy Elias studied Latin, Greek, poetry, and arithmetic at Lichfield's grammar school and church music at the cathedral. There is no direct evidence from this period indicating an awareness of dwelling in a "sacred landscape." However, Ashmole's later preoccupations and magnetic fondness for Lichfield leave little doubt that something of the sacred landscape was dwelling in him. His powerful desire to see Lichfield's religious monuments (especially the cathedral, or "temple," as he called it) restored, preserved, and filled again with song came from

Breadmarket Street, formerly Women's Cheaping. The original Guildhall stood at the far end of the street.

very deep within his being. This desire was more instinct than whim or predeliction; it marked him out, possibly, in spite of himself.

What if we try to get behind the boy Elias's eyes? What would those eyes have seen as his buckled shoes dodged the puddles and ordure of Lichfield's anciently paved streets?

Coming out of his family's house onto Women's Cheaping (now Breadmarket Street), he would immediately have found himself in the shadow of the Gothic tower of St. Mary's. The church was full of sepulchral monuments that the adult Ashmole was to record in detail; the monuments have disappeared but his records remain. The church was rebuilt in alien limestone in the eighteenth and nineteenth centuries and its subsequent transformation into a museum and community center gives little idea of the hoary grandeur that would have greeted Elias each morning.

Sixteenth-century building, Bore Street, now a tearoom and antique shop.

Glancing to his right, he would have taken in the black and white beams of the old Guildhall, resplendent on the south side of Borde (now Bore) Street. "Ye Gelde of ye gloriouse Virgin Marie of Lychefelde" was established out of two former guilds in 1387 by Richard II. The Guildhall itself was in existence by 1421.

The life of the Guild was entwined with the life of the Church. Suffering a considerable decline at the time of Ashmole's birth, the country's guilds had once wielded considerable influence on town life and demonstrated how intimately all aspects of life were, in pre-Reformation England, attached to religious festivals, symbols, ceremonies, and ethics. Guilds eagerly sought allegorical links between their trades and the Bible. Passages obscure to most of us held great meaning for guilds and confraternities.

St. Mary's Guild enjoyed the power to make bylaws for the maintenance of social order, employing its own dungeons, the remains of which survive to this day. Before its dissolution at the hands of Edward VI in 1547, the Guild had its own chaplains, who lived in a house on Women's Cheaping. Ashmole's family home may have been constructed on the site.

The Guild of St. Mary administered the Church's interest in the Christian relief of the poor, as well as taking care of its own members in the manner of a welfare system. The master and two wardens each held a key to the three locks of a chest, commonly called a "box," which would be opened on Boxing Day, among other occasions, for gifts to the poor. The dignitaries above all had to be present when the box was opened

Conduit Lands Trust Box for money and documents. Note the three keys.

to secure its contents. Relief from sickness and poverty came from the Guild's fines, rents, dues, and gifts, held in the box. The practice continued after the establishment of the Conduit Lands Trust in 1545, shortly before the Guild was dissolved.

The dissolving of the Guild left the town in financial straits. Probably as a result of the efforts of Minister of State William Paget (who owned a mansion at nearby Beaudesert), Lichfield was incorporated by royal charter in 1548. Having achieved a large measure of self-government (the Close was still an independent entity), Lichfield's City Corporation moved into the Guildhall. Not that the move required much furniture removal (Edward VI had plundered the city of silver and other valuables); the first bailiff and half of the Corporation's brethren had formerly been masters of the old Guild, while a further six of them had been Guild Wardens.

Queen Mary confirmed the charter in 1553, granting county status to a City of Lichfield that could now boast its own sheriff. By Ashmole's time, the trade companies, whose seniors occupied the ranks of the Corporation, appointed the all-important bailiffs. On March 1, 1633, Simon Ashmole had his fifteen-year-old son Elias enrolled as a freeman of the city's Company of Saddlers, Glovers, Whittawers, and Bridlemakers.

Turning away from the Guildhall to his left, young Ashmole would in a few short steps have found himself in the marketplace, which on a Tuesday or a Friday was filled with people and livestock come to market. Worsted cloths (produced at the city's mills), milk, cheese, meat, fish, vegetables, confections, spices, wine, pots, pewter, and paper were sold there as they are today, as well as cattle, poultry, game, and pigs.

Well-to-do people (one wonders what they would have thought of the word *consumer*) might also find leather carpets (to replace rushes), padded seats, tinderboxes, books, looking glasses, chests of drawers, silver and brass candlesticks, buttons, buckles, velvet waistcoats and cloaks, satin petticoats, and silk suits. The streets would be clogged with oxcarts and perhaps a stage-wagon: a heavy, lumbering cart, billowing and bulbous as a huge haggis, pulled by six, eight, or ten horses. The driver would walk alongside the horses, carrying a whip the size of a fishing rod.

Wives and servants would crisscross the market square. Veils, pearls, and furs were the height of fashion. Keen eyes followed maidens, who

EDWARD WIGHTMAN
OF BURTON-ON-TRENT
WAS BURNT AT THE STAKE
IN THIS MARKET PLACE
FOR HERESY
11TH APRIL 1612
BEING THE LAST PERSON
IN ENGLAND SO TO DIE

Memorial in Lichfield marketplace to Edward Wightman, burned for heresy there in 1612.

assessed the quality of the interest with discreet glances from behind simple white bonnets.

The air would have been thick with country accents and country smells. Perhaps some folk still found time to comment on the execution of Edward Wightman in 1612. Wightman had been accused of heresy; he recanted, then recanted his recantation, believing himself to be an incarnation of the Holy Spirit. He was burned alive in the marketplace.

The burning resulted from Lichfield still being the seat of the Bishop's Court. It had shocked many Lichfieldians. Poor Wightman was the last person to be burned in England for heresy but the people of Ashmole's Lichfield were not to know that; it could still happen to them, their friends, or their relations if they stepped too far out of line.

Much drinking was indulged; the country wasn't called "merry England" for nothing! Some decades before, there had been complaints that there were too many alehouses in the city, the cause of "much decay in the place."[2] Nevertheless, Lichfield was by far the richest town in Staffordshire, and with the money came the drinking.

Lawyers in broad-brimmed hats would converse with bailiffs, squires, and company men. Proud yeomen would meet fellow farmers and suppliers (such as saddlers) to pursue private transactions either beneath the stone market cross—a gift from Dean Denton in 1530—or in one of the many inns of Lichfield. Drinks might include *syllabub,* a sweet wine with cream; *mum,* a beer brewed with wheat, and *buttered ale,* beer served hot and flavored with cinnamon and butter.

We may imagine Elias dodging farmers and merchants as they made their way west from the Market Square, up Sadler Street (now Market Street) to one of the galleried inns in Bird Street, which runs at a right angle at the end of Sadler Street.

Looking to his right along Sadler Street, Ashmole would have recognized the large home of the influential and traditionalist Dyott family, roughly where Woolworth's currently stands. Behind the Dyotts' gabled home flowed a long garden. It ran parallel to other long gardens, extending down to the great pool that flowed from Bishop's Fish Pool (now Beacon Park) to the west into the marshy "Moggs" to the east of the town before becoming a large pool once more at Stowe.

Reflected in the pool (called Minster Pool) were the great sandstone walls of the Cathedral Close defenses, while from behind them, rising with a titanic thrust, the three great spires of the cathedral reached toward heaven.

LICHFIELD IN 1548, FROM THE BISHOP'S FISH POOL

Lichfield Cathedral as it would have appeared to the boy Elias. The Bishop's Fish Pool *(foreground)* has long since been drained. Note the battlements around the Cathedral Close.

As Elias's eye glided over the bristling thatch that nestles to the eaves above Sadler Street's fine houses, his ear would have been alerted to the sound of melodious pipes. Where today the pedestrian on Market Street might be swayed into rattling his pocket by the twanging and whining of a busker, the professed instruments of the seventeenth-century street musician and inn entertainer were the pipes. The piper's tune: the payer's choice. To young Ashmole's ears, the sonorous breath of the pipes held a special meaning—not only because in Old England the sound of the pipes suggested liberty, but also by reason of an old and cherished memory.

Fellow antiquarian John Aubrey (the historian of Wiltshire) related how Ashmole revealed to him that when he was a boy, a Lichfield piper had enchanted the young Elias with his music. The piper had also been enchanted, but not by another musician. He told the spellbound boy of how he was "entertained by the Fayries," that he "had oftentimes seen them" and that "he knew which homes of the Towne were Fayry-ground."[3]

Fayries, being rather more alarming creatures than the Edwardian image of them would indicate, were usually the denizens of an intermediate world between this one and the next. They were associated with hills, trees, pools, and departed spirits. Were there Fayries at the bottom of the Dyotts' garden? Or were they dancing on the rustling thatch, leaping from gable to gable and table to table, mad with the pipers' tunes? The piper had eyes that saw "out of the ordinary."

Ashmole's mature philosophy certainly held room for the secret life of these supposed strange, intermediate beings. It was customary to give fayrie-like characteristics to the spirits of the elements: of earth, *gnomes;* of water, *undines;* of air, *sylphs;* and of fire, *salamanders. A Midsummer Night's Dream* and *The Tempest* were modern plays when Ashmole was a boy.

But whereas the four traditional elements were everywhere and constituted everything, the "fayries" were quite particular about their chosen place. Not every house was suitable for fayries. It was a question of *location,* of *locus,* of *genius loci,* and of *locus genii.* Ashmole could hardly have been a stranger to the concept of the magick of place, whether that magick induced ecstasy or *panic* (remember the pipes of

Pan). *The pipes, the pipes are calling me . . .* The pipes called one over to the Other Side.

The pipes had told Elias that Lichfield was magical. Why, one wonders, did the piper choose to grace Elias's warm and highly musical ears with his account? Did he know a sensitive ear when he saw one? Such things of which the piper had to speak were not common knowledge. But, then, Elias had little interest in common knowledge.

Now standing outside the Swan (until very recently a hotel), Ashmole looked back across Bird Street to the George and Dragon (now the George Hotel). Both inns were built around cobbled courtyards, and both echoed with horses' hooves, the cries of ostlers, the cackle of fighting cocks, and the clanking and slapping of saddlery, which was the Ashmoles' staple income.

Looking to the north up Bird Street, Elias would have seen the low, narrow bridge built in stone by Bishop de Langton nearly 300 years earlier. The bridge gave access toward the cathedral fortifications and in doing so divided Minster Pool to the right from Bishop's Fish Pool (now drained and called Beacon Park) on the left. Crossing the bridge, Elias would approach the mighty gates, siege-proof walls, and the portcullis that guarded the western end of the Close.

Left: Remains of defensive tower at the entrance to the Cathedral Close.

Above: The bridge over Minster Pool as it is today, from the east.

Dr. Milley's hospital.

Walking northward up the hill, with the moat and defensive walls to his right and fields to his left, he would find himself in Bacon (now Beacon) Street. A few low cottages lined parts of this exit street from the city and we may be permitted to imagine the sound of truffle-digging swine that in their cooked state perhaps gave this street its name.

Near the top of the grassy hill, in a healthy, breeze-blown position above the denser, damper air of the town below, Dr. Thomas Milley had reendowed the almshouse founded by Bishop Heyworth in about 1424. Once rebuilt, Canon Milley's hospital for fifteen women had opened its doors to charity in 1504; it still stands and serves the needs of elderly ladies to this day. Perhaps a coterie of the old dears was perched on stools by Bacon Street watching the passing market traffic and gossiping about the good old days of Queen Elizabeth, or even—who knows?—the Virgin Queen's half sister, the Catholic Mary, named after the competing Virgin of England's spiritual imagination. Lichfield's population included a large number of Roman Catholics. Both the cathedral and the parish church were dedicated to Mary.

From the brow of the hill, Elias could see Bacon Street wind into the fork of Abnalls Lane and Cross in Hand Lane to the northwest as the cottages petered out into the rich farming land that surrounded the city.

Looking back down into Lichfield, he would be able to see the remains of the old ditch and bank raised by Bishop Roger de Clinton around the city's center, interspersed by the four city "barrs," or main gates. The first barr was below him on Bacon Street, just north of the cathedral gateway, opposite Gaia Lane, one of two main roads to the north that skirted the Cathedral Close's moat and defensive walls. The wooden gates would doubtless be open for market.

Looking across the depth of the town toward Greenhill to the south-

St. John's Hospital.

east, Ashmole would have seen another of Roger de Clinton's ancient barrs. Casting his eyes down to the right, his gaze would have been met by the neat row of imposing Tudor brick chimneys of the Hospital of St. John the Baptist, refounded and reendowed for thirteen almsmen by Bishop Smyth of Lincoln in 1495. Somehow, this hospital (which had been serving the needy since before 1208) had survived the desecration and destruction of Henry VIII's Reformation, which had reduced Lichfield's Franciscan friary just a bit further down St. John Street to ruins less than a century before.

St. John's stood outside the barrs of Lichfield—but only just. Beside the hospital stood another of Roger de Clinton's barrs, now permanently open to trade and travelers coming up from London and the south. Customarily, travelers could claim a kindly pot of ale from the hospital gates before pasing the barr and entering Lichfield. Failing that, the thirsty visitor might join locals at the Hartshorn Inn, adjacent to the hospital and temptingly close to the lips of Lichfield's grammar school boys. The grammar school was a further endowment of Bishop Smyth of Lincoln.

At the sight of this stone structure, Elias's eye would have good reason to linger, for this was his school and to it he had better hasten. And in returning—*festina lente, Elias!*—he had better harden his posterior for the master's rod that would soon descend for so abandoning his proper studies, to show us, his posterity, the stony lineaments of his glorious, gilded home, Lichfield, a pilgrim's dream at the center of Old England.

Site of Ashmole's grammar school and headmaster's lodgings, opposite St. John's Hospital. The grammar school was rebuilt in 1682.

THREE

London Calling

In spite of Elias's unwearied diligence as a gifted pupil of Lichfield's grammar school, his professional future was by no means assured. Merit was significant but social rank and its accompanying access to patronage were by far the more determinative factors in a young person's life in the seventeenth century. Ashmole's life was no exception to this general rule.

Elias had neither the intention of following in his father's somewhat erratic footsteps nor of joining the family firm of saddlery and local government. Even if the family had sufficient funds to send the youth to Oxford, there can be little doubt that an existence as "a poor parson of the town" would not satisfy this particularly precocious lad. The adult Ashmole's friend William Lilly later remarked that Elias was not assiduous in his religious duties; Ashmole's feel for the spiritual life belonged to a plane different from that largely occupied by conventional Protestant or Catholic religion.

Furthermore, Elias had intimate experience of the need for a proper income in order to stabilize life to the extent where personal ambition might find its outlet. It would take some years and not a little hard experience before he would come to grasp the full lineaments of his worldly and unworldly potential. Until then, he was more or less content to be a strong, would-be dashing, noble-hearted, brave, and very bright charac-

52

ter: not a bad start by any means. Ashmole enjoyed all of the romantic dreams to which young, gifted, healthy men are prone and which they must eventually qualify—for to remove all such dreams entirely is too sad a prospect; to take away a man's dreams, a sage once said, is to take away the man.

While Ashmole studied hard and dreamed easily, his mother had perforce to maintain a firmer footing on the turf of social and economic reality. Elias owed his mother a great deal for her perspicacity, wisdom, and solid common sense. A mother like Ann Ashmole has saved many a young man from attaining that bittersweet wisdom that derives from persistence in folly. The road of excess may indeed, as Blake maintains, lead to the palace of wisdom, but on entering, one can hear the door slam shut. Ann Ashmole probably saved her son for the nation and the world.

Mother's method was a polite cultivation of personal contacts and the action of chance—or as Elias Ashmole would surely add, the hand of destiny. That hand was now to play a trump card.

Ann Ashmole had a sister, Bridget. Bridget's second husband was James Pagit, Puisne Baron of the Exchequer of London. Bridget died in 1626 when Elias was six, but the Pagits enjoyed another Lichfield connection. James Pagit's sister Catherine was the wife of Dr. Charles Twisden, Chancellor of the Diocese of Lichfield. James Pagit's son Thomas (from a previous marriage) liked to visit his aunt in Lichfield and it was on one such visit that he became acquainted with the sister of his late stepmother. Ann Ashmole opened her household to her brother-in-law's son and it was there that Thomas met Elias; the youths became firm friends.

In due course Thomas told his father about his talented friend from Lichfield. James Pagit was particularly touched by Elias's serious interest in music, an interest in which the English excelled at the time; many on the Continent regarded England as the most musical country in Christendom. He was himself skilled in music, as were his sons, and he encouraged Ann Ashmole to see that her only son devote more time to its study.

Ashmole augmented his time as a cathedral chorister by persuading the organist to give him instruction on the virginals and pipe organ. One wonders if the piper of Ashmole's boyhood had espied faeries at the cathedral as well as in the houses of the town. Circa 1633, Elias added a study of dancing to his personal curriculum—his notes on the subject constituting his earliest extant writings. Such refined cultural accomplishments would *in potentia* gain him access to courtly life, both at its center and in its multifarious satellites.

Thomas Pagit kept his father informed of his friend's progress in music, and in the summer of 1633 James Pagit decided to invite the sixteen-year-old Elias to dwell at his London home. Perhaps the imminence of his departure to London accounts for the optimistic interest in dancing.

On July 2 Elias parted from his parents at Bassets Pole, seven miles south of Lichfield. He would never see his father alive again. One can only guess with what feelings Simon Ashmole was parted from his only son and with what tender relief Simon's wife must have greeted her boy's first step on fortune's road.

Ashmole himself would never forget the good fortune that brought Thomas Pagit into his life, later declaring his young friend to have been "the chiefe Instrument" of his "future preferment."[1] If there ever was some residual bitterness at being so "patronised" by the Pagits, he never voiced it. All patronage has its dark side, and in Ashmole's day "preferment" was all patronage. In Elias's case, it may be asked whether the price of patronage was the effective loss of his father. The "father image" would come to loom large in his life.

Preferment deriving from association with the Pagits certainly did lie in the future, for Elias Ashmole's translation to the capital was not altogether a happy one. Apart from inevitable homesickness and possibly—who knows?—guilt, life within the Pagit household was coarsened by the unpleasantness and mendacity of James Pagit's wife.

Mazaretta Pagit was neither a good mother nor a good hostess; the food was poor in quality and mean in quantity. Mazaretta did not take kindly to the honest boy from Staffordshire; she treated him as a servant. Elias fetched bread and in the mornings tended the cold, gray grate of Thomas Pagit's elder brother, Justinian.

Ashmole endured the life there for two years before moving out to lodgings at Mount Pleasant at the age of eighteen. He was learning to live by his wits.

Coat of arms of Philip Mainwaring and Ellen (née) Minshull (Mainwaring arms on left).

Careers in music were at this time reserved for a tiny number and both Elias and his friend Thomas Pagit pursued the study of law, to which James Pagit's copious contacts around London's Inns of Court afforded them ingress. Three years after moving out of the Pagit household, Elias Ashmole was soliciting in Chancery "and had" as he put it, "indifferent good practice."[2] He would need all the clients he could muster, for in August of the previous year (1637) Ashmole had journeyed to Smallwood on the Staffordshire–Cheshire border to ask the squire Peter Mainwaring for the hand of his daughter, Eleanor. The liaison with Eleanor Mainwaring appears to have been a love match, possibly initiated at the Pagits' house.

Ashmole's mother's family, the Bowyers, were distantly related to the great old Cheshire family of Mainwarings. The Mainwarings had come with William the Conqueror from Guarenne (or Varenne), near Arques in Normandy. The name was anglicized to Warenne, or Warren or Warin. Mein-Warin means the house of Warin, that is, Upper Peover in Cheshire. Ashmole would undoubtedly have been more than happy to restore a link with the Mainwarings.

On March 27, 1638, "I was," Ashmole writes in his personal records, "married to Eleanor Mainwaring eldest daughter to Mr Peter Mainwaring (and Jane his wife) of Smalewood in Com'Cest' [Cheshire] gent: She proved a vertuous and good wife. The marriage was in St. Benets Church neere Paules wharfe by Mr: Adams Parson there."[3]

Manor house and church of St. Lawrence, Upper Peover, once home to the senior Mainwarings.

Peter Mainwaring had one son and six daughters; one might unchari-tably imagine the squire to have been relieved to marry off Eleanor to practically anyone who could provide a roof and a silk handkerchief. Such cynicism would be misplaced, however. Elias was very popular in the Mainwaring family and he and his father-in-law became close, respectful friends. Perhaps Peter Mainwaring fulfilled something that had been lacking in Ashmole's relations with his own father.

Fourteen years older than her husband, Eleanor loved her young Elias greatly. Ashmole's characteristically succinct account of his wife makes

Whitmore Hall, Staffordshire, once the home of Edward Mainwaring III (right).

the affection between them quite explicit: "She was a vertuous, carefull and loving wife, her affection was exceeding great toward me, as was mine to her, which caused us to live so happily together."[4]

Nevertheless, the couple did not live together as much as both must surely have hoped. Ashmole needed to earn more money in order to establish a worthy house. In the meantime, Eleanor spent most of her married life living in the bosom of her family at Smallwood, Cheshire.

Smallwood Manor House used to stand adjacent to the old Smallwood Flour Mill by Martin's Moss, less than half a mile northwest of the nineteenth-century church and school at Smallwood. To the southwest, Mow Kop rises opposite Biddulph Moor on the Staffordshire border with the spire of Astbury church against Bosley Cloud to the west. One can well imagine Eleanor Mainwaring frequently looking over to the border, wondering when her husband would arrive home. Sadly, Smallwood Manor House no longer stands.

In the circumstances, Eleanor must have been delighted when a year after the wedding, Dr. Thomas Cademan, physician-in-ordinary to Charles I's wife Queen Henrietta Maria, became her husband's client. To add weight to Elias's good fortune, Peter Venables, baron of Kinderton—a distant relative of Ashmole through his mother—recognized the quality of his legal skills and put him in charge of his law business. The baron of Kinderton must have been watching the young man's progress

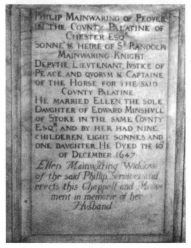

Above left: Effigy of Philip Mainwaring, lord of Peover, sculpted by a son of King's Master Mason Nicholas Stone: chapel at Upper Peover.

Above right: Philip Mainwaring's cavalry armor.

Left: Philip Mainwaring's memorial plaque.

and one senses the influence of Ashmole's mother in the arrangement.

The Venables of Kinderton, Cheshire, were also relatives of Eleanor Ashmole née Mainwaring. Eleanor's fifteenth-century forebear Margery Mainwaring was the daughter of Hugh Venables, baron of Kinderton. It was probably Margery who erected the unusual chapel at the church of St. Lawrence, Upper Peover (the home of the senior branch of Cheshire Mainwarings), over her husband Randle Mainwaring's tomb. Sir Randle (known as Handekyn the Good) died in 1456.

In April 1640, on taking over the management of the Venables law business, Ashmole took lodgings in St. Clement's Lane—one of life's little triumphs marred by tragedy: Elias and Eleanor's first child was stillborn.

Right: In Ashmole's day, people from Smallwood worshipped at nearby Astbury.

Below: Looking from Smallwood to the border with Staffordshire. The peak of Bosley Cloud can be seen between the trees.

In October, Ashmole moved to a chamber in the Middle Temple placed at his disposal by Thomas Pagit. Having been admitted to Clement's Inn and sworn in as an attorney in the Court of Common Pleas, Ashmole had a manservant sent from Lichfield; things were looking up.

A year of good business ensued and Eleanor may have wondered when Elias would have sufficient income for them to establish a family

Chambers in the Middle Temple, close to the Embankment.

home of their own—although it was normal practice in those days for married couples to share houses with their parents.

As the autumn of 1641 turned to winter, Ashmole the attorney planned a Christmas break to Lichfield and Smallwood. What he did not hear, as he made his preparations, was the news that plague had broken out in the town of Congleton near Astbury, only a mile from Smallwood. From the house of one William Laplove, the scythe of death, which had cut through most of Laplove's family, swung through this busy Cheshire village. By the end of the year, Astbury had seen no fewer than 330 of its inhabitants die from plague.

In the second week of December, Ashmole left London for the Midlands, doubtless looking forward to sharing some of the fruits of his growing career with his family. Perhaps he wanted to show off; perhaps he just needed a good rest and time to meditate among people who loved and cared for him.

Ashmole arrived in Lichfield on December 16. It was there, at the place of his birth, that he received the dark tidings. On December 5, Eleanor had fallen "sodainely sick about evening and died (to my owne great Griefe and the griefe of her friends) the next night about 9 o'clock."[5]

Above: The restored round Templar church, Middle Temple, London.

Right: Gateway to Middle Temple Hall.

By the time Ashmole passed through the southern barr of Lichfield, his beloved wife had already been interred, close to her deceased kin in Astbury church. A shadow fell over Ashmole's life.

On January 2, 1642, King Charles I went to the House of Commons to arrest Pym, Hampden, Hazelrigg, Strode, and Holles. The king offered the immortal soundbite "I see the birds have flown" on finding his parliamentary enemies absent. In spite of Ashmole's keen interest in such matters, this significant event in British constitutional history can barely have stirred the brokenhearted Ashmole from his grief. It would be a fortnight after arriving in Smallwood before he felt able to visit his late wife's grave.

Although he would marry twice more, Ashmole's memory of his dearest Eleanor never dimmed. Its flame was kept alive in his heart through regular visits to the Mainwarings of Smallwood. The affection was fully reciprocated. At Eleanor's funeral, her mother, Jane Mainwaring, told the Baroness of Kinderton that she loved Elias as her own son.

In August 1642, a lonely and unhappy Ashmole left London, strongly disapproving of the Long Parliament's erosion of the royal prerogatives of government. Sitting since November 1640, that historic Parliament had in January 1642 passed a bill to raise a militia and, when necessary, impose martial law: decisions that were historically the monarch's prerogatives. The militia was doubtless to "protect" the Commons from its rightful king. A Commons majority had also indicated its sectarian character by voting to remove bishops from the House of Lords; the underlying conflict between king and Commons was essentially religious.

The God of the Puritans did not approve of the king's religion. Since the God of the king held the same contempt for the religion of the Puritans, the bitterest antagonism was inevitable. The only resolution was to be sought in a confrontation of arms, whereafter the victor might claim that God had favored his cause, since there could neither be two Gods, nor the will of one God divided.

On August 22, King Charles I raised his standard at Nottingham, acknowledging thereby that a state of war now existed between the king and his Parliament. Seven days later, Ashmole returned to Smallwood from London. He began to write long poems. Like many men of conscience at the time, Ashmole looked deeply into his soul for his life's true compass. But there was little respite as the gathering storm spread about the country; fanaticism was in the air and men's thoughts darkened considerably. Signs were sought but the signs were everywhere. By the following spring, the war had arrived on the doorstep of Elias and the Mainwarings.

A few miles over the Cheshire–Staffordshire border from Smallwood, Biddulph Hall, garrisoned by Sir Francis Biddulph for the royalist cause, was destroyed by parliamentarian troops under the ruthless command of Sir William Brereton. Opponents of Parliament were *de facto* opponents of God's will; it would be impious to go soft on God's enemies.

From Biddulph, Staffordshire, one can clearly see the striking mount of Bosley Cloud, the site of a prehistoric temple (the "Bridestones" still stand there), to the northeast. The Cloud also dominates the northwest skyline from the hamlet of Smallwood. Between the Cloud and Smallwood rises the limestone spire of Astbury church. Beneath it, Eleanor Ashmole's cold remains lay in peace in the southwest aisle. That peace was soon disrupted by Brereton's Roundheads ("Roundhead" was a common nickname whose contemporary equivalent would be "skinhead").

While besieging Biddulph Hall, the Roundheads stabled their horses in Astbury church. They smashed the medieval stained glass, vandalized the stone- and woodwork, carried the organ and pre-Reformation furniture to a field, and burned the lot in a bonfire of self-righteous indignation. These furious acts of deliberate desecration must have played deeply on Ashmole's mind, but he may still have been reluctant to declare his allegiance. Perhaps one of the problems for him—as for so many others—was that opposing combatants were frequently related, either closely or distantly.

On March 21, 1643, for example, the Committee of Sequestrations at Stafford (on which sat Commissioner Edward Mainwaring of Whitmore Hall, Staffordshire) ordered that "the remainder of Biddulph House be preserved accordinge to Mr Biddulph's own desire, toward the repay-ringe of a little old house of his, not above two miles from it."[6] Sir Francis Biddulph was a direct descendent of the twelfth-century lord of Biddulph, Ormus le Guidon. Ashmole's mother's family could also be traced back to the Crusader (and possibly Templar) Ormus. The Mainwarings likewise were entwined with the great family tree that went back to Ormus and beyond.

Edward Mainwaring of Whitmore, a kinsman of Peter Mainwaring of Smallwood, must have enraged Staffordshire and Cheshire Royalist gentlemen with his enthusiasm for sequestrating their property and subjecting their purses to ruinous fines to pay for the parliamentarian army.

A contemporary portrait of Edward Mainwaring still hangs at Whitmore Hall, three miles south of Keele. After the Restoration of the monarchy and Parliament in 1660, the portrait was deliberately touched up. The lord of Whitmore underwent an image change: he was, to use a vulgar phrase, "repackaged." In a timely act of public relations, Mainwaring's parliamentary sash and breastplate were painted over. Edward Mainwaring was now loyal to the king; his past had been brushed out.

Back in the 1640s, the lord of Whitmore was not the only Mainwaring sympathetic to Parliament. North of Smallwood, Philip Mainwaring, lord of Upper Peover (near Jodrell Bank), would in September 1644 receive a letter from King Charles I (based at Chester) addressed to "Our trusty and well beloved Philip Maynwaringe," expressing concern that Mainwaring was "ill affected to us and our sayd service." He was called to serve, but should he "answer the contrary," travel across the country would be "at your utmost peril."[7] Philip was not cowed and would fight as a knight for Parliament. His cavalry armor may still be seen at the church of Upper Peover.

Philip Mainwaring's wife Ellen greatly assisted Cromwell's cause and permitted his troops to billet in the family church. After her death in 1656, notwithstanding her support for Cromwell, the Lord Protector-to-be, Protestant vandals lopped off her alabaster effigy's praying hands, taking them as signs of popish religion. As historian Steven Runciman has written, "Tolerance is a social, not a religious virtue."

Within a month of Commissioner Mainwaring's granting leave to Sir Francis Biddulph to repair a little house on what was left of his ancient estate, Ashmole made an attempt to leave the depressing devastation that was enveloping the Staffordshire and Cheshire he knew and loved. He decided to ride to London, accompanied by his late wife's cousin Henry Mainwaring of Karincham (today called Kermincham, near Swettenham, a few miles northeast of Smallwood).

Kermincham Hall, an Elizabethan manor house built in the shape of an H, must once have been a place of great enchantment. The hall was demolished in 1860; only the gatehouse survives to offer mute testimony to the adventures of Ashmole and his father-in-law's nephew. Three years later Henry Mainwaring and Elias Ashmole would make another fateful ride together, only this time it would be northward up the Warrington Road, as we shall see.

The two men arrived in London in April 1643 to witness sights every bit as disturbing as those that were becoming commonplace in the Midlands. Statues and pictures were being destroyed by the Trained Band, the bully boys of a Commons committee. If any doubts had still lingered in Ashmole's mind over political allegiances, they were now dispelled, for it was now clear to him that Parliament had become a syndicate running a property-stealing racket, enforced by religious fanatics and thugs both trained and untrained. The prospect of anarchy was real.

Elias Ashmole came to the fateful decision to declare himself for the

Top: The site of Colonel Henry Mainwaring's Hall at Kermincham, Cheshire, demolished in 1860.

Above: The gatehouse was part of the original Jacobean buildings. Ashmole would have passed by it regularly. (The author is indebted to the kindness of Ms. Sue Steer for permission to explore the site.)

royalist cause, ready and willing to defend that cause when the call came. The decision must have brought some respite to his long troubled mind: a chance to play the man and do his duty for the preservation of Old England against the hollow hysterics of constitutional innovators.

Elias Ashmole was at war.

FOUR

War

oth king and Parliament required money to prosecute the conflict. On May 27, 1644, the king's government, based in the loyal city of Oxford, appointed John Hill, James Povey, and a twenty-seven-year-old Elias Ashmole as commissioners for the gathering of excise in Staffordshire.

Before the storm: the lull. June found Ashmole taking part in martial training—or was it sport? He participated in tilts outside the walls of the city of Chester, so soon to suffer demolition at the hands of parliamentarians. He was fitting himself in body and mind for the arduous road ahead.

That road took him to Oxford at the end of 1644. There, together with excise collector John Hill, Ashmole entreated the royalist Parliament to pressure the governor of Lichfield, Colonel Richard Bagot, into ceasing his obstruction of the gathering of excise in the city. Behind these circumstances lay a micro-political battle that went back to 1604, when this story began. Those circumstances would indirectly change the course of Ashmole's life.

Readers may recall that in 1604 the Corporation of Lichfield was persuaded to surrender the lease of the Manor of Lichfield to the young Earl of Essex after courtiers of the Queen wrote a letter, delivered on Essex's behalf to Bailiff Thomas Ashmole. Robert Devereux, third Earl of Essex (1591–1646), appointed one Richard Drafgate as his steward in Lichfield to collect rents and dues; Drafgate became senior bailiff (mayor) in 1638.

On July 13, 1642, Essex was commissioned by Parliament as captain-general of its forces. He could now count on a parliamentarian faction squarely in the heart of Lichfield. That faction did not go unopposed. Drafgate would not have to walk far from the Guildhall to find Sir Richard Dyott; the latter's house stood in Sadler (now Market) Street. A Member of Parliament for Lichfield since 1637, Dyott had been chosen to act on the Council in the North "for the regulating of the disorders within our Middle Shires, with the power of Oyer and Terminer (and) to holde Gaol Delivery as there was occasion."[1] Dyott was the leader of Lichfield's royalist faction.

Problems in raising excise for the king seem to have stemmed from the curious situation of Lichfield's lease being held by the captain-general of Parliament's army with his agent, Drafgate, in charge of raising dues, while the garrison governor, Colonel Bagot, was himself hard-pressed. Bagot had only assumed the position on April 21 of the previous year after Prince Rupert of the Rhine had relieved royalist besiegers of a short-lived parliamentarian garrison. Bagot needed every penny he could get, obtaining financial levies from as far away as Walsall. He also received donations and money taken from the enemy, and claimed to have used his own money.

These complex political fissures served to bring Ashmole to an Oxford that would, forty years later, come to honor and fête him. Going to Oxford would also bring him to membership of a college cofounded by the same William Smyth, bishop of Lincoln, who had endowed Lichfield's Hospital of St. John as well as the grammar school that was to give Ashmole his second education, after his mother.

Ashmole entered Brasenose College in the heart of Oxford and in the midst of civil war. C. H. Josten believed that it was Brasenose's traditional openness to young men from Cheshire and Lancashire that made Ashmole's entry possible. In particular, it was "likely that Ashmole's family connections among the Cheshire gentry facilitated his admission."[2]

Anthony Wood, while compiling his history of the University of Oxford and her alumni, wrote to Ashmole in January 1673 to ascertain the circumstances of his admission to Brasenose. Ashmole informed Wood that "Doctor Yate [Thomas Yate, principal of Brasenose] can give you the best account of my admittance to Brazenose Colledge which I think was in 1645 [actually 1644] he entered my name in the House Booke."[3]

Residing at Brasenose, Ashmole studied natural philosophy (including botany), mathematics, astronomy, and judicial astrology, working in the college library and the great library (whose assembling was initiated by the extraordinary collector Sir Thomas Bodley in 1596).

Modern readers may be surprised to see Ashmole studying astrology in Oxford in 1644 while a war was raging across the country. There were more important things than political conflicts. Hermetic philosophy still enjoyed a significant following among the learned in the mid-seventeenth century, albeit not with everybody.

Isaac Casaubon's dating of the principal Hermetic philosophical dialogues had doubtless dampened scholarly enthusiasm for texts that had, in the time of Sir Thomas More, been regarded as the relics of pristine, divine wisdom. From an analysis of the Greek employed in the *Corpus Hermeticum* (published in 1614), Casaubon had shown that rather than being the survivors of antediluvian or pre-Mosaic times, the philosophi-

Brasenose College, Oxford (photo taken with the kind permission of the Principal and Fellows of Brasenose College, Oxford).

cal works of Hermes had in fact been written down in the late antique period—that is to say, after Christ. Since the works had formerly been seen as containing hoary prophecies of the Christian religion to come, their theological authority was stunted by Casaubon's study.

Nevertheless, Hermetic wisdom had been too closely bound to the enchantment that surrounded the works of Plato and the Neoplatonists to be discarded simply on chronological grounds; the Hermetic works had spiritual power. The real division in Oxford concerning Hermetic philosophy and its kindred art of astrology went back to the Middle Ages: the age-old antipathy between Aristotle and Plato, between realism and idealism, materialism and magick, the visible and the invisible, the measurable and the occult. The debate goes on quietly today, usually dressed up as a conflict between the "old" and the "new," or "traditional authority" versus "realism" and "modernism." 'Twas ever thus. Much that threatened the medieval Church was labeled "superstition."

Ashmole himself would have encountered little difficulty in locating classic astrological and Hermetic texts in either Brasenose's or Bodley's library. According to C. H. Josten: "Until Sir Isaac Newton promulgated the universal law of gravitation, astrology provided the only generally recognised universal law."[4] In fact, when Ashmole was at Oxford, judicial astrology was undergoing a revival following relaxation of censorship after years of suppression. Astrology was enjoying her last Indian summer of intellectual legitimacy. When that summer was over, Ashmole's intellectual relevance to posterity would, mistakenly in the author's opinion, be downgraded.

ASTROLOGY

At the crown of astrological theory stands the Hermetic principle: *That which is above is like that which is below,* or as William Blake expressed it, "God is in the lowest effects as well as in the highest causes." Or, again, as Elias Ashmole summarized the matter in his personal motto: *Ex Uno Omnia:* From the One, All.

Life on earth is part of, and reflective of, a vast cosmic pattern; the universe is bound by kinship or by "correspondences." Certain properties attract each other by analogy. For example, copper corresponds to the color green, as well as the planet Venus. This is simple enough. Copper ore (malachite) is green and the goddess Venus (love) is associated with vegetation (fertility). To attract the powers of Venus, one might therefore wear a copper implement and be dressed in green. If a person is "in love," he or she literally feels a "power of the universe"; no wonder people are apt to lose their heads!

Emblem from Malachias Geiger's *Microcosmus hypochondriacus sive de melancolia hypochondriaca*, Munich 1651, engraved by Jan Sadeler (1568–1665) (Bibliotheca Philosophica Hermetica, Amsterdam).

According to the theory, within all things there is a hidden substance ("occult virtue") that responds particularly to the action of "like" or kindred substances and processes, like a dog looking up at the distant arrival of its master. Poetry of course works by analogy, reinforced with incantatory rhythm. Common speech gains in force by the correct use of adjectives. Adjectives work by magical analogy.

For example, compare the following: "His speech was met by silence" and "His speech was met by a stony silence." The use of the *idea* (occult virtue) of "stone" *conjures up* (magick) a whole chain of correspondences: cold, still, implacable, impenetrable, gravelike, inert, dead, dry, hard, heavy, and so on. Politicians often use rhythms of three to hypnotize (if they're "bad") or "mesmerize" (if they're "good") their followers—if, that is, the followers have a will to follow.

Grasp of English has now declined to such a point that mere repeated nouns in threes "grab" headlines: *Education, education, education . . . Location, location, location . . .* Boring, boring, boring. Boring into your head like a steel wand, "grabbing" your attention. It would be good to meet such speech with the power of silence, even stony silence!

Astrology works on principles common to those that motivate people today and which have always secured the attention of human beings. Why do we say that a certain color "suits" one person and not another? People feel better or "more together" or "on form" on some days rather than others; "this is not my day" is a common complaint. A critic of astrology was apt to say "The fault is not in our stars, but in our selves," launching many a career in psychology. But many an astrologer would agree, because the "stars" *are* in our selves (the microcosm); the gnostic Anthropos (Man) contains the cosmos in himself—that is the ideal of growth that our educationalists (awful word) have utterly lost sight of, if indeed it had ever been in sight.

Seen from the earth, every planet and star is at an angle to everything else (its "aspect"); relationships may be calculated and quantified. Over thousands of years of observation, certain kinds of occurrences were noted as coinciding with stellar configurations. Holst's popular suite *The Planets* (based entirely on astrology) gives an excellent idea of what the planets were thought to represent, and, of course, all those powers evoked in the music—war (Mars), peace (Venus), old age (Saturn),

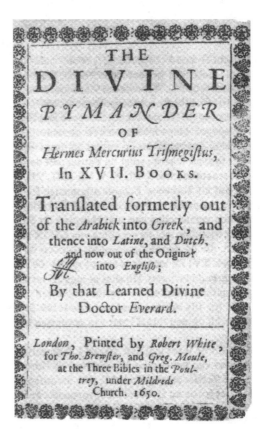

Above: Mercurius, or Hermes, as revealer of esoteric secrets in Achille Bocchi's *Symbolicarum Quaestionum, de universo genere, Bononiae, Soc. typogr. Bononiensis*, 1574.

Right: *The Divine Pymander* of Hermes Mercurius Trismegistus, translated by Dr. Everard, DD, in 1650.

jollity (Jupiter), the messenger (Mercury/Elias)—exist in ourselves. Into the unknown world of the cosmos, man projected, and found, himself.

Broadly speaking, astrology and alchemy represent a psychological science, requiring the art of interpretation, while modern science is external or measurable science.

In astrology, time is not a mere linear progress for purposes of quantitative knowledge ("in two hours from now . . ."). Time is not an amount of connected "nows." Time is a continuum that has variable qualitative potential; its reality and nature are not exhausted by its measurement (seconds). Time, as Plotinus thought, is the "moving image of eternity." The quality of time can be changed by the influence of the stars and planets or by higher agencies such as the divine will exercised by angels (messengers) or the stars' secret "governors."

But what does the world "look like" from the point of view of astrology? How does it differ from what most people today perceive to be normal?

Look at a field of grass. Some cows graze upon it. Beside the still cows runs a stream. Now close your eyes and imagine the same scene, only this time see the stars glowing in daytime, their light penetrating the blue; see the earth revolving slowly, the appearance of sun and moon, the orderly transits of planets producing new patterns, new intensities. Now see magic lines joining all of the dominant aspects of the scene together through their distributed elements—earth, air, fire, water—behind the scene, an invisible fire that touches the heart of things. Everything meets everything else; to see one aspect is to see the whole: the breath of the cow, the flow of the stream, the setting of the sun, the cows going to sleep, the sweet gaze of the moon on the water, the warm earth turning damp and cold. Now take your eyes higher and higher. Venus has risen from the earth bursting with night-light.

Feel the dew, the stars' rich secretion, forming on your toes as the silver guides twinkle in their silent progress. Then imagine a star within, within your mind, moving in its orderly way through the whole of your life as your conscious mind wanders, occasionally touched by the inner star forming questions: *Who am I? Where did I come from? Where am I going?*

This florid vision is only that which Elias Ashmole saw; the questions are only those that he asked three and a half centuries ago.

For help in answering these questions, perturbed humanity has visited sensitive men and women—and not a few insincere fakers—to have their birth charts calculated. For Ashmole, gazing above and beyond the crashing tumults of his times to the timeless principles that lay behind them, a message or imprint of the universe had been imparted in the earthly soul of every being at the time of birth.

Unique potentialities blended into a subtle system of more or less general principles of destiny and conduct. Within each person lived the image of a mini-universe, an inner reflection of the outer universe. This inner being was called the *microcosm* and it had its own special codes that bound it in relation to all of life's possibilities, being itself co-creative in those possibilities. The "real person" was a microcosm with every limb and organ corresponding to the external cosmos. God, according to Genesis, made the cosmos and then made man out of its substance. What we call *dust* is nonetheless "a heaven in a grain of sand." As Christ said, "The kingdom of heaven is within you."

As C. H. Josten observed of the theory of judicial astrology—that is, astrology relating to human personalities and their development: "Character and destiny were conceived as analogous effects of a higher reality transcending human comprehension."[5] Man really had no choice but to do "the will of God," though there was virtue in choosing to do so consciously. No man could know the whole will of God, but with deep care, one could find a portion of that will in oneself—as well as in nature and the stars above.

Astrology offered practitioners glimpses of the hidden order of life. The aim was to bring conduct into harmony with the hidden order (or *logos*). It was also legitimate to counteract negative influences: The universe being a duality, there were checks and balances, compensatory laws for all possible situations. The stars ruled but, perhaps paradoxically, did not compel. God had introduced a moral dimension into the system (He is with us always) to which the stars and their governors were themselves "indifferent." Man could choose, but the order as a whole was determined, insofar as it followed law. Love is also a law, a commandment.

Scripture gave some idea of ultimate purposes but no detail as to the mechanism. The astrologer could glimpse and make relative predictions but he could not prophesy, at least not from astrology alone. Astrology was an art of interpreting a certain science; it offered not revelation but rather a guide to possibility, probability, and potentiality.

THE INTELLIGENCER

Astrology did provide order in the wayward fortunes of life, and its attraction must therefore have been the stronger to an Ashmole who, at this time of his own journey, occasionally felt himself to be at sea, the misty, marshy, muddy horizon from Marston to Littlemore uncertain. In fact, the whole country was on tenterhooks and both sides of the conflict published newspapers with "Mercurius" in their titles, purporting to be authoritative messages from on high. The royalist weekly *Mercurius*

Aulicus, published in 1643, was swiftly followed by the parliamentarian riposte *Mercurius Britanicus* (later called *Mercurius Politicus* in the 1650s). Mercury of course always had another side: trickster, god of trade. The opposing Mercuries were propaganda.

While at Oxford in May 1645, Ashmole had the good fortune to meet the learned astrologer and cavalier George Wharton. They would become friends until Wharton's death on August 12, 1681. Ashmole and Wharton shared their knowledge and enthusiasm; neither man was going to let the war destroy his personal quest for understanding.

Two of Ashmole's personal gifts conjoined in astrology: first, his talent for observation, combined with an excellent memory. He observed people, nature, objects, and documents closely. He sought and, more often than not, he found. Second, he had a remarkable talent for bringing together disparate material, sensing a hidden pattern, and reducing it to an order. This talent would make him what at the time was sometimes dubbed an Intelligencer, as useful in war as in peace.

Ashmole's biographer C. H. Josten expressed the matter thus: "His greatest gift was to penetrate rapidly into abstruse and difficult matters, to collect facts as well as objects in a careful and judicious manner, and then (to use his own phrase) to 'digest' them 'into one body,' whether this was a memorandum, a book, or a museum, which would, not unlike a catalyst, impart a significant stimulus to others without manifestly making an original contribution to the resulting change."[6]

This account from one intelligence officer with respect to another is very insightful. Like the wind, you cannot see it, but when it passes, the trees bend. Ashmole, the Geminian soul, was born under an air sign: Ariel and Prospero combined. Hermes and Elias were both messengers from the heavens, almost interchangeable in significance.

Ashmole saw himself as "human mercury," an agent for transformation, moving swiftly twixt earth and heaven, almost invisible: a presence. In the frontispiece to his translation of *Fasciculus Chemicus* (1650), he hides his face behind his astrological birth chart. The *essential* Elias was a kind of incarnation of the Hermetic principle; the real man could be found in the stars, albeit with his feet on the ground.

Men such as Ashmole are few in number, and vitally necessary. Like the Englishman of George Santayana's observation, "It will be a black

Frontispiece of *Fasciculus Chemicus* (An Alchemical Posy), translated by Ashmole and published by him in 1650.

day for the human race when scientific blackguards, churls, and fanatics manage to supplant him." Men of Ashmole's cast stimulate the conditions that enable the genius of an Einstein, Newton, or Mozart to flourish. He was a master's master, most recognized by the few, not subject to that democratic assessment whose choices lie invariably between mediocre and superficial options. Democracy has always been a means chosen by the sick to control the healthy.

If these gifts of Ashmole's were obvious to discerning scholars in his antiquarian works, they were no less intrinsic to his continuous engagement with drawing up astrological "figures" or "schemes" (as he called them) for himself and others. What appeared first as advice to ladies seeking husbands (there were many more young widows in Ashmole's day) would eventually serve the deliberations of the monarch and his senior ministers.

Readers may want to know a little more about the principles governing Ashmole's countless schematic responses to what he referred to as "horary questions."

Ashmole's "figures" showed the positions of the sun and the moon as well as the seven known planets within the familiar twelve signs of the zodiac. The zodiac was divided into twelve "houses," six above and six below the horizon, six east and six west of the meridian. The "cusp" or beginning of the first house (the "ascendant") always coincides with the eastern point of the horizon, the seventh house cusp, with its western point. The cusps of the tenth house ("mid heaven") and the fourth are determined by the meridian.

The distribution of the cusps of intermediary houses varied depending on the system employed by the several authors. It should be emphasized that while there was science in astrology (astro-*nomy,* the law of the stars), interpretation (astro-*logy*—the *logos* or "word" of the stars) was an art, and like all art required experience and individual human sensitivity. It is therefore inappropriate for a scientist to dismiss astrology for not being science; man cannot live by bread (law) alone.

Horary judgments were based on "favorable" or "unfavorable" positions (or "conjunctions") of planets in the zodiac and in the twelve houses. Harmonious and disharmonious characteristics of certain angles ("aspects") at which the sun, moon, and planets "beheld one another" were also taken into consideration. Plotting the angles or aspects required some knowledge of geometry. The when and how of constructing a significant building involved both an astrological and a geometrical aspect. A *sign*ificant building contained a "sign," a celestial signal.

Different aspects of the celestial pattern touched planet Earth in different ways at different times, as did the rays of the sun and the moonlight that had such a demonstrable effect on planetary existence. These aspects might condition any significant detail of life. For example, a horoscope of the time in which a letter arrived could inform the astrologer of the writer's sincerity or hidden intentions. Horoscopes could be used to decide on the advisability of a projected meeting or "scheme," or even the laying of a foundation stone.

Furthermore, one might plan one's future activities around propitious times. A number of projected scenarios could be set up as "figures." The

Above: Detail from the frontispiece of *Fasciculus Chemicus*, 1650.

Right: Engraving of Ashmole by William Fairthorne, 1656.

resulting figures were called "elections." According to Ashmole's *Theatrum Chemicum Britannicum*: "by Elections we may Governe, Order and Produce things as we please: *Faber quisque Fortunae propriae* [Every man is the maker of his own fortune]."[7]

ASHMOLE'S PERSONA

Astrology also provided Ashmole with insights into psychology. Like any psychologist today, he had to analyze himself according to the ancient Greek dictum *gnothi seauton*, know thyself. In Ashmole's nativity figure, he discerned that Mercury was the most powerful planet. Further delight would have stemmed from the observation that it was favorably disposed in Gemini and in near conjunction with the Sun. Any contemporary astrologer might from this alone construct a picture of Ashmole's dominant psychic characteristics.

Ashmole's later close friend the parliamentarian astrologer William Lilly also analyzed Ashmole's horoscope, with the added advantage of knowing the man personally. Lilly (who was to predict astrologically the execution of the king) arrived at conclusions demonstrated by history. He was happy to pass them on to Ashmole's first literary observer, Anthony Wood.

Ashmole, wrote Lilly, was "of an hott and moyst complexion, very near into a perfect sanguine, not tall but of an upright, slender and well proportioned stature." He had "a good lovely face" with a scar, good eyesight, beautiful eyes and skillful hands. His hair "was of a kind of red or sandy color." In his middle age he was "of a brown ruddy complexion."[8]

Ashmole's manner was "of a certain gravity . . . commixed with a kind of pleasantness or decency therein." He could be "accidentally choller-ick." All his actions were governed "by reason and judgement." "Not-withstanding the sharpness of his natural fancy [humor or imagination] is much quickened," he would incline to "counsell and discretion." That is to say, while he was wont to express great enthusiasm, he would judge, take advice if necessary, and act with his feet firmly on the ground. What a "privileged blend" was Ashmole! His Staffordshire upbringing with its native common sense along with his mother's firm influence doubtless played their part in shaping his attitudes and demeanor.

Ashmole did not reveal himself to all and sundry; he was not inse-cure. He would, according to Lilly, "open his heart only to few persons and for the most part, keep to himself that which really occupied his mind."

In Lilly's assessment, the conjunction of Mercury with certain fixed stars gave Ashmole "profound judgement," sagacity, "prodigious parts in all human learning," and a good memory. The combination of "aspects" made him very industrious, "Curioing [sic] together with much Carefulness and Fearfulness" made him "such a person as would know all things, having an itch after Noveltys."

While Ashmole's wisdom was well rooted and watered in the past, he delighted in the flora of futurity. He was open to and interested in new things, fascinated by invention and ingenuity. He believed in the better possibilities of humankind, knowing the extraordinary depth and wealth of our hidden—and largely unexplored—spiritual and techno-logical potential. He did not cry about mankind's hideous catalog of failings; rather he rejoiced in our species' successes, and tried to put our negativity into the larger, wholesome perspective. It had more than once crossed his mind that the Earth looked different from above.

The study of astrology gave Ashmole a more refined sense of bal-ance than common sense alone. All of Ashmole's qualities, noted Lilly, "excited him unto so high and deep learning as he is Master of, and hath been ever from his infancy or primary studyies."

The favorable position of Mercury in Gemini also endowed Ash-mole with "admirable sharp fancys" (excellent wits and imagination), "extreme studious and capable of learning, guileful or wily, wise, wary, divining well, or giving good advice, acting all human affaires with great dexterity and judgement." Lilly concluded that Ashmole's genius "natu-rally inclined" to the "Mathematicks, Astrology, Eloquence, to Magick and also to Musick." He would "learn any Art with much ease."

Booking into Brasenose College in 1644, Ashmole was psychologi-cally well suited to being the Renaissance Man. But what does the Ren-aissance Man do in times of war?

He takes the seat of Mars, and he fights—while, beneath the breast-plate and the plume, he thinks, he studies, he observes, he seeks.

DEFENDING OXFORD

At his friend George Wharton's suggestion, Ashmole was commissioned as captain in the king's cavalry in May 1645 and became one of four Gentlemen of the Ordnance in the Oxford garrison. He was ordered to attend a fortified position to the east of Magdalen College.

In March 1643, the river Cherwell had been dammed to protect the city's eastern flank. The raised walk at Magdalen College, now called Addison's Walk, with its water ditch, was probably constructed at this time. The walk leads to a bastion commanding the Cherwell. That bas-tion was called Dover Pier, after the Earl of Dover who first commanded it. Elias Ashmole was given charge of the eastern artillery defenses and stationed at Dover Pier. His knowledge of mathematics would have helped him achieve the posting, since artillery's effectiveness depends on

The site of Dover Pier, Ashmole's artillery defense position to the east of the city of Oxford.

accurate calculation of height, distance, weight, and reaction, as well as earth construction.

Ashmole, not surprisingly, was also involved in intelligence work. He devised codes used for carrying messages between royalist headquarters in Oxford and the Lichfield garrison. These coded messages were received and deciphered by John Hill, Ashmole's fellow commissioner of excise.

Ashmole began keeping a diary, in cipher, in 1645; it ran for four years and is the source of valuable knowledge of his activities. According to Josten, himself a government officer before becoming curator of the Museum of the History of Science at Oxford, Ashmole seems to have learned cipher between 1643 and 1645.

It was possible for Josten to translate the cipher because a copy of magus and cryptographer John Dee's *Monas Hieroglyphica* of 1564[9] also appeared in a cipher version.[10] It transpired that the cipher system was identical to that invented by John Willis in the fifth revised edition of his book, *The Art of Stenographie* (1617). It may be asked whether Ashmole's interest in cryptography first brought him to acquaintance with

Monas Hieroglyphica (1564) by John Dee.

the reputation and achievements of Dee, Queen Elizabeth I's famous astrologer and polymath. Deep interest in Dee would punctuate Ashmole's adult life, even at his busiest.

Commanding the ordnance in Oxford was Lieutenant General Sir John Heydon. Ashmole would have found much in common with his senior officer. Heydon was also a mathematician and mystically inclined. As they shored up the earth and wicker defenses about their cannon and gazed over the flatlands to the east of Oxford, did Ashmole and Heydon discuss the relative merits of different authors concerning the distribution of cusps of the eighth and ninth zodiacal houses? Could they have been simultaneously in the midst of the stars above as well as in the English Civil War below?

DREAMS AND SPIRES

Within a month of Ashmole's commission, the king's army suffered defeat at Naseby (June 14, 1645). While shock waves reverberated about royalist Oxford, Ashmole began to record his dreams. In the seriousness he attached to the life of the unconscious, he might well be regarded as having been considerably ahead of his time. C. H. Josten sent Ashmole's notes on his 1645–50 dreams to the great Swiss psychologist (and gnostic) Carl Jung. By doing so, Josten wisely linked Ashmole's unique life to the rediscovery of the value of the gnostic tradition in the twentieth century.

Jung believed and demonstrated that the Hermetic gnostic spiritual traditions held insights and knowledge of signal importance to the science of psychology as well as to the revival of genuinely spiritual religious consciousness. Jung himself was happy to inform Josten that Ashmole's dream records were "of the greatest interest to historically inclined psychologists, especially as no comparable seventeenth century series of dreams is known to be extant."[11]

Jung's interpretation of Ashmole's dreams rather confirms the author's analysis of Ashmole's childhood influences. Jung noted that Ashmole's dreams at this period revealed an attempt to suppress the *anima*—the feminine aspect of the soul or psyche—in favor of a one-sided masculinity.

It is tempting to see Ashmole's psychodrama played out against Oxford's drizzly backdrop of low-level mist, marsh, mud, and murky dampness that has whisked away many a young man on the black wings of tuberculosis. With only the penetrating spires and towers to cast doubt on the depression of the landscape, this dual atmosphere has always conspired to induce a corresponding dreaminess in sensitive students.

Ashmole was, on the one hand, a fairly mature scholar studying the *heimarmene* ("night-cloak") of the stars—the "body" of the goddess Sophia (Wisdom) whose "seven pillar'd worthy house"[12] was supported by the seven heavenly bodies—while on the other, he was a saber-wielding tutor of artillery, expected to do a man's work for king and country.

The saber and the military arts were the tools of Ashmole's father's absences on foreign campaigns. Ashmole's learning and intuitive development came from his mother, the Sophia of his infancy. The subconscious conflict may well have caused him intense inner conflict, and it is therefore not surprising for the psychologist to find Ashmole's life at this point characterized by strong dreaming. It is also highly likely that

Ashmole sought some measure of understanding and insight consistent with the conscious mind's encounter with the disturbing life and images of the unconscious. He would undoubtedly have found such consistency in alchemy.

According to Josten, Ashmole's first extant notes on alchemy derive from the period 1640–50. He could easily have gained access to alchemical writings from the Bodleian and, possibly, Brasenose College Library (Neoplatonism and Hermeticism were well represented in Brasenose's old library, now secreted).

A group of Ashmolean notes from the Rawlinson Mss. consists of passages from well-known figures of alchemical history. The notes refer to Ashmole's contemporary Cornelius Drebbel, to *Poimandres* (the most famous Hermetic philosophical dialogues), and to the alchemical writers de Nuisement, Cosmopolita, Hero Alexandrinus, Dionysius Halicarnasseus, Xenophon, Polybius, *Lipsius in Polybium,* Vegetius, and Thucydides.[13]

The Bodleian Library, Oxford.

An image of the hermaphroditic *Rebis*, so central to alchemical symbology, from *Aurora Consurgens*, a fifteenth-century manuscript (Knihovna University, Prague, Ms. RO. VI. Fd. 26).

The *Magnum Mysterium* of alchemy (when that phrase does not refer to Nature herself) is concerned with the harmonization of opposites and their idealized transcendence into a new unity. This process is sometimes expressed as the "chemical wedding," or *mysterium coniunctionis*, frequently imaged as the copulating couple Sol (sun) and Luna (moon). Masculine and feminine aspects come together to form an ideal hermaphroditic *rebis,* sometimes depicted with wings. (A good example of a highly refined rebis figure is Leonardo da Vinci's enigmatic *John the Baptist.*)

In short, taking up arms was bound to have an effect on the magus-to-be's psychic life. Intriguingly, the resulting drama is, in the author's opinion, idealized five years later in the aforementioned frontispiece to Ashmole's first book, *Fasciculus Chemicus: or Chymical Collections Expressing The Ingress, Progress, and Egress, of the Secret Hermetick Science* (1650).

The highly individualized and stylish engraving—surely directed by Ashmole himself—depicts a riot of images in a liberated style placed upon and between two pillars. The left pillar is covered with the instruments of peace and creativity: a freemason's square and compasses, a

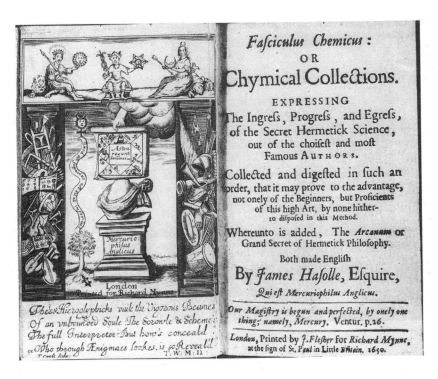

Fasciculus Chemicus, frontispiece and title page.

globe, alchemical instruments, and mathematical and geometrical diagrams. The right-hand pillar predictably illustrates trumpets of war: a cannon, drum, pike, sword, standard, breastplate, and helmet.

Between the opposites: a bust of Ashmole on a plinth, his face obscured by a horoscopic "scheme" with the inscription *Astra regunt homines* (the *stars* rule men)—not, one might infer, Oliver Cromwell, who himself is but a player in the quiet stellar drama's reflection below. As well as being a truism of astrology, the statement may well have been a clever message to sad and disaffected royalists distributed across the country. (It is significant that Ashmole sent a fresh copy of the book to Sir Richard Dyott, the leading royalist figure in Lichfield.) Ashmole's true face was, in these days of Cromwellian hegemony, hidden.

The "scheme" is unfolded as a scroll by a hand from above the clouds. The inscription on the plinth gives us Elias Ashmole's new nickname, Mercuriophilus Anglicus. This is no user of Mercury to dispense propaganda, but a true suitor of the Mercurial principle. Ashmole has become the English Mercury Lover. To the left of the plinth, suspended in the sky like a sudden, sparkling manifestation of invisible fire, is the alchemical sign of Mercury (☿). The symbol is linked by a narrow scroll to the earth below, to an ash tree and a little mole (*Ash-mole* of course), with the Latin inscription *That which is superior* (above) *is like that which is inferior* (below). Above the duality set up by the twin pillars, Hermes is enthroned on a dais with his caduceus and alchemical Azoth symbol. To his right, Sol, to his left, Luna. Monarchy may not temporarily rule the government, but it most certainly rules nature both visible and invisible; Hermes is King.

This charming illustration, with its many-layered meanings, also shows Ashmole's ideal resolution of the psychic struggle between, in Jungian terminology, *animus* (the "masculine" aspect of the soul) and *anima*. The conflict between the life of learning (harmony) and the life of war (conflict)—or of mother (moon) and father (sun)—is transcended on a higher plane where opposites are wed in a new Hermetic being.

As he stood by his cannon in Oxford in the autumn of 1645, it may only be guessed how far Captain Ashmole was from realizing the secret mystery contained in the words inscribed at the foot of the frontispiece to *Fasciculus Chemicus* five years later:

> *These Hieroglyphicks vaile the Vigorous Beames*
> *Of an unbounded Soul: the Scrowle and scheme's*
> *The full Interpreter; But how's conceald*
> *Who through Aenigmaes lookes, is so Reveal'd*
> T:W:M:D

WOMEN

In order to understand Ashmole's burgeoning state of mind further, it is worth noting that he had been a widower for nearly four years. Many's the time he must have sought his soul's partner.

However, for psychic wholeness to emerge (the "unbounded Soul"), it is necessary for the psyche to find its harmony within the "Self." What is more often the case is that the "romantic" seeks his soul's correlate in the being of another, "substitute" self. In this process, nature in her most fundamental, procreative aspect is only too willing to thrust the troubled lover into the arms of a woman, whether spiritual or not; the soul is always seeking its own reflection.

In 1645, Ashmole, no different from the general rule, entered a prolonged period of involvements with a number of women. A true soul guide might have told him that what he (unconsciously) sought in another he would better have found first in himself. But was Ashmole ready to interpret his dreams, to listen to his true soul guide?

The quest to find a lady to fill the perceived hole in his life—and his pocket—would in the end come to disrupt severely his alchemical and magical development. As Jimi Hendrix sang, "Loneliness is such a drag." Very soon, Ashmole would himself express, in the grandeur of contemporary poetry to be sure, the self-same message.

In October 1645, only a month after he began to keep a record of his dreams, Ashmole first set eyes on a certain Mrs. March in the library of Brasenose College, a natural venue, one might think, for a wandering consciousness to gaze up from a difficult or tedious text. Elizabeth

The library as it is today. (Photos by kind permission of the Principal and Fellows of Brasenose College, Oxford.)

March was a widow with six children; her capricious character would later cause much vexation for Elias.

Ashmole enjoyed—though "suffered" might be better—a number of flirtations with other ladies. They did not disappear simply because there was a war on. Indeed, the number of young widows was likely to increase. Bridget Thornborough was only eighteen, the granddaughter of the late bishop of Worcester. Ashmole cast her horoscope—a highly useful strategy for fascinating ladies—only to discover that she would fall ill, "either of too much eating or too much lechery." Whether the droll Ashmole informed her of the prospect we know not; such knowledge would hardly have suited his purposes, if indeed Jung's assertion that the period marked an attempt of a "one-sided masculinity" to gain control over the mysterious *anima* is to be credited.

What does the Renaissance Man do in times of war?

Why, sir, he falls in love.

WORCESTER

In October 1645, the Royalist High Command at Oxford appointed Ashmole commissioner of excise for the City and County of Worcester. The posting, which may have involved intelligence work, seems to have been the idea of a fellow mathematician, Sir John Heydon.

Heydon gave Ashmole a letter of introduction to Lord Jacob Astley, lieutenant general of the king's forces in Worcestershire, Staffordshire, Shropshire, and Herefordshire. In the letter, Heydon described Ashmole as "an able, diligent and faithfull man": someone who could be trusted.

Ashmole left Oxford, owing Brasenose College four quarters' worth of unpaid battels (accounts for provisions), and under favorable stars. He predicted riches to come by honor and preferment, as well as "much mirth and happiness."

Most of us tend to confuse pleasure with happiness; Ashmole was no exception. According to William Lilly the younger, Ashmole was remiss in the duties of religion, "more to mind his pleasure than the service of God." Ashmole's duties in Worcester left him leisure to philander.

A cipher note for March 6, 1646, records a "conjunction" (expressed in symbols) of Mercury and Venus, with someone whose name began with "Mur-." Ashmole used the Mercury symbol (☿) to denote himself. As Josten observes of this 8:15 p.m. encounter, "the conjunction he records was probably not astrological."[14]

Between the lecherous embraces, big events were taking place. On April 27, Charles I was compelled to flee Oxford in disguise, leaving the city to an advancing parliamentarian force. He headed for Scotland to try to raise another army. Six weeks later, the parliamentary army began a bombardment of Worcester's defenses. On June 12, Ashmole took up command of ordnance in the fort, but his mind was occupied with other things.

Ashmole had fallen in love with Lady Thornborough, the "very covetous" mother of the aforementioned Bridget Thornborough whom he had met in Oxford.[15] Both ladies asked him the significance of their dreams. This was an intimate road. On May 3, 1646, Lady Thornborough sent for Ashmole at 11:30 in the morning: "I went to her and found her in bed," he wrote. "Then she told me her dream."[16]

On June 15, Lady Thornborough departed from Worcester, leaving Ashmole heartbroken. He was also in love with her daughter, and he dreamed of both.

As the royalist garrison negotiated surrender terms with the besiegers, Ashmole proposed to the irresistible Miss Bridget Thornborough. She refused; Ashmole composed a touching elegy.

He bade farewell to "the glory of those former days" when he enjoyed learned conversation and the joy of good books, when his health was excellent (Oxford would not have improved it), when his mind was filled with "noble Speculations," untainted by "Ambitious thoughts"; "When the whole yeare seem'd Spring," when Nature's "choycer Rarities" delighted, and "vanquisht stars" resigned their "weaker light" to the "grand power" of Venus, the Morning Star:[17]

> . . . Then, then all Houres lookt lovely, and each free
> Delight, seem'd th'pledge of long Felicity.
> But since those glorious Joyes have fled my Heart
> Since Desolation seiseth every parte,
> Since my sad Soule left lost to all Content,
> Farewell, blest dayes; (Fates pleasure I'le adore,)
> Such I once saw, but such must see no more.

Site of Smallwood Manor,
Cheshire, home of Peter
Mainwaring and his family.

Oxford surrendered to parliament on June 20. Lichfield held out until July 14. Worcester was the last garrisoned city to fall—and with it the royalists' fortunes—on July 24.

Ashmole swore an oath to resign from the fighting and was allowed to go home. But where was home now? He decided to head for the hearth of his beloved father-in-law, Peter Mainwaring, at Smallwood, Cheshire.

FIVE

Defeat and Rebirth: Freemasonry

O ne week after Worcester's surrender, Ashmole entered the devastation that was now Lichfield, her cathedral ruined, its central spire demolished by parliamentarian cannon. Going to his mother's house in Women's Cheaping, Ashmole was met by the dejected vicar of St. Mary's, opposite Ashmole's birthplace, who informed him that his mother was dead. Ann Ashmole had died on Friday, July 9, one of over 800 victims of the plague that had ravaged the city during the cruel siege.

Yet again, Ashmole was too late to comfort his dearest in the fatal hour of need. He was twenty-nine years old, and in despair.

Ashmole had not been long in Smallwood when feelings of guilt emerged through the medium of dreams. He dreamed that his mother came to his room to tell of her deep disappointment in him. She told her only son of how she had walked from Lichfield to Brereton (about six miles to the northwest). There she waited, in vain. Giving up hope of seeing him, she returned to Lichfield to die without his comfort. Ashmole was distressed; the hole in his life grew greater still.

Perhaps because he was driven to fill that hole as hastily as possible, an encounter with a distant relative, the twenty-four-year-old Elinor

Minshull, quickly developed into a romantic obsession. Elinor was the second daughter of Captain Peter Minshull of Erdeswick Hall, Minshull Vernon, Cheshire. The Cheshire Minshulls were relatives of the Mainwarings, and as such he referred to her as his "cousin."

On August 15, 1646, Ashmole recorded another dream: "About an hour before sunrising that Elinor Minshull came into my office and seemed very big with child and had a hat on which I imagined she put on that strangers should think her a married wife because she had a great belly and yet this was at a time when she should be married to me, and notwithstanding I could not but love her and thought to marry her though she was got with child by another."[1]

Ashmole wanted to be taken seriously as a suitor of eligible Cheshire ladies, but was stricken by his lack of adequate funds: a not untypical scholar's dilemma, especially now that his brief military career had collapsed in defeat. On October 9 he recorded another dream involving Elinor: "Morning, that Elinor Minshull came and told me she was married to Humphrey Carter and showed me 3: to 4: pieces of gold that he had sent her and implied that if I had given her gold, or that I had been rich, I might have had her."[2]

Ashmole's pride was taking a battering from all sides. Perhaps, he wondered, the most acceptable course would be to take ship and quit his homeland. On August 22 he cast an astrological "figure" to answer the "horary question": "4.30' after noon whether it will be best for ☿ [me (denoted by the sign for mercury)] to go beyond sea or stay in England."[3]

Just over a week later, he told his cousin Mullins that he would give his house to some of his uncle John's youngest sons "if I went beyond [the] sea."[4] Where exactly he proposed to go beyond the sea is not recorded, though crossing the Channel seems too little a distance to warrant the phrase. Perhaps he was thinking of the West Indies or New England. His mind, it seems, was already at sea.

At 6:30 on the afternoon of September 6 he asked the horary question whether he should marry "Jane Tak[. . .]k."[5] The lady with the unusual surname has not been identified. On the same day, similar indecisiveness and confusion appear to have led him to the ministrations of a fortune-teller.

The results of the occult consultation were definite:

> [T]hat I shall set forth my journey toward London upon a Monday/ because I am in danger of waters/ and not to travel either upon the Wednesday nor Friday following not to make complaint or claim to my house as yet [his uncle in Lichfield seems to have taken possession in Elias's absence]/ that I love women and to be careful of my choice that I left my wellwishers in Worcester, and have resolved to speak to Mrs: Minshull/ but not to have any more to say to her/ I shal first see her again on a Sunday in London and be married upon a Monday within 12 months/ 'tis best to go in crimson apparel.[6]

Three days later, "Between 4 and 5: after noon I took leave of my cousin Elinor Minshull and told her that she then part[ed] with the truest friend that she ever had or should have and at 8 a clock and 8 30' after noon I took a second leave."[7]

On September 12, Ashmole's amorous attentions found yet another object. It is not recorded whether he was wearing crimson apparel at the time. "About 4 after noon I first saw the Lady Fitton at Gosworth."[8] This lady was Felicia, daughter of Ralph Sneyd of Keele, second wife and widow of Sir Edward Fitton, Second Baronet, of Gawsworth Hall, Cheshire. (Gawsworth Hall still stands on the Congleton-to-Macclesfield Road.) Lady Fitton's forebear Mary Fitton was the supposed "Dark Lady" of Shakespeare's sonnets; such a one might have been eminently suitable for Ashmole's peculiar interests.

Gawsworth Hall, Cheshire.

An idea seems to have been growing in his mind—hardly an original one in this period of fortunes hurriedly gained and quickly lost. If he had not the means to marry, then by marriage he might find the means. Ashmole made a horoscope for the "annual revolution" of his nativity. The planets' position in the eighth house, "the house of women's substance," showed that "I shall labour for a fortune with a wife and get it . . . without pains and easily."[9] This fateful assurance would come at a price.

Perhaps jumping the gun somewhat, Ashmole consulted the stars on September 26, 1646, as to "whether I should marry Lady Fitton"—after which time, Lady Fitton drops out of Ashmole's amorous cast and the scene of his life's play changes abruptly.[10]

> 1646
>
> Oct: 16. 4.30. p.m. I was made a Free Mason at Warrington in Lancashire with Coll: Henry Mainwaring of Karincham in Cheshire.
>
> The names of those that were then of the Lodge,
>
> Mr: Rich Penket Warden, Mr: James Collier, Mr: Rich. Sankey, Henry Littler, John Ellam, Rich: Ellam & Hugh Brewer.[11]

Of all Ashmole's extensive esoteric interests, his decision to become a "Free Mason" has perhaps aroused the greatest controversy. His brief

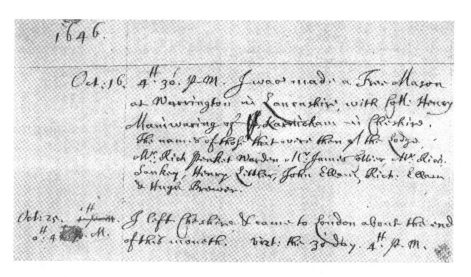

Ashmole's record of his initiation (Bodleian Library, Ashmole collection).

memorial note has long been considered to be the first record of initiation into "speculative Freemasonry," its date of 1646 strangely in advance of the generally accepted date for the establishment of "speculative Free-masonry" as an organization. A "Grand Lodge" is first mentioned in Reverend James Anderson's *Constitutions* of Freemasonry, 1723, refer-ring to the year A.D. 1716.

The adjective speculative has been used since the nineteenth century to distinguish symbolic and ritual Freemasonry from the "operative" trade of masons and freemasons (builders, architects, sculptors). However, recent researches into the origins of Freemasonry have suggested that at least in the seventeenth century, no appropriate contemporary distinc-tion may be supposed between "symbolic, ritual" freemasonry and the so-called "operative" craft. What, then, had Elias Ashmole joined in his darkest hour?

FREE MASONRY

All of the English seventeenth-century evidence points toward Ashmole's having passed through an "Acception" ceremony, following which rit-ual or rituals he became a "Fellow" of the Craft. The Acception was run from within the world of the Freemasons' companies that had emerged out of the medieval guild system. Accepted Free Masons appear to have constituted a kind of upper echelon or club in the freemasons' world.

Accepted brothers were encouraged to operate according to close ties of mutual loyalty, concentrating on the universal and symbolic meanings of architecture, especially the historical, spiritual, and religious content of masonic traditions, which were very great and, in a religious world, greatly significant.

Looking at the evidence for Accepted Free Masonry cannot help but give us important clues as to Ashmole's inner world, for so much of the tradition ties in closely to his general outlook, both antiquarian and spiritual. There is also evidence that Ashmole himself intended to write a history of Freemasonry.

According to C. H. Josten, the best short account of Ashmole's life was that by John Cambell, LLD (1708–85). Dr. Campbell's biographical article on Ashmole states that Ashmole collected material for a history of Freemasonry, the notes for which existed among Ashmole's papers in 1687. Campbell's account reads as follows:

> As to the ancient history of Freemasons, about whom you are desir-
> ous of knowing what may be known with certainty, I shall only tell
> you, that if our worthy brother E.Ashmole Esq; had executed his
> intended design, our fraternity had been as much obliged to him
> as the brethren of the most noble Order of the Garter. I would not
> have you surprised at this expression, or think it at all too assum-
> ing. . . . What from Mr E.A's collection I could gather, was, that
> the report of our Society's taking rise from a Bull granted by the
> Pope in the reign of Henry III, to some Italian architects, to travel
> all over Europe to erect chapels was ill-founded. [The "Comacene
> theory" of Masonic origins: The architects were supposed to have
> come from around Lake Como, survivors of the fall into barbarism.]
> Such a Bull there was, and those architects were Masons; but this
> Bull, in the opinion of the learned Mr. A was confirmative only, and
> did not by any means create our fraternity, or even establish them
> in this kingdom.

Dr. Campbell suggested inquirers look into the stories of St. Alban and King Edwyn, in whose time masons were supposed to have been active. Campbell furthermore asserted that Mr. Ashmole was more understanding of, and better acquainted with, these stories of masonic origins than those who would ascribe a late date to Freemasonry. Campbell bases his view on the existence of some of Ashmole's manuscripts wherein were to be found "very valuable collections relating to the history of the Free Masons." This text is footnoted, "What is hinted above, is taken from a book of letters, communicated to the author of this life, by Dr. Knipe of Christ-church."[12]

One of the letters, dated June 9, 1687, is from a "Dr. W" to Sir D. N. (possibly Sir Dudley North, 1641–91), and contains a long passage relating to the early history of freemasonry. Marginal note no. 4 reads "History of Masonry, p.3" while two further notes accompanying later passages of the text of Dr. W's letter to Sir D. N. refer to pages 19 and 29 of the same "History of Masonry."

It follows that there must have been in existence in 1687 a manuscript or printed document of no fewer than twenty-nine pages, and Josten concludes that this was "a lost manuscript volume containing Ashmole's collections on the subject, which may formerly have been among the Ashmolean manuscripts at Oxford." It is to be greatly regretted—not for the last time—that such a text, if it ever existed, is now lost: destroyed, mislaid, or stolen.

So, it seems likely that Ashmole believed he had entered into an ancient fraternity. What else do we know of this fraternity apart from the fact that he perceived its lineage to be of antiquarian interest?

After Ashmole established his famous museum in Oxford, he approved the appointment of Dr. Robert Plot as its first curator. Plot was to be the author of *The Natural History of Staffordshire,* published in 1686. In chapter eight, he gives an account of "Free-masons" in the moorlands of Staffordshire:

> To these add the Customs relating to the County, whereof they
> have one, of admitting Men into the Society of Free-masons, that

Title page of Dr. Robert Plot's *Natural History of Staffordshire* (1686). Note the caduceus, square, and dividers, placed to the figure's right.

in the moorelands of this County seems to be of greater request, than anywhere else, though I find the Custom spread more or less all over the Nation; for here I find persons of the most eminent quality, that did not disdain to be of this Fellowship. Nor indeed need they, were it of that Antiquity and honor, that is pretended in a large parchment volum they have amongst them, containing the History and Rules of the craft of masonry. Which is there deduced not only from sacred Writ, but profane story, particularly that it was brought into England by Saint Amphibal, and first communicated to S.Alban, who set down the Charges of masonry, and was made paymaster and governor of the Kings works, and gave them charges and manners as St. Amphibal had taught him. Which were after confirmed by King Athelstan, whose youngest son Edwyn loved well masonry, took upon him the charges and learned the manners, and obtained for them of his father a free-charter. Whereupon he caused them to assemble at York, and to bring all the old books of their craft, and out of them ordained such charges and manners, as they then thought fit: which charges in the said Schrole or parchment volum, are in part declared: and thus was the craft of masonry grounded and confirmed in England. It is also there declared that these charges and manners were after perused and approved by King Hen.6. and his council, both as to Masters and Fellows of this right Worshipfull craft.

Into which Society when they are admitted, they call a meeting (or Lodge as they term it in some places) which must consist at lest of 5 or 6 of the ancients of the Order, whom the candidates present with gloves, and so likewise to their wives, and entertain with a Collation according to the custom of the place: This ended, they proceed to the admission of them, which chiefly consists in the communication of certain secret signes, whereby they are known to one another all over the Nation, by which means they have maintenance whither ever they travel : for if any man appear though altogether unknown that can shewe any of these signes to a Fellow of that Society, whom they otherwise call an accepted mason, he is obliged presently to come to him, from what company or place soever he be in, nay tho' from the top of a steeple, (what hazard or inconvenience soever he run) to know his pleasure, and assist him; viz. if he want work he is bound to find him some; or if he cannot do that, to give him mony, or otherwise support him till work can be had; which is one of their articles; and it is another, that they advise the Masters they work for, according to the best of their skill, acquainting them with the goodness or badness of their materials; and if they be in any way out in the contrivance of their buildings modestly to rectify them in it; that masonry be not dishonoured: and many such like that are commonly known: but some others they have (to which they are sworn after their fashion) that none know but themselves, which I have reason to suspect are much worse than these, perhaps as bad as the History of the craft it self; than which there is nothing I ever met with, more false or incoherent.[13]

Plot's references to Free-masons operating in the Staffordshire moorlands makes much sense when one considers that the entire area had until the Reformation been dominated by three Cistercian monasteries built and maintained by freemasons: Croxden, Dieulacres, and Abbey Hulton. Furthermore, we know that freemasons (the trade) were indeed active in the Staffordshire moorlands during Ashmole's lifetime.

Biddulph Parish registers (Stafford Record Office) contain many names of people connected with quarrying and masonry. For one unique year, Biddulph's Rector gives us the occupations of those named. Thus we learn that "in 1600. Baptismata. Mar. 6 Joanna, fa. Rumbaldi DURBAR, freemason." Rumbald Durbar was interred in Biddulph Church on April 23, 1610. Biddulph in the Staffordshire moorlands is only three miles southeast from Smallwood across the Staffordshire–Cheshire border, the home of Ashmole's father-in-law.

But what was a "freemason"? The first appearance of the expression "freestone mason" (later shortened to freemason) occurs in London in 1212: *Sculptores lapidum liberorum,* referring to a sculptor of freestone.[14] Freestone is a kind of stone suitable for carving by virtue of its grain and relative softness. On mastering the craft of freestone masonry, these masters were also the architects (as we understand the word today) of Britain and Ireland.

Dr. Plot's account chimes in well with what Dr. Campbell wrote on the views of Ashmole concerning St. Alban and King Edwyn. Indeed,

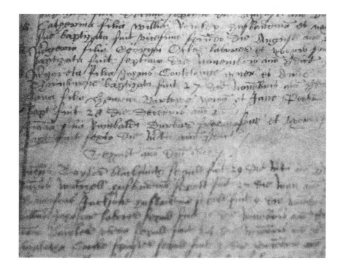

Biddulph Parish register for the year 1610, referring to *"Rumbaldus Durbar, freemasone."* (Stafford Record Office)

one might have reason for thinking the historical account came from the same source—that is, Ashmole himself. The historical information that Plot dismisses (some references are plainly fanciful and legendary) coincides with a document that has come down to us from the Sloane Collection. By a curious coincidence, the manuscript copy dubbed the "Constitutions of Masonry" formerly in the possession of Sir Hans Sloane ends with the following autograph : *"ffinis p.me Eduardu : Sankey decimo sexto die Octobris, Anno domini 1646"*—the very day on which Ashmole and his late wife's cousin Colonel Henry Mainwaring were made Free Masons. Warrington church registers record the baptism of "Edward son to Richard Sankeay [*sic*], gent., 3 ffebruarie, 1621/2." It seems highly likely that this was the son of the Richard Sankey recorded by Elias Ashmole as having been present at his initiation. We may be permitted to imagine Edward Sankey writing out the Charges—perhaps from memory—as part of his father's preparation for the ceremony. Edward Sankey wrote as follows:

> Good brethren & ffellows, our purpose is to tell you, how and in what manner; this Craft of Masonrie was begun; and afterwards founded by worthy Kings and Princes; & many other worshipful men; and also to ym that are heare; wee will declare to ym the Charge yt doth belonge to every true Mason to keep ffor good sooth if you

take heede thereunto it is well worthie to bee kept; or a worthie Craft and curious science, ffor there bee seaven liberall sciences;

before Noes flood was a man called Lameth as it is written in ye 4 chapt of Gene, and this Lameth had 2 wives; ye one was called Adar; ye other Sella: and by Adar hee begott 2 sonnes The one was called Jabell ye other Juball; And by ye other wife hee had a sonne & a Daughter; and these foure children found ye beginninge of all Crafts in ye world; This Jabell was ye elder sonne; and found ye Craft of Geometry;

and these children did knowe that god would take vengeance for sinne eather by fire or water; Wherefore ye writ ye Sciences wch weare found in 2 pillars of stone; yt ye might be found after the flood; The one stone was called Marble that cannot burne wth fire; The other was called Letera that cannot drowne with water; Our intent is to tell you truly how & in what manner these stones weare found; where these Crafts were written in Greek; Hermenes that was sonne to Cus, & Cus was sonne to Shem wch was ye sonne of Noath: The same Hermenes was afterwards Hermes; the ffather of wise men, and hee found out ye 2 pillars of stone where ye Sciences weare written, & taught him forth.

when Abraham and Sara his wife went into Egypt; there weare taught the seaven sciences unto ye Egyptians; And hee had a worthy Schollar called Euchlid and hee Learned right well and was Maister of all ye 7 Sciences;

And there was a King of an other Region yt men called Hyram and hee loved well Kinge Solomon; and gave him timber for his worke; And hee had a sonne that was named Aynon & he was Mr of Geometry; and hee was chiefe Mr of all his Masons; and Mr of all his graved works; and of all other Masons that belonged to ye Temple; & this Witnesseth the Bible in libro 2 Solo capite 5.

And soe it befell that a curious workman; who was named Nimus Graecus & had beene at ye makeinge of Solomons Temple; and came into ffrance; and there taught ye Craft of Masonrie; to ye man of ffrance that was named Charles Martill;

And all this while England was voyde both of any charge or Masonrie; until ye time of St.Albans; And in his time ye King of

England that was a Pagan; and hee walled ye Towne wch is now called St. Albans;

until ye time of King Athelstone; yt was a worthy King of England; and hee brought ye Land into rest and peace againe; and hee builded many great workes & Castles & Abbies; and many other Buildings; and hee loved masons well; and hee had a sonne yt was named Hadrian:

And hee held himself assembly at Yorke and there hee made Masons, and gave ym Charges and taught them Mannrs of Masons; and commanded that rule to bee holden ever after: And to them took ye Charter & Commission to keepe;

And from time to time Masonrie until this day hath beene kept in yt forme & order, as well as might gov'ne ye same; And furthermore at dyvrs assemblies hath beene put to and aded certaine Charges; more by ye best advices; of Mastrs and fellowes; Heare followeth the worthie and godly oath of Masons; Every man that is a Masonn take Heede right well; to this charge; if you finde yo'self guilty of any of these; yt you amend you; againe especially you yt are to bee charged take good heed that you may keepe this Charge; for it is a great perill for a man to foresweare himselfe on a book[.][15]

These are almost certainly the exact words that Elias Ashmole and Colonel Henry Mainwaring heard at their initiation into Accepted Free Masonry. The story of Freemasonry contained therein was central to the oldest documents of freemasons' companies. These documents were called the *Old Charges* and were used to justify the masons' special status as being linked to the creative purposes of the Almighty and His Son, the "foundation stone" of a Church earthly and heavenly.

Plot refers to Free-masons being called "a Fellow of that Society, whom they otherwise call an accepted mason." He does not tell us what precisely he means by an "accepted" mason. There is some mystery here.

The most significant early reference to an "Accepcon"(Acception) occurs in the Renter Warden's Accounts of the *London company of ffreemasons,* 1638, now held in the Guildhall Library, London. Records for 1638 describe a meeting that took place sometime between March and midsummer 1638, the year, incidentally, in which Elias Ashmole married Eleanor Mainwaring.

Five freemasons, already members of the company, paid ten shillings for the privilege of being "accepted"—or perhaps as a contribution to a post-ceremonial feast. We have no idea how long this ceremony had been practiced, as records for the London Freemasons Company before 1619 do not exist.

> Pd wch the accompt [accountant] layd out
> Wch was more than he received of them
> Wch were taken into the Accepcon
> Whereof xs [ten shillings] is to be paid by
> Mr. Nicholas Stone, Mr Edmund Kinsman
> Mr John Smith, Mr William Millis, Mr John Coles.

Readers may note the name of Nicholas Stone. Stone was no footnote to history. King's master mason, close-working colleague of Inigo Jones, architect of the magnificent Banqueting House, Whitehall, "ffreemason

Sculpture of John Donne, St. Paul's Cathedral, by Nicholas Stone the elder. (Photo: Matthew Scanlan)

and citizen of the City of London," sometime Master of the London Company of Freemasons, sculptor of one of the finest sepulchral monuments known to seventeenth-century history (the effigy of John Donne, St. Paul's), Stone was learned in classical mythology and theological symbolism, and encouraged his son to travel to Italy to further such and related practical and theoretical studies.

And yet, for all this, Stone, along with the four other men referred to in the Renter Warden's accounts, while still a member of the London Company of Freemasons, had yet remained a stranger to the "Accepcon" until 1638. In that year he and his colleagues were prepared to pay the large sum of ten shillings for the privilege.

Incidentally, Stone's son, Nicholas Stone the younger (a royalist), was the author of the *Enchiridion of Fortification* (1645). This is a most suggestive title when one realizes that in the year prior to publication, Elias Ashmole was put in charge of Oxford's eastern defenses and a year later made a Free Mason.

The name Stone was not unknown to the Mainwaring family. Two years after the initiation of Colonel Henry Mainwaring and Elias Ashmole, Ellen (née Minshull), the widow of Sir Philip Mainwaring, erected a mortuary chapel at the church at Upper Peover. The life-size marble effigies of herself and her husband were the work of either freemason Nicholas Stone the younger or one of his brothers, John or Henry.[16]

SECRET SIGNS

Dr. Plot's statement in his *Natural History of Staffordshire* that the admission of accepted Free-masons "chiefly consists in the communication of certain secret signes, whereby they are known to one another all over the Nation, by which means they have maintenance whither ever they travel" is attested by seventeenth-century documentary records.

The earliest known English freemasonic catechism, *Sloane Ms. 3329* (British Library), has been dated to c. 1700 or a little earlier, only fifty years or so after Ashmole's initiation.[17] This manuscript (almost certainly referring to operative practices) was bound up by Sir Hans Sloane (1660–1753) in a large volume described as "Loose papers of mine concerning curiosities." Like Ashmole, Sloane was a member of the Royal

Society and, being thirty-two when Ashmole died, he had ample opportunity to encounter the grand old man of British antiquarianism.

In his "Narrative of the Freemasons Word and signes" Sloane gives details of various means by which freemasons recognized one another. The grips for fellow crafts and masters are not those employed today (it is significant that the grips for fellows and masters are different). Sloane says that the former grip was made by thrusting the thumbnail "close upon the third joint of each others' first finger."

Practices seem to have varied; Sloane gives two forms of the master's grip, his information apparently being secondhand, so to speak. Sloane does mention the placing of the feet in a manner identical and familiar to Freemasons today. He then gives an example of "their private discourse" that is worth relating in full, as it seems likely that something very similar to it was experienced by Ashmole and Mainwaring on (possibly) passing to fellow craft on October 16, 1646. (I have put the words in modern spelling and added punctuation—which is almost entirely absent from the original—not having been designed to be written down, but rather memorized.)

Question: Are you a mason?

Answer: Yes, I am a freemason.

Q: How shall I know that?

A: By perfect signs and tokens, and the first points of my Entrance.

Q: Which is the first sign or token? Show me the first and I will show you the second.

A: The first is heal and Conceal or Conceal and keep secret by no less pain than by cutting my tongue from my throat.

Q: Where were you made a Mason?

A: In a just and perfect or just and Lawful Lodge.

Q: What is a just and perfect or just and Lawful Lodge?

A: A just and perfect Lodge is two interprintices, two fellow crafts and two Masters, more or fewer, the more the merrier, the fewer the Better Cheer, but if need require, five will serve, that is, two interprintices, two fellow Crafts and one Master, on the highest hill or Lowest Valley of the world, without the crow of a Cock or the Bark of a Dog.

Q: From whom do you derive your principals?

A: From a greater than you.

Q: Who is that on earth that is greater than a freemason?

A: He it was carried to ye highest pinnacle of the Temple of Jerusalem [note the Christian reference].

Q: Whither is your lodge, shut or open?

A: It is shut.

Q: Where Lies the Keys of the Lodge door?

A: They Ley [sic] in a bound Case or under a three-cornered pavement, about a foot and a half from the Lodge door.

Q: What is the Keys of your Lodge Door made of?

A: It is not made of Wood, Stone, Iron or steel or any sort of metal, but the tongue of a good report behind a Brother's back, as well as before his face.

Q: How many Jewels belong to your Lodge?

A: There are three. The Square pavement, the blazing Star and the Danty tassley [a corruption of "perpend ashlar"].[18]

Q: How long is the Cable rope of your Lodge?

A: As Long as from the Lop of the Liver to the root of the tongue.

Q: How many Lights are in your Lodge?

A: Three. The sun, the master, and the Square.

Q: How high is your Lodge?

A: Without foots, yards, or inches it reaches to heaven.

Q: How Stood your Lodge?

A: East and west, as all holy Temples Stand.

Q: Which is the master's place in the Lodge?

A: The east place is the master's place in the Lodge, and the Jewel resteth on him first, and he setteth men to work. What the masters have in the foornoon [sic], the wardens reap in the Afternoon.

In some places they discourse as followeth (Viz)

Q: Where was the first word given?

A: At the Tower of Babylon.

Q: Where did they first call their Lodge?

A: At the holy Chapel of St. John.

Q: How stood your Lodge?

A: As the said holy Chapel and all other holy Temples stand. (Viz.) east and west.

Q: How many lights are in your Lodge?

A: Two. One to see to go in, and another to see to work.

Q: What were you sworn by?

A: By god and the Square.

Q: Whither above the Clothes or under the Clothes?

A: Under the Clothes.

Q: Under what Arm?

A: Under the right Arm.

Sloane's notes also include reference to the "master's word," which we may suppose might have been given to fellow crafts such as Ashmole and Mainwaring. It is noteworthy also that the word *degree* does not occur in Ashmole's diary entries, nor in the Sloane Mss.

> Another [salutation] they have called the master's word, and is Mahabyn, which is always divided into two words and Standing close With their breasts to each other, the inside of Each other's right Ankle Joints the master's grip by their right hands and the top of their Left hand fingers thrust close on ye small of each other's Backbone, and in that posture they Stand till they whisper in each other's ears ye one Maha- the other replies Byn.

> THE OATH
>
> The mason word and every thing therein contained you shall keep secret. You shall never put it in writing directly or indirectly. You shall keep all that we or attenders shall bid you keep secret from Man, Woman, or Child, Stock or Stone, and never reveal it but to a brother or in a Lodge of Freemasons, and truly observe the Charges in ye Constitution. All this you promise and swear faithfully to keep and observe without any manner of Equivocation or mental Reservation, directly or Indirectly, so help you god and by the Contents of this book. So he kisses the book &c.

The key word Mahabyn has been compared to the Arabic—and particularly Sufic—greeting *muhabba*—that is, "love." This might make sense of a record from John Sleigh's *A History of the ancient Parish of Leek*.[19] Sleigh refers to a tradition that a crusader-knight who was lord of Biddulph returned from the Holy Land in the twelfth century to Biddulph Moor with "paynim" (Saracens) who established themselves there and were the ancestors of the dark-skinned "Biddulph Moor men" who have survived to this day. According to Sleigh, one tradition maintained the Saracen was a mason; contemporary carvings extant in the church of St. Chad in Stafford have been observed to show striking and enigmatic Oriental influences.

Carvings in the church of St. Chad, Stafford, twelfth century.

Saracen knowledge undoubtedly informed the knights of this period who built castles and chapels in Staffordshire and Cheshire. The Crusades were of course a period of great interchange of knowledge between East and West, much of which was practical, esoteric, geometrical, mathematical, scientific, and architectural. The Earl of Chester (c. 1200) was much involved with building, and his favored knights no doubt had access to new processes, or at least to those who could operate them. That some ancient practices from the Middle Ages had been passed down to Ashmole's time is in no way unreasonable, and the key word related above may be one such remnant of a great age of Oriental influence on the West.

For a man such as Ashmole with a deep longing to be acquainted with the records and practices of the past, a man driven by earnest instincts for preservation, a man whose personal concept of salvation seems to be synonymous with *recovery of what was lost:* for such a one, fraternity with the Free Masons must have contained great personal resonance.

To all that, add the references in the *Old Charges* to the ancient, pristine knowledge having been handed down to masons past by the work of Hermes, "the father of wise men," patron of the astro-psychical and alchemical cosmos so dear to Ashmole, and one can begin to grasp the significance of the Craft for him.

Ruins of Beeston Castle, Cheshire, built by order of the crusading knight Ranulphus de Blundeville, Earl of Chester, early thirteenth century. The architecture of Beeston has been compared to the crusader castle at Sahyoun, Syria.

Ashmole was not alone in seeking a link between his own shattered times and the pre-Reformation world. The entire Renaissance had been built on the Platonic idea that education was *remembrance*—what the soul had enjoyed when it danced among the *Ideas,* before projection into earth. Progress lay in the recovery of what was lost, not in the embrace of novelty.

Those who suffered in the process of Parliament claiming and exercising prerogatives formerly held in trust by the king would also find, in the spiritual and practical traditions of Free Masonry, some reassurance and steadying perspective. They might also find signal inspiration for science, or, as Ashmole and his generation called it, "natural magick."

Does the membership of Ashmole's lodge at Warrington tell us anything about what attracted some men to "acception" within the Society of Free-masons?

First, the little lodge at or near Warrington on the Lancashire–Cheshire border was not a coven of esotericists, at least as far as we can tell! Nor was it a discussion group for the latest philosophical "discoveries." What we see is a cross section of the upper middle to higher end of Cheshire and Lancashire society.

The Warrington lodge was largely made up of landed gentlemen from Cheshire and that county's border with south Lancashire: royalists and parliamentarians both, with a significant number from families with traditions of faithfulness to the "old religion," Catholicism. It is reasonable to conclude that for Ashmole, the contact came through the Mainwaring family and its connections with gentry (and probably craftsmen) to the north of the old County Palatine of Chester. But why Warrington?

If, as seems most likely, Ashmole's reference to "Mr Rich: Penket Worden" means that Richard Penket was warden of the lodge (he is mentioned first), then the Penket family name may give us a clue. Friar Thomas Penketh (d. 1487: one of the Penkeths who held lands from the lords of Warrington, the Boteler [Butler] family) was Head Hermit at the Priory of St. Augustine, Warrington. The Penketh coat of arms used to adorn a window in the Warrington Friary and a window in Warrington parish church. The Penkeths also patronized the church at Farnworth, to the west of Warrington.

We see here a suggestive connection between gentleman-landowners and the monastic and parochial system. This was also the case with respect to the Mainwarings in Cheshire and Staffordshire. The adherents of the old religion would have the greatest concern with old family chapels and their ornamentation—never mind the pre-Reformation monastic world to which fifteenth-century members of the Mainwaring family were bound by deeds of confraternity.[20] Puritans and Protestants generally devalued (at best) the physical representations of God's houses.

The Penkeths lived at Penketh Hall, Penketh (a hamlet of Great Sankey), in the time of James I, as they had done since at least the early 1200s, but after 400 years, Richard Penketh sold Penketh Hall to Thomas Ashton, in 1624. The sale appears to have marked the demise of the family's fortunes. It is perfectly possible that this Richard Penketh (or perhaps his son) was the same Richard Penketh who was warden of the lodge Ashmole describes as having gathered at Warrington.

Ashmole refers to a Henry Littler as having been present at his being made a Free Mason. The Littlers were a family of Cheshire gentry.

The Sankeys held mesne manors under the lords of Bewsey at Great and Little Sankey and were of sufficient consequence to have had their arms emblazoned in the windows of the Warrington church. The old family seat was the Hall at Sankey Parva or Little Sankey. Once a hamlet of Warrington, it may be that the lodge joined by Ashmole and Colonel Henry Mainwaring on that late October afternoon came alive at that place.

Penketh Hall today. The hall was rebuilt in 1757.

View from Penketh Hall of surviving farmland.

We have mentioned the Edward Sankey who wrote out the Masons' Charges in October 1646. Born in early 1621, he was possibly the son of Richard Sankey. It is also possible that this was the Edward Sankey described by William Beamont in his *The Chapelry of Sankey*.[21] Beamont called Sankey "the last of his ancient house of whom we hear, a man well born and well educated, and who had lately been abroad and seen something of military affairs."

Having joined Sir William Brereton's regiment of horse in 1642, this Edward Sankey received a commission to command a company. He was one of the party that, on New Year's Day 1643, searched the house of Mr. Davenport of Bramhall. He also joined in the attack upon Withenshaw, the house of Mr. Tatton.

Edward Sankey even appears in a contemporary lampoon verse—a verse that, intriguingly, includes a Mainwaring at arms. This could equally have been Edward Mainwaring of Whitmore, Thomas Mainwaring of Peover, or Colonel Henry Mainwaring of Karincham:

> *Lancaster's mad,*
> *And Eaton's as bad,*
> *Mainwaring looks like an ape;*

The remains of parkland, formerly part of Sankey Hall, leading down to Sankey Brook.

Oxley is naught,
And Sankey was caught
When he was in a captain's shape.

One can only speculate as to what might have kept Edward Sankey from joining his supposed father at a lodge that might well have been convened at the family home. Since Edward Sankey almost certainly wrote out the copy of the *Old Charges* used at Ashmole's initiation, it is practically certain that the scribe was an accepted Free Mason. On the other hand, Edward Sankey may have indeed been present and Ashmole simply omitted his name for some reason of his own.

Ashmole recorded that one Hugh Brewer attended the initiation. Hugh Brewer may have been the man of Lancashire yeoman stock who distinguished himself as a sergeant major in Lord Derby's royalist regiment of horse (the burial of a Hugh Brewer is recorded in Warrington Parish records on May 29, 1658).

Mr. James Collier may have been the James Collier of Newton, gentleman, reported in a certificate taken by Randle Holme (*Deputye to the Office of Armes*). This Collier, on June 3, 1640—at the age of thirty-two—married Elizabeth, daughter of Sir Edward Stanley of Bickerstaffe,

Lancashire, whose grandfather was Sir Randle Mainwaring of Peover—
a relative of Colonel Henry Mainwaring, and thereby a distant relative
of Elias Ashmole himself.[22] Whether or not this was the man, it seems
likely that the James Collier of the Warrington Lodge did come from
Newton and was a royalist.

The case of John Ellam's brother, Richard, is particularly interesting.
It shows how the Warrington lodge did not operate independently of
the operative world of freemasons but was controlled by its customs and
regulations.

Seventeenth-century Cheshire wills records reveal a Richard Ellom of
Lymm, with a brother called John. Richard Ellom's will (September 7,
1667) describes him plainly as a "freemason," and shows that he had
property to dispose of in a gentlemanly fashion. Freemasonry could be
reasonably lucrative, as one might expect of such a vital craft. If this was
the same Richard Ellam referred to by Ashmole, it seems likely that his
singular presence at a lodge of accepted gentlemen fulfilled a stipulation
of contemporary trade practice.

When a number of London Free and Accepted Masons attempted
to establish a system of lodges beyond the control of craftsmen freemasons between 1720 and 1730, a chief instrument in their purposes
was the publication of the Rev. James Anderson's *Constitutions* of Free
and Accepted Masons (1723). As if to preempt Anderson's work, Free
Mason J. Roberts—about whom nothing else is known—published
another set of Constitutions in 1722. Significantly, he repeated the
Charge of Grand Lodge MS. No. 2 that a properly constituted lodge
must contain at least five Accepted brethren and a minimum of one
Brother who was an active master of the trade.

Grand Lodge MS. No. 2 is a copy of the *Old Charges,* held by the
United Grand Lodge of England. It dates from the 1660s and is possibly
a product of an Assembly of Masons believed by both Roberts and
Anderson to have been held in 1663. Ashmole's "mother lodge" at Warrington in 1646 conforms to the rule regarding a properly constituted
lodge. It also shows that the leaders of the trade craft of freemasons
encouraged the existence of lodges constituted primarily of gentlemen for
purposes other than training apprentices; a symbolic and learned Free
Masonry running side by side with the trade seems to have been intended.

John Ellam was almost certainly the statutory working freemason.

Ashmole's introduction to this system must surely have come from his kinship with the Mainwaring family. He did, after all, ride up the road that joins Smallwood to Warrington with Colonel Henry Mainwaring, his father-in-law, Peter Mainwaring's nephew.

Colonel Mainwaring was the squire of Karincham (now called Kermincham and pronounced by locals as "Kermidgum"). Kermincham is close to Swettenham, where Mainwarings were interred for many years. Records from the Consistory Court in Chester reveal that Henry Mainwaring of Karincham, the colonel's grandfather (and Ashmole's father-in-law's father), was involved in a dispute over burial places and seats at the church of St. Luke, Goostrey, two miles away. Henry Mainwaring was permitted to build an out aisle or aisles on the north side of the chancel. One wonders who undertook the masonry.

The Advowson of Goostrey, incidentally, had been held by Dieulacres, a great abbey of the Staffordshire moorlands founded by Ranulphus, earl of Chester, in 1214. Roger de Mein-warin (Mainwaring), along with William de Venables, witnessed the earl's instruction to his barons regarding its founding. As we have seen, Ashmole was a distant relative of the Venables family, as was his first wife, Eleanor Mainwaring.

Eleanor's forebear Margery Mainwaring was the daughter of Hugh Venables, baron of Kinderton, and it was Margery who erected the unusual chapel at the church of St. Lawrence, Upper Peover, over the tomb of her husband Randle Mainwaring, who died in 1456. There are, as we have seen, numerous other monuments in St. Lawrence's that testify to a long-standing relationship with fine sculptors and architects—freemasons—from the Middle Ages right into Ashmole's time.

Six miles north of Upper Peover (on land given by William the Conqueror to the Venables family) is that church's mother church of Rostherne, some six miles southeast of Warrington. In 1578 an arbitration award was made to Thomas Legh against Sir Randle Mainwaring, who had claimed possession of the Legh chapel in Rostherne church. According to Raymond Richards: "The Legh Chapel at Rostherne stood ruinous in the sixteenth century for want of glass, [and] Sir Randle Mainwaring repaired it at his own expense," assuming possession for himself and

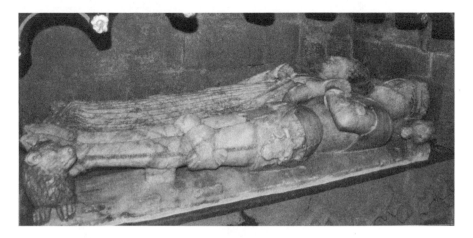

Tomb of Margery and Randle Mainwaring, who died in 1456 at Upper Peover, Cheshire. Margery was the daughter of Hugh Venables, baron of Kinderton, an ancestor of Ashmole's first wife.

his family "only to be turned out by Thomas Legh."[23] The passion for building continued. In 1585 the stately home of Peover was completed. It still stands, unspoiled, in the midst of Peover Park, overlooking the church of St. Lawrence.

One further fact regarding Ashmole's initiation may be noted. Colonel Mainwaring had in 1643 taken a leading role in the defense of Nantwich against the royalists, with 2,000 men and a furiously constructed but well-designed trench-and-earthwork system. Mainwaring's later commitment to the parliamentarian cause seems to have wavered considerably, as the plot thickened, but he was, like all the fighting-age Mainwarings of whom we have knowledge, associated with Parliament.[24]

There is no record that Ashmole regarded Mainwaring's disloyalty to the person of Charles I with censure. Perhaps there was something in him that he felt to be above such partisan concerns. In the lodge to which he would be fraternally bound he encountered a Catholic, an Anglican, a parliamentarian, and a royalist: himself. Following the afternoon of October 16, 1646, what did they all have in common?

As far as we can tell, Elias Ashmole stayed in fellowship with Accepted Free Masonry to the end of his life. There were indeed more important things than political conflicts. As Ashmole wrote, "The stars rule mankind."

SIX

Return to London

We do not know whether it was concern for Ashmole's state of mind that encouraged a member or members of his acquired family to point him in the direction of Free Masonry. Whatever the exact circumstances, the sight of the two returning soldiers, fresh from Warrington and united in fraternity, must have warmed the heart of old Peter Mainwaring at Smallwood. The first Civil War was over and many prayed for brotherhood to be restored among all Englishmen once more.

In spite of the fact that Ashmole's natural state subsisted in a posture of warm, if wary, self-confidence, the task of finding a wife and rebuilding his fortune would nonetheless require all the faith, energy, and wit he could muster. Reinvigorated, it would appear, by his discreet experience of Free Masonry, Ashmole elected to return to London, regardless of the fact that he was a known royalist captain and, as such, an object of suspicion in the capital.

"About 12 o'clock my cousin Manwaring [Colonel Henry Mainwaring, Ashmole's masonic Brother] lent me three *l* [pounds] and Manwaring gave his word for a horse for me."[1] On October 15, Ashmole saddled up his new mare at Congleton and began his journey to London, his body wrapped in a striking red cloak he had had sent up from Worcester.

Ashmole had been in London for less than three weeks when he met a man destined to become one of his closest friends. On November 20—a Friday evening (one might imagine they were at a tavern)—Jonas Moore (1617–79; knighted 1663), a royalist mathematician, introduced Ashmole to William Lilly, an ardent Roundhead (chiefly on religious grounds). The combination of talents seems strange at first sight. Jonas Moore would become mathematics tutor to the duke of York the following year; Lilly would serve the cause of Parliament—a commitment that would on subsequent occasions enrage Ashmole. What did they have in common?

C. H. Josten speculated that it might have been Free Masonry that sealed these new associations. "Perhaps," wrote Josten in his biography of Ashmole, "his newly acquired masonic connections had influenced Ashmole's decision [to return to London]. Certainly on his return to London, his circle of friends soon included many new acquaintances among astrologers, mathematicians, and physicians whose mystical leanings might have predisposed them to membership of speculative lodges, yet it is not known of any of them that they belonged to the craft."[2]

Such absence of knowledge would hardly be surprising. Only a handful of names could be summoned from the surviving records of seventeenth-century England and attached with confidence to a concern with Free Masonry. Ashmole was most unusual in his commitment to preserving records; his *personal* record of initiation is unique. However, even that brief record was in cipher, not intended for public consumption, at least in his lifetime.

The dynamic of Masonry required the full observation of the classic Hermetic posture, a firm finger against the lips: *He who speaks, does not know.* The key is in the mind. Such peace has passed the understanding of those disposed to suspect Masonry of secret wickedness.

Critics apt to condemn the Craft might pause to consider that if membership of Free Masonry aroused suspicion among the ignorant, many in the seventeenth century regarded interest in astrology and the now respectable mathematics as positively culpable. Mathematical figures suggested magical pacts with incomprehensible, unseen forces. Numbers were magical; manipulation thereof was fraught with potential trespass on the territory and governance of angels.

According to Josten, "To many orthodox minds the study of mathematics and astrology, which to all intents and purposes still were but two aspects of one discipline, savoured of heresy and atheism, a suspicion which might easily have fostered the formation of mathematicians' lodges or other secret societies, yet no evidence supporting such a conjecture is known."[3] No evidence is known, but Josten did not withdraw the conjecture.

Sir Jonas Moore would, like Ashmole fourteen years later, become a Fellow of the Royal Society, a pioneering exoteric institution of science. Before the Royal Society, men of scientific talent tended to gather about the precincts of Gresham College.

Founded in 1597 by City Mercer and royal agent Sir Thomas Gresham (who also founded the Royal Exchange), Gresham College was housed in his mansion in Bishopsgate until 1768. Originally, there were seven endowed chairs: Divinity, Music, Astronomy, Geometry, Physic (medicine), Law, and Rhetoric. The college provided accommodation for the early life of the Royal Society.

Whereas Royal Society rules discouraged discussion of spiritual and religious subjects—unfurling an early banner for the utilitarian principle—meetings and discussion at Gresham College could openly entertain such as might interest its denizens.

On Valentine's Day 1647, Ashmole sought a response from the stars as to whether he should "go to the Feast of Mathematicians at Gresham Colledge."[4] Two days later, "The Mathematical Feast was [held] at the White heart in the old Baily, where I dyned."[5] Perhaps it was at the same tavern where he first met Lilly; perhaps it was the site of a lodge.

A serious interest in mathematics would have put Ashmole on the "underground" or unspoken avant-garde of London intellectual society. Ashmole's long climb to high intellectual and social respectability had begun; it would not be a tale of overnight success.

WOMEN AGAIN

Readers may recall Ashmole's first encounter with the attractive power of a certain Mrs. March in Brasenose College Library while he was studying at Oxford. The lady had reentered Ashmole's life, and on December 31, 1646, she informed Ashmole that she would entertain no other suitor but he: until, that is, she should hear from a preferred Frenchman, Mr. Lollies. If there was a *grave* accent on that final *e*, Ashmole omitted it; he owed nothing to his rival. He was particularly "stuck on" Mrs. March, to be sure, but there were other eligible widows who had also taken a fancy to Captain Ashmole (retd.).

On November 18, Ashmole first records seeing Mrs. Wall, inquiring of the stars in no-nonsense fashion "whether I shall have her or not."[6] A fortnight later he was asking the same question with regard to Mrs. Mary Coachman.

On December 3, between 10 p.m. and midnight, Ashmole "discoursed with Mrs Wall in her bedchamber where still all her discourse beat upon her fear that she would marry not to pl[ease] her friends."[7]

On January 1, 1647, Mrs. March wishes Ashmole had only made his suit sooner. "Upon my request to her for a kiss, she then gave it to me for a New Year's gift, and told me that if she did not infinitely love me, she would have been sparing in her assurance to me."[8] Mrs. March was having her cake and eating it; so was Elias Ashmole.

At 1:15 p.m. the next day, he consulted the stars as to "whether Mr Lollies or myself shall have Mrs March."[9] She had gotten under his skin. That night, he had a dream: "I dreamed that Mr Lilly had assured me, he would procure me Mrs March by his art."[10] This art must have been a particular magick art, such as a sigil, talisman, or charm made to attract the opposite sex. Did the God-fearing William Lilly call the spirits to his service? It may be supposed that he did.

Advice to Young Gentlemen, a broadsheet ballad of the period.

The heady mix of sex and magick seems to have quite overtaken all other interests in this Sturm und Drang period of Ashmole's life. On January 5, whether by occult means or not, Mrs. March warmed further in the astrologer's direction: "I had this day divers kisses from her and she lent me her picture to wear next day to my heart. She then put her hand into bed to me and protested she had never done so much since her husband [Francis March] died, and she told me she hoped that I was confident there was nothing she could afford me but I might command it, and the *consummatum est* was not passed with the other, and bade me still hope."[11]

Twelve days passed. "This day she lay in bed, and I was with her all the day. In the morning I felt her breasts and belly, and in the afternoon lay by her with my hand on her breast while she seemed to sleep, and stole kisses while she lay so."[12]

Was Ashmole's interest in Mrs. March entirely sexual? Mrs. March owned a profitable brew house. Ashmole reckoned it an income until Parliament decided on the degree of his "compounding" (fine) for having taken up arms against it—or until such time as he might be ready to return to his legal practice. He was living, we may say, by his wits.

On January 30, he drew up a "figure" to ascertain whether Mrs. Anne Corbet (of an ancient Shropshire family) "shall marry the gentleman she now loves."[13] Did Ashmole take money for astrological readings? We have no record of money changing hands for this purpose but ladies may have chosen to grant him favors other than kisses and portraits of themselves.

In the weave of Ashmole's difficult love life (is there any other kind?), Mrs. Mary Coachman reappeared, this time in a dream. "This morning between 6: and 7: [February 11, 1647] I dreamed that being with Mrs Mary Coachman, I pressed her to marry her, and she consented, and went to dress her[self], but I repented myself and knew not how to get off being we were to be married [*sic*] as soon as she was dressed."[14]

The day after he attended the aforementioned Mathematicians' Feast at Gresham College, a new interest appeared. On February 15, Ashmole consulted his art to ascertain "whether my Lady Mainwaring bestow these favors to me out of an end to marry me."[15] Ashmole's involvement with Lady Mainwaring would be most fateful—for good and ill—in Ashmole's life.

In a sense, she appears as though magickally summoned or evoked from out of the tapestry of London society, to play the wished-for role in Ashmole's life of wife and provider of fortune. One imagines Ashmole's large eyes surveying each lady in turn with the question, "Is it she? Or, is it *she?*" He seemed to know that someone would heed his inner call; the universe answers the yearning soul. His expectation may have made him somewhat incautious.

As to what favors Lady Mainwaring bestowed, it was most likely money: an investment for a suitable and agreeable husband. Widows could—and indeed had to—pay their own "dowry," as it were. They could not, after all, bring virginity to the altar—though Lady Mainwaring could certainly offer plenty of experience. As things transpired, she brought what we would now call a good deal of "past baggage" as well.

LADY MAINWARING

Mary Mainwaring was the only daughter of Sir William Forster, K.B., of Aldermaston, Berkshire. Born on December 28, 1597, she was just under fifty at the time she and Elias began their courtship. She had been married three times and widowed thrice. On November 1, 1611, she

The last remains of Bradfield Manor (photo courtesy of Bradfield College).

Part of Bradfield College, Berkshire, on the site of Bradfield Manor, incorporating elements of the original stonework.

A view of the park, Englefield Hall, adjacent to the manor of Bradfield.

married Sir Edward Stafford of Bradfield. This was to be the most significant marriage in terms of its ramifications in Ashmole's life. She bore Sir Edward five children. At his death in November 1623, Sir Edward's legacy included the advowson of the rectory and parish church of Bradfield in Berkshire, as well as the manor house there and sundry lands. Visitors to Bradfield may still be struck by the extensive manor's great beauty.

Mary's next husband, John Hamlyn, died on November 1, 1633. The widow then married Sir Thomas Mainwaring in July 1634. He was distantly related to Ashmole's in-laws. Mainwaring, a lawyer of the Inner Temple, was Recorder of Reading (east of Bradfield) and one of the Masters in Chancery. He died in July 1646.

That the lady was a Mainwaring, like his first wife, might have appeared particularly significant to Ashmole. There were a number of other attractions. William Lilly described Lady Ashmole as "very handsome, of a goodly structure, Low, merry, and cheerfull, but accidentally very much Saturnine [that is, occasionally melancholic]."[16]

Before the death of her third husband, Mary had demised her jointure lands at Bradfield (held until her death and then to revert to the Staffords) to her eldest son from her first marriage, Edward Stafford, for fifty years at a rent. This arrangement in due course generated a lawsuit between the lady and her son. By 1647, Edward Stafford's rent was in arrears—to the tune of £602, sixteen shillings—a considerable sum. In fact, Lady Mainwaring was in such straits as to have to pawn her rings; Ashmole was concerned for her. On February 24, 1647, he posed the horary question as to "whether the Lady Mainwaring shall get the better in her suit with her son Stafford."[17]

An hour after seeking celestial assurance, Ashmole posed another question, at four in the afternoon, "whether the profession the Lady Mainwaring made to ☿ [Mercurius—the symbol Ashmole used for himself] be real, and whether it will be best for him to accept her favours to go into the county [of Berkshire] with her."[18]

On March 1 Ashmole took the plunge and proposed marriage. He "received a faire answer though no condescention [final decision]."[19]

Meanwhile, though not in his matrimonial sights, Mrs. March was still occupying a hearth rug amid the fires of his subconscious. Two days after his proposal, he had a dream: "In the morning I dreamt that ☿ [Mercurius] put his hand into Mrs March's placket ["a slit at the top of a skirt or petticoat for convenience of putting on or off," according to the Oxford English Dictionary] and then to her next petticoat and then to her third petticoat and then to her smock, and then pulled it up, and with very little struggling felt her bare cun[?] and see[ing] that it was so easy to be done prayed her to let him lie with her which she consented to, and then he went with her hand by to find out a private place to do it, but could find none, and did not do it, though she was willing, and he vexed."[20]

I should take his inability to locate his desire precisely as a sign of guilt, as well as obvious frustration.

On March 5, Lady Mainwaring called Ashmole "my dearest friend." Writing again in the third person, "He answered he would wear that epithet in his heart as long as he lived. She said that he might do."[21] Mary Mainwaring was putting Elias Ashmole through his paces.

Ashmole's use of the third person to describe his amorous activities suggests that he was not deeply comfortable with the very intimate nature of what he—the supposed cavalier—was involved with. One might think he was projecting a persona and transferring responsibility for his actions thereby. Otherwise, his reticence may have been conventional when dealing with sexual matters.

There is another intriguing possibility, that Mercurius (soon to be paradoxically revealed as the "faceless" cartoon of Mercuriophilus Anglicus in his first book) was a kind of resonant caricature of himself. Mercurius operated in the world as a secret actor but one whose invisible Self was yet hidden, even perhaps, from himself.

It is not unusual in serious occult thinking to distinguish between the essential Self (the "daemon" belonging to a spiritual world) and the actor "self" (ego) rooted in the world of action and thereby attached to it. Of course the genius of "Mercurius" (whose symbol is a symbol of a name) is that "he," being the transformative principle itself, may not only "fly" (with winged head and feet) between the two worlds, but also alchemically join them.

The Ash and the Mole are of the earth but are happily joined to the higher Mercurius who could echo Salvador Dali's famous phrase with respect to surrealism: "L'Hermétisme? C'est moi!" The cheeky Mercurius who attempts to unravel the ladies' garments in search of a secret that mere Ash-mole cannot grasp is at once a projected self, a gamester, and at the same time the active *will* (or true will) of the hidden Self. As troubadour Raimon de Miraval sang of the love god in the twelfth century: "He *must* accomplish His desires!"

Ashmole's spiritual life in this period was in a state of alchemical flux.

Ashmole *knew*, it seems to this author, that it was all leading somewhere, but his conscious mind was not altogether sure where. There is a lesson for our own times here: we put too much trust in the opacity of consciousness. Hurried speakers try in frenetic rap to reflect precisely what they see and think at the time. We receive a deceptive reflection, a surface, but no depth; we skate on thin ice, dismissing the interior voice.

The unease between the poverty of Ashmole's consciousness and the wealth of his unconscious led naturally to disquiet. He suffered conscious twinges of guilt and anxiety. *"Not I, but another,"* he might have apologized, was leading him on. In fact, he had little to worry about. A conventional courtship with Lady Mainwaring was in progress, the aim of which was to acquire a new social base and income boost, as well as to heal his lonely heart—and yet he was still unsure what was his best course. Only five days after Lady Mainwaring called Elias "my dearest friend," Ashmole was speculating whether he (☿) "shall have Mrs Marth[a] Hook."[22]

Ashmole needed spiritual guidance. He sought it and, eventually, he found it.

He also had acute money worries. Careful to acquire funds and careful to share them as conscience dictated, he was nonetheless prone to great anxiety should the prospect of losing them occur; he was not cavalier with his pocket. His upbringing had, not surprisingly, scarred him with the tremor of insecurity. These fears were doubtless extreme at times, but he believed sincerely that he could heal his nervous fears by acquiring wealth and position from without (*fame* would come from within). We are, not infrequently, as others treat us, but the fear of poverty, born in childhood, is with us forever.

It might be argued that Ashmole should have had absolute confidence in the spectacular gift of his interiority, his extraordinary feel for the reality and prodigious depth of his inner life, his *daemonic* intelligence. He should, in short, have kissed good-bye the world and its values and donned the mantle of the poor scholar or alchemical gypsy, guided solely by his soul's light, like a Joachim Morsius or a Heinrich Khunrath, who stalked the secret places of late-sixteenth and early-seventeenth-century Europe.

We must, however, put a brake on all this elevated mystical idealism and recall that which latter-day troubadour John Lennon sang shortly before his murder: "It's your mother, man! Don't forget your mother; she what bore you in the back bedroom!"[23]

One should never forget the presence of the departed Ann Ashmole. She had taught him well and hard about the real demands of life. There were two sides to every question: two pillars, as the Free Masons believed, to hold up the celestial universe. The world in its clamor and folly required attendance. Elias would have to do better than his father. And he had a secret self to do his bidding. Mercurius was at work in the world, separating and binding together, weaving a magickal life by the power of the caduceus and silence.

Above—or, perhaps, below—all, Ashmole's eyes could look up to see a blade of Damocles hovering over his long, ruddy brown hair, pressuring his powerful will with the threat of disaster. As a royalist captain and man of some (limited) means, he was in the sights of the government's "compounding and sequestration" program.

Lesser royalists (like Ashmole) might, if they were fortunate, be fined one sixth of their estate. Adding to the humiliation was a form of "self assessment"; tax is always taxing. Those summoned to undergo what the government called "compounding" (the state can always come up with a novel euphemism for theft) had perforce to attend Goldsmiths Hall and declare their income and property. In order to avoid ruinous sequestration, those called could opt for a "mercy of the state," conditional on the royalists' swearing the "Negative Oath," that never again would they bear arms against Parliament. Having stolen "rights" by force, Parliament now proceeded to dispose them. Having fashioned the laws, it could call itself just.

For some reason, Ashmole did not want Lady Mainwaring to know of his fate, whatever it might be, at the hands of the compounders. On March 12, 1647, he wrote: "13 hours after noon, whether the business I project concerning my compounding will be carried privately without the Lady Mainwaring's knowledge of my end in it."[24] One should recall that Ashmole was a lawyer and had an influential parliamentarian friend in astrologer William Lilly.

On March 30, 1647, at 10:15 a.m., Ashmole "took the Negative Oath" to free his property from the threat of sequestration.[25] This painful act must nonetheless have brought considerable personal relief.

Ashmole's courtship proceeded regardless. April 1, 1647: "2 hours after noon upon discourses with the Lady Mainwaring, she told me that no wife should love me better than she did, and taxing her that she concealed herself from me she said she had so opened herself that she had really hid nothing from me, but before a 12 month came about, she would see if she could get anything that would cross her love, or make her not to love me so well."[26]

Perhaps it was Ashmole's gathering attendance to worldly matters that made him wonder, on June 22, "whether ☿ [Mercurius] shall ever attain to a perfection in magick or astrology."[27] Note that word, *perfection*. He was on his way. While Ashmole dreamed of becoming the complete magus, the government was busy consigning the adoration of the Magi and all that Christmas then contained to the refuse heap of superstition. The feasts of Christ's Nativity (as Christmas was then called) were abolished by order of Parliament on June 8: a fine business for midsummer, one might think. Also abolished were Easter, Whitsuntide, and other feasts "heretofore superstitiously used and observed."

On Christmas Day 1647, Ashmole would write an elegy, "Upon the neglect of celebrating Christmas."[28] The hotheads have not disappeared from English life.

Mania was entering Ashmole's own, usually painstaking deliberations. Two days after waiting on the king at Caversham Lodge (near Reading), he awoke on the morning of July 11 with the thought that he might "have Dol [Dorothy Mainwaring, his first wife's younger sister] live with me as my wife."[29]

Something seems to have been trying to get a message through to Ashmole that marrying the Lady Mainwaring might yet be attended by some inconveniences. As if to give horrific form to such immaterial fears, Ashmole became victim of an attempted murder.

Ashmole had moved into Berkshire to help sort out the Lady Mainwaring's legal and family problems, renting rooms at the house of Mr. Antipas Charington at Englefield, close to Bradfield. He first visited Bradfield House, where Edward Stafford was living, on May 26, in an attempt both to reconcile the family and insist on the payment of rent for Edward's mother's welfare. The Staffords simply regarded Ashmole as a gold digger and worthless interloper.

Ashmole was still at Charington's on July 30 when it happened: "About 2 H: PM . . . Mr Humfry Stafford, the Lady Mainwaring's second son (suspecting I should marry his Mother) broke into my Chamber and had like to have kild me, but Christ: Smith witheld him by force, . . . in regard it was thought I was neere death, and knew no body. God be blessed for this deliverance."[30] Ashmole was ill with fever at the time and it cannot have assisted his recovery to discover that all about him sided with Humphrey Stafford.

Mania was in the air. In January 1648, Ashmole noted how his king was finally deprived of all liberty. He consulted his friend William Lilly's book of predictions, *England's Propheticall Merline* (1644). In Lilly's entry for January 30, 1649, stood the prophetic words: "Woe is me, a very great man comes to an untimely end: a rot of sheep and men. Is any Nobleman beheaded? What if may be? Justice took place."

Ashmole's relations with Lilly were strained, most likely for political reasons. On January 5, 1648, he paid an evening call on Lilly: "I delivered to Mr Lilly *Picatrix* and was reconciled to him."[31]

Picatrix (also known as *The Aim of the Sage*) was a powerful compendium of magick. Emanating from the Sabians of Harran, it had appeared in Spain in the eleventh century before being translated into Latin in 1256. It gave a complete theory and guide to the making of talismans, set in the context of Hermetic and Neoplatonist philosophy. The book showed the essence of "sympathetic magick" as the art of attracting *spiritus* into *materia* through the construction of appropriate talismans.

Did Ashmole require a magickal service of Lilly? The rapprochement did not last. On March 14, Ashmole's other close friend, royalist astrologer George Wharton, was arrested and imprisoned in Newgate. Ashmole suspected that Lilly the parliamentarian astrologer was implicated in this attack on his astrological and political rival. Astro-politics had begun, and Ashmole closely observed the storm.

On March 31, Ashmole again plied his suit with Lady Mainwaring. "Lady Mainwaring told me that she could wish she were married to me."[32] Ashmole could glimpse the prize: emotional and financial security. On May 22, Lady Mainwaring sealed Ashmole a lease for the "Parkes at Bradfield." The next day, Ashmole was thirty-one, and wrote of his "pleasant Hermitage."[33] The choice of the word *hermitage* is telling. He clearly intended to devote his life—now that his "nasty" material struggle seemed over—to a study of alchemy, a study he knew required great solitude and single-minded devotion. Bradfield, at first sight, should have been perfect for the task.

On July 8, we have the first definite date to indicate Ashmole's immersion into the great and not so great alchemical authors. One Nicholas Bowden of Reading gave him a book on the philosopher's stone and "The Supercelestiall, Celestiall, and Terrestrial Divine Lights of Nature."[34]

On January 30, 1649, for a few terrible seconds, the course of English history stopped, then spurted out and splashed onto a Whitehall scaffold amid the groans of the onlookers. King Charles I was martyred; England had become a republic.

Eleven months later, on November 22, at a date "elected" by astrological means, Elias Ashmole and Lady Mainwaring were married at Silverstreet, London. If he thought his troubles were over, he was wrong.

A contemporary illustration of the king's martyrdom at the Banqueting House, Whitehall.

SEVEN

The 1650s (I)

The Philosopher's Stone

W
hat is alchemy? Through centuries of experience in the smithy and the jeweler's fire, the intuition developed that metals were animated, living things, subject to change and transformation. Metals were seen directly, visibly, and invisibly to be affected by water, air, earth, and fire. In the larger astrological context, metals were deemed subject to the stars like everything else. But above all, they were subject to the *will* of the skilled operator. And nowhere were these technicians more skilled than in Egypt.

The Greek word for alchemy simply means "the Egyptian art," from *chemia*, the black earth—the Greeks' name for an Egypt whose black, fertile, muddy land was the result of the Nile's annual inundation.

In ancient Egypt, operating with metals came under the patronage of the god Thoth, called Hermes after the Greek invasion of Egypt in 331 B.C. Hermes presided over the magick of transformation. The element mercury or *mercurius* (Latin form of the Greek Hermes) with its swift transformation from solid to liquid states symbolized the possibilities of change from one state to another. Metals were like minds; they could change and be changed.

As we describe someone lacking in knowledge as "dim" or "dense," so metals in their lowest state were called "black" (*nigredo*). Comparing the rise in quality from dull blackness to the unique, refined, incorruptible state of gold was like glimpsing the ladder that could take man from earth and death to heaven and eternal life. Speculation on chemical transformation in the ancient world led to the conviction that the full transition to gold could be most easily effected if one had a quantity of the "stone" or "philosopher's stone." This "stone," frequently understood to be a powder, served as a dynamic catalyst.

While alchemical writings offered "recipes" to "project" this mysterious and magickal substance, and much alchemical practice was concentrated on its generation or manifestation, its essential, paradoxical qualities remained mysterious. That mystery was—and still is—an enormous attraction.

The stone is always presented as something from without that is produced within that effects within and manifests without. You can write songs and poems about this riddle, but producing it would prove as elusive as is the manufacture of stable quantities of fusion energy today. That does not stop people from trying, and in terms of seventeenth-century knowledge, Ashmole's profound interest in the subject was a vital component of the most farsighted, albeit suspected, science and philosophy.

Nevertheless, it would be a mistake to think that alchemy was all about finding the philosopher's stone (*philosopher,* by the way, was simply another word for "alchemist"). The essence of the art was *Change.* That is why Hermes, the archetypal "quick-change" artist, was its psychopomp, or president.

The key to change rested in the principle that it was possible to separate "body" from "soul." One only has to think of a common match or "lucifer" (as matches were first called) to get the idea. A spark produces the flame, the "visible" and intangible sign of soul. It rises upward, leaving the powdery remains of the "body." Since bodily illnesses were frequently ascribed to weaknesses or dis-ease in the soul, substances ("chemicals") might be used to right imbalances by providing corresponding boosts or "elixirs" to the invisible soul-frame of the person.

Likewise, a person might be thought of as being representative of a metal, governed by a planet. The metal could become sick due to unfavorable planetary alignment. A balancing regimen of correspondingly good influences might help matters.

There was also a moral dimension. "Evil" or bad influences could be understood as part of an improving process. A potentially good metal could "suffer" much hard work in the process of bringing forth its hidden strength, like hot metal being hammered into shape, then plunged harshly into a "screaming" bath of cold water. The greater the potential, the more suffering one could expect.

The idea of necessary, even exalted, suffering (willingness to be acted upon) invited Christian alchemical images of crucifixion and resurrection. It is often wondered whether alchemy in Ashmole's time was a physical practice or a form of spiritual psychology. It is clear that it was both.

Indeed, it is from both aspects (the *lab*-oratory and the oratory; the "ergon"—work—and the "parergon" or by-product) that the benefits of alchemy have come down to us today. Alchemical concepts suffuse medicine and psychology as well as chemistry. The drug industry was begun by alchemists, as was the alternative medicine school. In common parlance, we know what we mean when we say that a man has "nerves of steel" or a woman is an "iron lady"; a determined person has "fire in the belly," a kind one has a "heart of gold." Jungian psychology is, to all

Left: Alchemists at work in Georgius Agricola's *De re metallica libri XII . . . animantibus subterraneis liber . . . Basileae, Froben, 1556.* (Ravenna, Biblioteca Classense; 50.9.l)

Right: Oratory and Laboratory; Ergon (work) and Parergon (by-product), from *Speculum Sophicum Rhodo-stauroticum,* Daniel Mögling, Germany, 1618.

intents and purposes, a form of alchemy, as Jung himself realized.[1]

Nevertheless, it would be doing alchemy a great disservice to reduce its scope to what we have inherited as part of our understanding or what conforms to contemporary scientific knowledge. The same caveat may also be applied to Ashmole's day.

As C. H. Josten asserted in his biography of Ashmole: "An evaluation of astrology and alchemy in terms of their usefulness to modern developments does by no means exhaust, or even touch upon, their significance as remnants of a lost spiritual discipline which, even in Ashmole's time, may no longer have been fully understood by the *adepti*."[2] Ashmole himself was aware of the loss of knowledge experienced by those honestly encountering alchemical knowledge. As he would write in the *Prolegomena* to his *Theatrum Chemicum Britannicum:* "They are Mysteries Incommunicable to any but the *Adepti,* and those that have been Devoted even from their Cradles to serve and wait at this Altar."

The adepti had observed that what occurred in metals had direct correspondence or analogy to the bodily and, above all, spiritual nature of man. It was then deduced that human beings too were part of a cosmic alchemy, and alchemy must therefore offer knowledge of the Creator's essential power and creative method. The earthly operator experienced this dangerous power as a reflection or *microcosm* of the greater working, the *macrocosm.*

It was also understood that due to the fundamental nature of alchemical principles, alchemy should be employed in association with geometry (the word *projection* is shared by alchemists and geometers) and with mathematics, the science of quantity. Alchemy's links with astrology were intrinsic. Alchemy was, as Ashmole would write in *Theatrum Chemicum Britannicum,* an art favored by freemasons, among other craftsmen.

While it is clear that alchemy provided the experiential basis for chemistry in general, its strictly "scientific" reputation had long been sullied by its attraction to charlatans obsessed with the single exploit of getting gold from lead: that is, something for nothing. To add to the confusion and obscurity, alchemy also employed recipes whose expressive admixture of strange and often polyvalent symbols with quantities of known, tangible substances were used to conceal vital knowledge from the "profane." Much time and money were wasted as a result.

However, throughout the early seventeenth century, the reputation of alchemy had steadily increased among private individuals with money to dispose on penetrating its mysteries, and stories abounded of successful transmutations. It is possible that the idea of mysteries within nature compensated for the loss of mystery in Protestant religion.

Alchemy was of particular interest to men who suffered from the effects of the fissures in religious life resulting from the Reformation. There was a subconscious hunger to recover the principle of *unity* behind all things. Among such men, and Ashmole was one of them, the spiritual potential of alchemy was as compelling as its physical possibilities, though Ashmole may not have admitted such a distinction as absolute.

The spiritual potential of alchemical thought was increased as a result of the fact that since the age of the Egyptian alchemists in late antique times (first to fifth centuries A.D.), the processes had been expressed within the terminology and cosmic understanding of a Neoplatonic and Hermetic *gnosis*.

The gnostic idea that there is a divine "substance" (*pneuma*) hidden or occulted within the gross "body" of the potentially gnostic person

The alchemist has been spiritually resurrected into the golden state, raised above earth in a "new" body, leaving the earthly body below. From Jean-Jacques Manget's *Bibliotheca Chemica Curiosa*, Cologne, 1702. (Biblioteca dell' Accademia dei Lincei, Rome; Verginelli-Rota n. 211)

chimed in very well with the alchemical art, and soon became practically inseparable from it, if, indeed, theory and practice had ever been separated. Readers who want to further explore the links among alchemy, gnostic thought, Free Masonry, and seventeenth-century Rosicrucianism may consult my book *The Golden Builders.*

There existed among the more intelligent practitioners of alchemy the idea that somehow alchemy had, in the past, been "badly handled." Bad or corrupt men had been blinded by the lure of gold. But for those who looked beyond the nefarious activities of the "puffers" and "accursed gold-makers," it was clear from the ancient alchemical authors that something Very Big indeed was implied within the "Great Work."

"That which is above is like that which is below" intoned the ancient, antediluvian message of mystagogue Hermes Trismegistus. And what was the purpose of this divine cosmic analogy? Hermes' "Smaragdine Table" (written on emerald in distant times) expressed it succinctly: "To work the miracle of the One Thing."

The alchemical symbol for the sun.

EX UNO OMNIA

Now consider Ashmole's motto, *Ex Uno Omnia*: From the One, All. The possibilities encoded within the alchemical universe were as endless as the imagination and, it was deemed, long unexplored. If one were to come to grips with alchemy's full potential, one would need to refine the manuscript tradition and, if possible, get back to the original insights and states of mind that initiated the alchemical quest in the first place. This kind of work was very much within Ashmole's sphere of gifts, and very much in tune with his deepest needs and ideals.

In pursuit of these laudable aims, it was observed that as the metals needed to be transformed from within, then the *artifex*—the operator—

would also need to become a more spiritual being, pleasing to God. After all, one was presuming to gather crumbs from the Grand Artifex's table, or at least get a glimpse of His laboratory, His Oratory of Labor. The clamor of the world would need to be stilled so that the voice of divine inspiration could enlighten the artifex. Becoming a fully fledged magus meant rising on a path of holiness. In short, alchemy could produce a new kind of being and, thereby, a new kind of world. Ashmole was acutely, even painfully, aware of this.

Ashmole's alchemical ideals were fully expressed on paper within a year of his marriage to Lady Mainwaring. In his introduction to *Fasciculus Chemicus* ("an alchemical posy"), published in 1650, he noted that in all alchemical writings "the Golden Thread of the Matter is so warily disposed, covertly concealed, and so broken off and disperst" that even "the best principled student" will not find "its scattered ends . . . unless the Father of Illuminations prompt, or lend an Angels hand to guide." This illumination is "a Havn [*sic*] towards which many skilful Pilots have bent their course, yet few have reached it." "Many are called, but few are chosen."

The few who are by divine grace chosen to be the "Adepted Priests" "celebrating the ceremonies of so divine a Miracle" will be conspicuous for "a most virtuous life"; "being so qualified, they straightaway lay aside ambitious thoughts, and take up a retiredness; they dwell within their Root; and never care for flourishing upon the Stage of the World." No "corrupt or sinister thoughts can grow up in them," as the possession of the secret, which God will never suffer "to be revealed to any but those that can tell how to conceal a secret," will free them from "the root of all evil"—namely, covetousness.

This was all a very tall order for Ashmole, who was undoubtedly ambitious and was not at all averse to flourishing on the stage of the world. The spirit was willing . . .

Furthermore, in spite of his marriage to Lady Mainwaring, Ashmole was still very much involved in the dramatic incidents of earthbound existence. As Ashmole and the Lady Mary were wed in Silverstreet on November 16, 1649, his astrologer friend George Wharton was languishing under parliamentarian lock and key. The president of the Council of State, John Bradshaw, wanted the royalist Wharton hanged. On

November 22, Ashmole went to William Lilly to effect Wharton's eventual release. This was accomplished through Lilly's patron, Balstrode Whitelock (1605–75), one of the three commissioners of the Great Seal and a member of the Council of State.

Nevertheless, in spite of the fact that Ashmole later claimed that worldly concerns (especially the legal tangles surrounding Lady Mainwaring's disputed estate) kept him from a deeper involvement with the practical side of alchemy, his presence in Berkshire did yield substantial spiritual contacts.

The two most significant new stars on Ashmole's horizon were the alchemist and inventor William Backhouse (1593–1662) and the Rev. Dr. John Pordage, rector of Bradfield (1605–81). The interests of both of these extraordinary men provided foci for engaging with the central concerns of Continental spiritual and esoteric-scientific thought.

Backhouse was a learned devotee of the Continental "Rosicrucian" movement, while the eccentric Pordage was one of the first Englishmen to seize upon the significance of the theosophical works of the German mystic Jacob Böhme (1575–1624) and write about them to great effect.

Left: Dr. John Pordage, from *Gottliche und Wahre Metaphysica*, Frankfurt and Leipzig, 1715.

Right: The gnostic theosopher Jacob Böhme, the source of Pordage's inspiration, from Edward Taylor's *Jacob Behmen's Theosophick Philosophy Unfolded*, London, 1691.

Indeed, it seems somewhat extraordinary that Ashmole should find such contacts at the very moment he took up his lordship of the manor of Bradfield. Unfortunately, we only receive hints of what specifically took place between Ashmole and these men, but such as we do receive (especially concerning Backhouse) leaves us in no doubt that the confluence of these powerful interests—and minds—would shape and intensify Ashmole's headlong quest for magickal enlightenment.

On May 20, 1650, Ashmole posed the horary question "Whether I shall ever have the Philosopher Stone, or whether the matter and fire I think of be true."[3] Ashmole needed spiritual guidance.

Five weeks later, he asked, "Whether I shall ever receive [h]urt or good from General Cromwell, while he is General." It may be supposed that the response to this question would encourage him to abandon, at least temporarily, the worldly stage and devote himself to profound studies. Furthermore, the same month in which Ashmole pondered his chances under Cromwell's rule saw him embark on a journey that would eventually change his life and grant him the fame on which his name now chiefly rests.

On June 15, 1650, Ashmole, his wife, and his beloved friend Dr. Thomas Wharton (a leading physician and discoverer of Wharton's duct) paid a visit to John Tradescant the younger (1608–62) at South Lambeth. Tradescant, the famous antiquary and naturalist, had given over his home to extensive gardens of great botanical fascination and his house to a mighty collection of artifacts and natural curiosities from around the known world. His gardens and collections captivated Ashmole's attention and deeply stimulated his imagination.

Without the temptations of the old Stuart court and its satellites, the 1650s would see Elias Ashmole synthesize the full scope of his interests: alchemical, astrological, antiquarian, and natural-philosophical. He and other learned men of his day called this line of interest "Natural Magick," of which he would write in *Theatrum Chemicum Britannicum*; his words possibly showed the influence of Jacob Böhme via John Pordage.

According to Ashmole, Adam (the primal Man) was before his Fall "so absolute a philosopher" that he possessed "the true and pure knowledge of Nature (which is no other than what we call Natural Magick) in the highest degree of Perfection."[4] According to Josten, "Natural Magic as conceived by Ashmole is therefore, in modern terminology, Science."[5]

Unlike the mystic—or gnostic—William Blake (who, born a century later, was also a reader of Böhme and of Pordage), Ashmole was more interested in the "true and perfect knowledge of Nature" contained in Adam's breast than he was in Adam the Ancient Man and Gnostic Anthropos. Ashmole was never overwhelmed by mythology; his eye was shrewd, his imagination served. He was more inclined to look *through* the mystical to the material world than the reverse. This makes him a man of a new era as well as of the old: a herald—and an enigma.

FASCICULUS CHEMICUS

Ashmole's immersion into the alchemical universe was balanced by interest in his seigneurial rights at Bradfield. On April 29, 1650, he inquired of the stars whether the wife of the rector, Mrs. Pordage, "had best sell her houses or keep them."[6] He seems to have gotten involved with Pordage family business (public and discreet). A month later he was giving astrological advice as to "Whether Mr. [blank] Por[da]g[e] shall have the Mr[s.] he affects."[7] This Mr. Pordage was probably Dr. John's son, Samuel (1633–91?), unless, that is, one was to suspect the eccentric rector of adultery, in addition to a most extraordinary style of ministry.

That style was laid out for public disgust in *A Most faithful relation of two wonderful passages which happened very lately . . . in the Parish of Bradfield in Berk-shire.* Local gentleman Mr. William Foster observed the rector emerging from his church "bellowing like a Bull, saying that he was called and must be gon."[8]

Going to the Pordage home, with which his wife was intimate, Foster was amazed to see "Mistress Pordich [sic] Clothed all in White Lawne, from the crown to the Head to the sole of the Foot, and a White rod in her hand." She was hailed as a prophetess by those dancing country dances about her "making strange noyses." Explaining that they were rejoicing "because they had over come the Devil," Dr. Pordage then appeared "all in black Velvet" and pressed Foster and his wife to join in. Foster made his excuses, to Pordage's disappointment, and the dancing went on around the parish "expecting when they shall be taken up to Heaven every hour."[9]

Top left: Bradfield church today, just below the site of the old manor hall.

Top right: The interior of Bradfield church as it is today.

Left: The porch of Bradfield church from which John Pordage emerged "bellowing like a Bull."

What Ashmole thought of this premature manifestation of the spirit of 1969 is not recorded, nor whether he was in deep sympathy with the thoughts of Jacob Böhme, whose works appear to have freed Pordage and his family's mind, certainly from conventional inhibition, and perhaps, at times, from reason too.

It is worth noting that gnostic movements tend to carry two moral extremes: strict asceticism (the body being an obstruction to the spirit) and sexual indulgence (love knows better than society; women are not property; the spirit should be free). Ashmole was not the ascetic type. Perhaps he was indulgent of a little discreet, free, holy love. He was certainly, like many cavaliers, tolerant of adultery. On May 19, 1650, he posed the horary question "Whether ☿ [Mercurius] shall ever enjoy Mrs Martha Beale."[10] Whether or not he did, we do not know.

Dr. Pordage certainly encouraged a sense of liberty, perhaps license, in his verdant, richly endowed parish. He had been there since 1647 and many of the parishioners appear to have gotten used to a surprising new order of things. Pordage experimented with theology, followed his inner Christ, and communed with what he took to be the Holy Spirit and His angels. His ministry in some respects presaged a breakdown of order that accompanied the demise of the king and the dismemberment of his church.

During 1650, Ashmole went to Bradfield on at least seven occasions to obtain rents from tenants for himself and his wife. These attempts were frequently unsuccessful. By the end of March, Ashmole had heard that Humphrey Stafford had told the tenants to withhold rents from his mother and her new husband. In this matter, Humphrey Stafford and his brother Edward were aided and abetted by Lady Mainwaring's brother, Sir Humphrey Forster, who conceived a great hatred for Ashmole. Ashmole himself continually sought reconciliation in the family and was unafraid of confronting his enemies face-to-face.

On having his and his wife's rights upheld in court after much legal antagonism, Ashmole held courts baron at Bradfield in January and March 1653 as lord of the manor. In spite of his friend Sir George Wharton's help in raising rents, Ashmole's courts, in the main, failed; the population of Bradfield mostly ignored him.

This experiment in Ashmolean squirearchy does not seem to have lasted long. One suspects that it began in seriousness, became a bit of a pose, then collapsed in boredom and suppressed embarrassment. The citizens had more to get excited about than the Staffordshire-born *arriviste* from London. There was utopian hope and excessive optimism in the air, as well as harsh government repression. Ashmole himself felt the tug of that solitary holiness of life that should characterize the devoted alchemist.

The day after wondering whether he could enjoy the comforts of Mrs. Martha Beale, he drew up a list of recipients of his first book, *Fasciculus Chemicus*. As well as putting Dr. John Pordage on his list, Ashmole, interestingly, added the name of the chief royalist in Lichfield,

Sir Richard Dyott, chancellor of the County Palatine of Durham and Steward of Lichfield (d. March 8, 1659).

Fasciculus Chemicus was the first appearance—or disappearance—of Elias Ashmole in print. As readers will recall, the frontispiece showed his face obscured by his natal scheme. He also obscured his name. According to the frontispiece, the book was authored by one "James Hasolle." This anagram of Elias Ashmole may have been observed as an alchemical and Rosicrucian convention; alchemical texts rarely carried the real names of their authors. In this case, the name was doubly pseudonymous. While "James Hasolle" contained Elias Ashmole, *Fasciculus Chemicus* contained the work of Arthur Dee (1579–1651), the son of Dr. John Dee (1524–1608), the famous Elizabethan astrologer and court scientist.

In spite of obscuring the author on the title page, the frontispiece is in fact a profound revelation of his, shall we say, *astral* identity. As Josten writes, the frontispiece "appears to proclaim that, as heavenly Mercury is among the Gods, metals, and planets, such is Elias Ashmole, alias *Mercuriophilus Anglicus,* on Earth."[11]

Ashmole wrote the introduction and translated Arthur Dee's work, thinking the latter was dead. On discovering that this was not the case, that in fact Dee had only been abroad in Moscow—as the much respected physician to the czar—Ashmole wrote to him requesting permission to publish. Dee, now residing in Norwich, replied that he did not object to "James Hasolle's" use of his work.

Friends of Ashmole met Dee in London but Elias missed his own opportunity, for Dee died the next year (1651). Dee left a son, Rowland,

Dr. John Dee (1524–1608), mathematician, astrologer, polymath, summoner of angels. The portrait, which belonged to Dee's grandson Rowland, now hangs in the Ashmolean Museum, Oxford.

who was a merchant in London and who gave Ashmole a family pedigree in 1674 during a prolonged period of Dee-interest in Ashmole's life.

ONE HIEROGLYPH—NEW BEING

The figure of John Dee was extraordinarily significant to Elias Ashmole. He saw depths of possibility and understanding within Dee's life and work that almost nobody else in his time glimpsed. He seems to have seen Dee not only as his personal ideal (immensely learned, judicious, scientific, mystical, mathematical—and yet also holding high place in the state), but also as his prototype. That is to say, it appears that Ashmole saw himself as something of a fulfillment of Dee's prophetic promise.

In order to get a glimpse of what this promise involved, one need only consult C. H. Josten's excellent introduction to his translation of Dee's *Monas Hieroglyphica*, a work that Ashmole also transcribed and which inspired him greatly.

Josten writes:

> It would seem, therefore, that the aim of the secret discipline which Dee wished to express, as well as to conceal, in his treatise was the elevation of certain chosen and most rare mortals to an existence transfigured by direct participation in astral and supracelestial influences, an existence in which they would be masters of Nature and free from the humbling limitations of ordinary life in the body. Those alchemists of his own time who were merely trying to produce gold, therefore, appeared to him as impostors and as the unworthy heirs of a doctrine whose essential parts were not only unknown to them, but also beyond their reach.

Ashmole would have read this passage with alacrity. Like Friedrich Nietzsche over two centuries later, he was taken up in the vision of nothing less than the appearance of a *new kind of being*. This vision drove him from deep within himself. He expected to see in his lifetime a profound renewal and illumination of esoteric science (Natural Magick) in tune with the original Rosicrucian and Paracelsian prophecies of revelation of natural secrets before "the last light."

In his optimism he differed from John Dee himself, who implied in his *Monas Hieroglyphica* (1564) that spiritual illumination was on the wane, as the world sank into new barbarism and a darker age. Furthermore, as Josten notes in his introduction:

> In another dark passage, which alludes to the philosophers' mercury and its replacement by the Sun, i.e., gold, Dee asserts that this operation (which is the final stage in the transmutation of metals) can no longer be performed in the present age, as it was in the past performed by some great experts, unless indeed one let the work be governed by a certain soul which has been severed from its body by the art of controlling the fire (*ars pyronomica*), a work very difficult and fraught with dangers because of the fiery and sulphurous fumes which it occasions.
>
> This passage defies complete and certain interpretation, but indicates beyond doubt that, in Dee's view, the chances of alchemical success in the external world are diminishing as that world, by progressing in time, descends into spiritually darker ages, and that any palpable success in the transmutation of metals may, if at all, be hoped for only after the successful completion of a most unusual and dangerous work. If one assumes that the soul, which in this dangerous adventure is to be separated from its body, is the human soul (or part thereof), then the *ars pyronomica* by which the work is to be performed must be primarily spiritual alchemy, the very *astronomia inferior* of which the monad is Dee's chosen symbol.[12]

Was there any likelihood of Ashmole's fulfilling Dee's somewhat tortuous conditions? Ashmole was certainly ambitious in matter and spirit, but had God fitted him for the task? As the English herald of a new age, what would he have to know? On July 13, 1650, he asks, "Whether I shall ever attain to the knowledge of making such a glass as Paracel[sus]: makes mention of in his 5th book, p. 143."[13]

The passage from Paracelsus's *Archidoxa* referred to by Ashmole concerns the making of three magick *specula* in metal. The first was so as to render visible the images of all men and animals past and present. The second was to gain access to all things spoken and written in the past—and why. The third was to become intimate with all secret things that were ever written down. The specula were to be made specifically for the nativity of the individual who desired to use them. With intelligence like this, would there be any need for intelligence?

Five days later, Ashmole employed magick for a more mundane purpose. He made magick sigils during a conjunction of Saturn and Mars for the purpose of driving out flies, fleas, and caterpillars. "The Figures of the Caterpillars and Flyes Fleas and Toades, were all made in full pro portion, in litle, and cast off in Lead. Without [magickal] Characters."[14] This is the earliest reference to Ashmole casting sigils. One might think he would be above such activities. Would he not soon write in *Theatrum Chemicum Britannicum* that the teachings of magick should not offend "the Eares of the most Pious"? "[F]or here" declares Ashmole, piously, "is no incantations, no Words, no Circles, no Charms, no other fragments of invented Fopperies nor needs there any; Nature (with whom free Magicians deal) can work without them, she finds Matter, and they Art, to help and assist Her, and here's All."[15] He was of course writing in a period of witch trials, so it paid to be discreet.

Nevertheless, "James Hasolle" was not so guarded in his *Prolegomena* to *Fasciculus Chemicus:* "Characters, Charms, or Spells" are "low and inferior assistants . . . yet these have their several powers, if judiciously and warily disposed and handled."

Ashmole was nothing if not judicious, and he was always wary. On October 19, he made an astrological figure to ascertain "Whether good to let Dr. Por[da]g[e] go to dwell in my house at Bradfield."[16] This wariness presumably coincided with the publication of the exposure of Pordage's spiritist ministry and the beginnings of investigations into his activities. Pordage would not leave his Bradfield ministry until 1654, though he continued to be the largest renter of property there.

THE THEATER OF BRITISH CHEMISTRY

By the end of 1650, Ashmole had already embarked on his next major project: a collection of the works of English alchemical authors, long since unavailable, and many never seen before in print. The *Theatrum Chemicum Britannicum* would become Isaac Newton's most heavily consulted alchemical text when he came to search for the single divine principle through a thorough working of alchemical experiments. It is now believed that without the imaginative stimulus of alchemy, Newton may never have reached the summits of his mathematical and natural philosophical genius. Ashmole deserves some long overdue credit here.

On December 7 Ashmole completed transcribing manuscripts by a favorite alchemical author, Sir George Ripley (c. 1415–90?), a canon of Bridlington monastery and an official in the service of King Edward IV. Ripley's pupil was Thomas Norton, author of the *Ordinall of Alchemy,* also to be included in Ashmole's *Theatrum.*

Studying the significance of the monastic tradition in providing a home for alchemical and related studies made Ashmole even more acutely aware of the damage wrought by the Reformation and its seismic aftereffects (through one of which he was living) and the need for preservation and antiquarian exactitude.

Ashmole began to wonder if some remnant of alchemical expertise had not been hidden away in the monastic grounds before Henry VIII's despoilers arrived for demolition duties. On February 19, 1651, he posed the question "Whether there is any of the medicine [philosopher's stone] hid in the abbey of Reading which is now pulling down and in what part and whether I shall find it."

Ashmole's mind was filled with alchemy. On February 16, 1651, he

Page from Ashmole's *Theatrum Chemicum Britannicum* (1652). The engraving shows the Alchemist giving instruction to his "Son," heir to his knowledge.

noted the transcription of another alchemical text, *A Naturall Chymicall Symbol Or a short confession of Henry Kunwrath* [Heinrich Khunrath, d. 1603] *of Lipsicke* [Leipzig], *Doctor of Physick,* dated December 12, 1597, and a poem by the same, dated December 23, 1597. The poem is entitled *A philosophical short song of the incorporating of the Spirit of the Lord in Salt.* (Salt is frequently a symbol for the material body in alchemy.)

It is possible that the title of his English alchemical compendium (the *Theatrum*) was based on the title of Khunrath's *Amphitheatrum Sapientiae Aeternae* (Amphitheater of Eternal Wisdom, published in 1595 and reprinted many times).

During 1651, Ashmole obtained a large collection of books, including alchemical texts by the following authors: Democritus Abderita, Trismosinus, Artephius, Basilus Valentinus, Michael Maier, Heinrich Khunrath, Petrus Arlensis, Camillus Leonardus, Alphidius, and Jean Dastin. Ashmole noted how he found some of them in books and manuscripts from the libraries of William Backhouse, Dr. [Levin?] Flood, and D[avid] Ramsey. He also obtained other books on precious stones, Kabbalah, and Etruscan antiquities.

Ashmole first met Dr. Flood on a visit to Maidstone with Dr. Childe, "the Phisitian," on March 7, 1651.[17] Dr. Robert Childe must have been a man of great note in British esoteric circles at the time, for no less a work than J. Freake's 1651 translation of Henry Cornelius Agrippa's *Three*

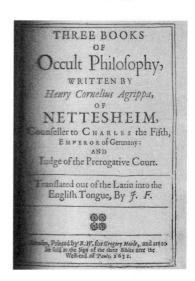

Henry Cornelius Agrippa's *Three Books of Occult Philosophy,* dedicated to Dr. Robert Childe.

Books of Occult Philosophy was dedicated to him—and in what terms!

"See it is not in vain" writes Freake of Dr. Childe, "that you have compassed Sea and Land, for thereby you have made a Proselyte, not of another, but of your self, by being converted from vulgar, and irrational incredulities to the rational embracing of the sublime, Hermeticall, and Theomagicall truths. You are skilled in the one as if Hermes had been your Tutor; have insight in the other, as if Agrippa your Master."

Ashmole was finding himself in most excellent company for his purposes. Freake's translation of Agrippa was one of the main publications of the 1650s Hermetic "blitz" that made that decade possibly the richest donor of literary crops in the history of British Hermetism. It was certainly the decade wherein British Rosicrucianism came out of the woodwork—and we find Elias Ashmole at center stage.

His links to the movement were ingenious. For example, on March 21, 1651, a fortnight after his trip to Maidstone with Dr. Childe, Ashmole received the grant of an imprimatur for his *Theatrum Chemicum Britannicum*. The document was signed by John Booker and by Philip Stephens. Booker, one of two licensers of mathematical books since 1643, was himself an astrologer and a friend of Ashmole. Booker also contributed verses to Freake's Agrippa publication, condemning those who failed to see the depth and lasting value of Agrippa's *Occult Philosophy:* "They are indeed mysterious, rare and rich, And far transcend the ordinary pitch."[18]

For good measure, the encomium on the magus Agrippa was penned by one of the deepest of the British Rosicrucian philosophers, Thomas Vaughan (1622–66), publisher of the first English printing of the *Fame and Confession* of the Rosy Cross Fraternity (1652).

ASHMOLE AND THE ROSICRUCIANS

On April 3, 1651, at half past midnight, "Mr : Will : Backhouse of Swallowfield in Com. Berks, caused me to call him Father thence forward."[19] This was, according to Josten, "an alchemical initiation," an example of the "Hermetic adoption" discussed by Ashmole himself in the pages of his *Theatrum*.[20]

The relationship of "father" to "son" may well be in imitation of the traditional relationship between Hermes Trismegistus and his pupils Asclepius, Tat, and Ammon. Ashmole was clearly seeking spiritual initiation. As Pico della Mirandola asserted in his epoch-marking *Oration on the Dignity of Man* (1486), the mystic doctrines had always been passed on "from mind to mind, through the medium of speech." Deeply impressed by Backhouse's service to him, Ashmole wrote a poem dedicated to my "worthily honour'd William Backhouse Esquire Upon his adopting me to be his Son."

> *From this blest Minute I'le begin to date*
> *My Yeares & Happines . . . & vow*
> *I ne're perceiv'd what Being was till now.*
> *See how the power of your Adoption can*
> *Transmute imperfect Nature to be Man.*
> *I feele that noble Blood spring in my Heart,*
> *Which does intytle me to some small parte*
> *Of . . . Hermes wealth . . .*
> *. . .*
> *Since my crude Mercury's transmute to Gold.*

The poem goes on to emphasize that it is alchemy's power to transmute the man rather than the metal that has led him to offer his fate over to what he calls the "Hermetick Tribe." He asks the stars to give:

> *. . . good direction that shall lead*
> *My Father's hand with's Blessing to my Head*
> *And leave it there. His leaves of Hermes tree*
> *To deck the naked Ash beqeath to me;*
> *His legacy of Eyes to'th blinde Mole spare*
> *And (though a younger Son) make me his Heire.*[21]

What do we know of this Backhouse who chose Elias Ashmole to be his spiritual son and heir, giving the "Mole" new eyes and the "Ash" fresh leaves?

William Backhouse (1593–1662), a younger son of Samuel Backhouse Esq. (1582–1626) of Swallowfield Park in Berkshire, entered

Christ Church, Oxford, as a commoner in 1610, at the age of seventeen. Leaving without a degree (as was not uncommon for gentlemen in those days), he devoted his time to occult studies and became a renowned alchemist, "Rosicrucian," and astrologer.

Backhouse's eldest brother, Sir John Backhouse, K.B., died on October 9, 1649, aged sixty-six. William Backhouse succeeded him as the owner of Swallowfield Park. Among the properties bequeathed him by his brother, William inherited what Samuel Hartlib, the great enthusiast for "Rosicrucian"-style Baconian reform, described as "one of the best Thermometers or Weather-glasses which also K[ing].Charles saw and was mightily pleased with it. Hee hath also a long Gallery wherein are all manner of Inventions and Rarities."[22]

William Backhouse was also a collector of mechanical marvels and, by the way, inventor of the *Way wiser,* a kind of pedometer for attachment to a coach by means of which the distance traveled could be determined.

Above: Swallowfield church.

Right: Swallowfield Park, Berkshire, today—more a haven for anglers than for alchemists.

Backhouse married Anne, the daughter of Brian Richards of Hartley Westpall, Hampshire, by whom he had two sons (who predeceased him) and a daughter, Flower. Flower first married William Bishop (d. 1661) of South Warnborough, Hampshire. Her second husband was her father's kinsman Sir William Backhouse, Bart. (1641–69). Her third husband was Henry Hyde (1638–1709), the second Earl of Clarendon, who rebuilt Swallowfield Park in a style admirable to this day.

On October 22, 1685, Ashmole's acquaintance, the famous diarist John Evelyn, accompanied Lady Clarendon to her house in Swallowfield. Evelyn's description of Swallowfield Park gives some idea of the joy that must have entered Ashmole's heart when he rode or strode through the park to his spiritual father's house:

> This house is after the antient building of honourable gentlemens' houses when they kept up antient hospitality, but the gardens and waters as elegant as 'tis possible to make a flat (site) by art and industry and no mean experience, my lady being so extraordinarily skilled in the flowery part and my lord in diligence of planting so that I have hardly seen a seat which shows more tokens of it than what is to be found here, not only in the delicious and rarest fruits of a garden, but in those innumerable timber trees in the grounds about the seat to the greatest ornament and benefit of the place.
>
> There is one orchard of 1000 golden and other cider pippins, walks and groves of elms, limes, oaks and other trees. The garden is so beset with all manner of sweet shrubs that it perfumes the air. The distribution of the quarters, walks and parterres is also excellent.
>
> The nurseries, kitchen garden full of the most desirable plants, two very noble Orangeries well furnished, but above all the canal and fishponds, the one fed with a white, the other with a black running water, fed by a quick and swift river, so well and plentifully stored with fish, that for pike, carp, bream and tench, I never saw anything approaching it.
>
> We had at every meal carp and pike of size fit for the table of a Prince, and what added to the delight was to see the hundreds taken by the drag out of which, the cook standing by, we pointed out what

most we had a mind to, and had carp that would have been worth at London twenty shillings a-piece.

The waters are flagged about with *Calamus aromaticus*, with which my lady has hung a closet that retains the smell very perfectly. There is also a certain sweet willow and other exotics, also a fine bowling green, meadow, pasture and wood. In a word all that can render a country seat delightful. There is besides a well furnished library in the house.[23]

Ashmole left no record of the carp, but he did make excellent use of the library.

Dying at Swallowfield on May 30, 1662, Backhouse left a number of manuscripts: *The pleasant Founteine of Knowledge: first written in French 1413, by John de la Founteine of Valencia in Henault*, translated into English verse in 1644; a translation of *Planctus Nature: The Complaint of Nature against the Erroneous Alchymist*, by John de Mehung; *The Golden Fleece, or the Flower of Treasures, in which is succinctly and methodically handled the stone of the philosophers, his excellent effectes and admirable vertues*; and, *the better to attaine to the originall and true meanes of perfection, inriched with figures representing the proper colours to lyfe as they successively appere in the pratise of this blessed worke. By that great philosopher, Solomon Trismosin, Master to Paracelsus*—a translation from the French. We have already observed Ashmole collecting a work by Trismosin, presumably from Backhouse's library. He should have been in seventh heaven in the company of one such as Backhouse, the confluence of their mutual interests being so remarkable.

According to his *Ephemerides*, Hartlib inquired of William Petty concerning Backhouse.[24] This was the William Petty who frequented John Wilkins's rooms at Wadham College, Oxford, between 1648 and 1651, at which meetings the core idea of the Royal Society was established (according to Sprat's official history of the society).

Petty described Backhouse to Hartlib as "an Elixir man," and it is difficult to tell whether this designation for an alchemist dedicated to finding the "Elixir of Life" had any pejorative meaning attached to it. One intuits here that Ashmole was not a member of the core group whose associations fostered the Royal Society but was of great interest to at least some of them.

One thing Ashmole certainly had in common with Samuel Hartlib and a number of his friends was an appreciation of those mythic, secret hierophants of alchemical transformation, the fantastic Fraternity of the Rosy Cross (see my book *The Golden Builders* for a thorough account).

THE ROSE CROSS FRATERNITY

Briefly, the Fraternity of the Rose Cross first appeared in manuscript c. 1610. A brilliant and profound satire, the work of Tübingen writer and theologian Johann Valentin Andreae (1586–1654), the *Fama Fraternitatis* (the Fame of the Fraternity) promised the revelation of a new age of scientific and spiritual understanding based on the profoundest wisdom from the East. All this could become a reality, the *Fama* implied, should the wise of Europe awake to the need for cooperation, openness, and the highest spiritual virtue.

Illustration showing the mythic *Collegium Fraternitatis*—the House of the Holy Spirit—from *Speculum Sophicum Rhodostauroticum* by Daniel Mögling (1618).

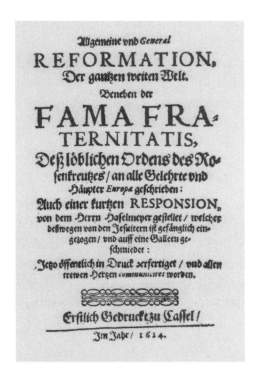

The first printed edition of the
Fama Fraternitatis, Cassel, 1614.

J. V. Andreae (1586–1654), creator
of the virtual Rose Cross Fraternity.
Note the family coat of arms: a
cross with four red roses.

The fraternity's influence would blow away the old world of corruption and scientific incompetence once and for all; men would come together and share the discoveries that God, "the Father of Lights," would reveal to them. Printed in 1614, the *Fama* appeared as a clarion call for every farsighted person of learning and Hermetic-Christian idealism to enter the ranks of the invisible fraternity—invisible, that is, to the blind eyes of the world.

Intended, it seems, as a "virtual fraternity"—membership was by consciousness only (the fraternity would "know" who was with and who against)—it also attracted a large number of cranks to the point that its author withdrew his support from the clamor. However, in England, the Rosicrucian furor arrived rather late, in dribs and drabs, in the form of the covert interest of Paracelsian scholars, physicians, and antiquarians. The Rosicrucian promise smoldered in fitful starts, encouraged by foreign visitors such as Comenius and the Pole Samuel Hartlib.

In Britain, the "Rosicrucian" excitement was channeled and restrained, but no less potent in the long term for that. British aficionados of the

Rose Cross mythology tended to be of the view that the Rose Cross Brotherhood did in fact exist somewhere, somehow, across the Channel, though "good form" prevented one from daring to contact such an august body. Proper form was to associate oneself with its work by an inner commitment to spiritual magick or science. In Britain, the "virtual fraternity" concept worked very well, without much of the bitter aftertaste that afflicted the Continental movement.

Ashmole seems to have concerned himself quite a lot about trying to get authentic knowledge of the Rosicrucians, for it is from about this period that we also get a note, mostly written in cipher from Ashmole's Bodleian papers, offering this surprising snippet: "The Fratres RC : live about Strasburg : 7 miles from thence in a mon[a]st[e]ry."[25] The name "Doctor Molton" is written in the margin of the manuscript, a little above the note, so one may think this snippet came from this (unknown) person. The top of the page is inscribed "Notes out of Dr. Child's book." Clearly Ashmole had not wasted his trip to Maidstone with "Doctor Child the Phisitian" in March 1651.

Ashmole almost certainly believed that the Fraternity of the Rose-Cross actually existed in some form or other. In the Bodleian Library's

THE
FAME
AND
CONFESSION
OF THE
FRATERNITY
OF
R: C:
Commonly, of the
Rofie Crofs.

WITH
A Præface annexed thereto, and a fhort
Declaration of their Phyficall
Work.

By EUGENIUS PHILALETHES.

Jarch: apud Philoftrat:
Καὶ γὰρ κρόσG εἴη, μήτε πιςεύΐν,
μήτε ἀπιςεῖν πᾶσιν.
Veritas in Profundo.

London, Printed by J. M. for Giles Calvert, at th
black fpread Eagle at the Weft end of Pauls. 1652

The first English printed version of the *Fama*, translated by Thomas Vaughan (1652).

Ashmole manuscript collection there exists, appended to a hand-written copy of the *Fama Fraternitatis,* a fervent petition to "the most illuminated Brothers of the Rose Cross" that he, Elias Ashmole, might be admitted to their fraternity.[26] The original English translation from which the copy of the *Fama* was taken lies elsewhere in Ashmole's papers.[27] W. H. Black's *Catalogue of the Ashmole Manuscripts* (1845) notes that the original was "written in an early 17th century hand . . . certainly not later than the reign of Charles I."[28] The original copy of the *Fama* is different from that which Vaughan published (under the name Eugenius Philalethes) in 1652, and may have been in the possession of Backhouse.

Professor Frances Yates believed Ashmole's Latin address, headed *Fratribus Rosae Crucis illuminatissimis*, was an entirely private "pious exercise," a kind of prayer. He was aware that the convention for approaching the fraternity was to understand that the Brothers of the Rose Cross could detect the true will of the aspirant without themselves seeing any written petition. Unfortunately, we do not know for sure the date of this petition, but it would seem to belong to the early 1650s, and it would be reasonable to suggest that Backhouse encouraged the petition.

Certainly by the time his *Theatrum Chemicum Britannicum* was published in 1652, Ashmole was familiar with the contents of the *Fama* and those who encouraged it, such as Count Michael Maier (1568–1622).

On January 26, 1652, Ashmole recorded how "the first of my Theat: Chem: Brit: was sold to the Earle of Pembroke."[29] Ashmole's *Theatrum Chemicum Britannicum*, product of a brilliant research inquiry into the English alchemical tradition, claimed his experience of the field had never passed the stage of speculative inquiry. Spending so much time with Backhouse, he can hardly have been entirely without experience in the matter. It may be that he was trying to avoid violation of his privacy or an attack such as that organized through a mob against Dr. John Dee's library while Dee was on the Continent (September 23, 1583).

Ashmole was fully aware of the treatment England afforded to her alchemists as a rule, and used a story from the *Fama* as an example in his *Prolegomena:*

> Our English Philosophers generally, (like Prophets) have received
> little honour . . . in their owne Countrey : nor have they done any

mighty workes amongst us, except in covertly administering their Medicine to a few sick, and healing them . . . Thus did I.O. (one of the first foure Fellowes of the Fratres R.C.) in curing the Earle of Norfolke of the Leprosie. . . . But in parts abroad they have found more noble Reception, and the world greedy of obteyning their workes; nay, (rather than want the sight thereof) contented to view them through a Translation, though never so imperfect. Witnesse what Maierus [Michael Maier] . . . and many others have done; the first of which came out of Germanie, to live in England; purposely that he might so understand our English Tongue, as to translate Norton's Ordinall into Latin verse, which most judiciously and learnedly he did: Yet (to our shame be it spoken) his Entertainment was too coarse for so deserving a scholar.[30]

Ashmole may have wanted to know whether John Dee—a man with whom he clearly identified—was a member of the fraternity. Shortly after the publication of the *Theatrum,* a Mr. Townesend wrote to Ashmole to inform him that Dee "is acknowledged for one of ye Brotherhood of ye R. CR by one of that Fraternity, who calleth himself Philip

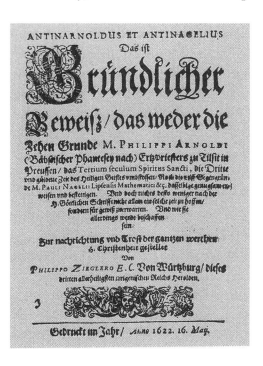

Philipp Ziegler, *Antinarnoldus et Antinagelius . . . o.O.,o.D.,* 1622 (Bibliotheca Philosophica Hermetica, Amsterdam).

Zeiglerus, Francus."[31] Whether or not Ashmole considered this information credible is unknown. We can be fairly certain, however. Ziegler was a German nutcase who declared himself to be the "King of the Rosicrucians" in the 1620s.

Ashmole was certainly fired up sufficiently to want to undertake an even deeper and more expansive study of the alchemical tradition. He hoped for a volume to succeed the *Theatrum*. However, as he would maintain in his preface to *The Way to Bliss* (1658), his studies thereto "received most unfortunate Interruptions, from the Commencement of several vexatious suits against me." These came from Sir Humphrey Forster, Ashmole's brother-in-law, and concerned the tenure of Bradfield. Ashmole had to withdraw himself to some extent from profundities, since "She" [Hermetic Philosophy, or Wisdom] requires "a serene Minde, quiet Thoughts, unwearied Endeavours, indeed the whole Man."

Nevertheless, the studies continued. A month after selling his first copy of the *Theatrum,* he "began to learne Hebrew, of Rabby Solomon Frank."[32] Ashmole was clearly interested in the tradition of Jewish *gnosis* known as Kabbalah, or Cabala, or Qabalah (the Arabic spelling). The idea was that while Moses received an exoteric tradition on Sinai (the Law), he also received an esoteric tradition that was handed down by word-of-mouth and mind to mind. Hence the word *kabbalah* refers to that which has been *received*. Rabbi Solomon Frank was one of the earliest members of the Sephardic community in London that met at a synagogue in Creechurch Lane.

On March 10, Ashmole recorded how "This morning my Father Backhouse opened himselfe very freely, touching the great Secret."[33] As if smelling something interesting going on, 11 a.m., June 14, 1652: "Doctor Wilkins and Mr Wren came to visit me at Blackfriars. This was the first tyme I saw the Doctor."[34] Both men were active members of the core group that, according to Sprat's official history, went on to form the Royal Society.

John Wilkins, DD (1614–72), warden of Wadham College and according to John Evelyn a collector of "artificial, mathematical and magical curiosities," had previously been chaplain to Prince Rupert's brother, Charles Louis, Prince Elector of the Palatine. The prince's son, Charles, would become one of Ashmole's greatest admirers.

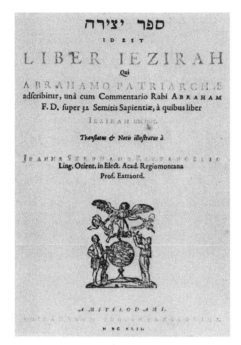

Left: The *Sefer Yezirah* or Book of Creation, a classic of Jewish gnosis. *Sefer Yezirah id est Liber Iezirah qui Abrahamo Patriarchae adscribitur, . . .* Trans. Joannes Stephanus Rittangelius (1606–52), Amsterdam, 1642.

Right: *Artis Kabbalisticae, sive Sapientiae divinae Academia; in novem classes amicissima cum brevitate, tum claritate digesta.* Pierre Morestel (c. 1575–1658), Melchiorem Mondière, Paris, 1621. (Bibliotheca Philosophica Hermetica, Amsterdam)

Wilkins, in his *Mathematical Magick* (1648), based on Dee's *Mathematical Preface* (1570), gives an example of "mathematical magick" in his reference to an underground lamp, comparing it to the lamp "seen in the sepulchre of Francis Rosicrosse, as is more largely expressed in the Confession of that Fraternity." "Francis" is an error made presumably by misreading a manuscript copy of the *Fama* and *Confession;* he takes *fra.*, meaning *frater,* as "Francis."

"Mr. Wren" was of course Christopher Wren (1631–1723), whose chief interests were biology and optics. At this time, Wren was a fellow commoner of Wadham. Royalists Ashmole and Wren would enjoy years of mutual respect, sealed by their common interests in science and the Order of the Garter.

Ashmole's reputation as a walking encyclopedia and man to be consulted and respected grew tremendously quickly after publication of the *Theatrum Chemicum Britannicum*. In 1653, Richard Sanders dedicated his book *Physiognomie, And Chiromancie, Metoposcopie, The Symmetrical Proportions of Signal Moles of the Body &c.* to "the Truly and Vertuously Noble Universally Learned Mycaenas (My Much Honoured Friend) Elias Ashmole Esquire." The letter of dedication praises Ashmole as "a real mercurial Encyclopaedia."

As veneration for mathematics was a central element of British Rosicrucian interest and of burgeoning scientific enthusiasm, it is noteworthy to reproduce a poem on Numbers, written by Ashmole in 1653 and sent to "my vallued Friend Mr : Noah Bridges":

> *For Number is the Mother and the Key*
> *Of Arts; gives lyfe, and opens to a Sea*
> *Of knowledge, whence a Diving hand*
> *May bring whats'ever it conceales to Land.*
> *Number is that whereby Created Things*
> *Subsist, and from whose Roote their vertue springs.*
> *The Patterne in our great Creators Minde,*
> *Whence all things did both Forme and Matter finde.*
> *Nay, 'tis presum'd, the Soul's a Harmony*
> *Fram'd out of Numbers blest Concordancy!*
> *The strickt Observer, by their power, may Skrew*
> *Into the Creatures properties, and view*
> *Their distinct vertues, Nature, Forms, and tell*
> *The uninstructed World, where Secrets dwell,*
> *And by Materiall Things, still upward rise*
> *To th'height of Immateriallities.*[35]

And by Materiall Things, still upward rise / To th'height of Immateriallities. On May 13, 1653, Ashmole at last became privy to the "Great Secret": "My father Backhouse lying sick in Fleetestreete over against St: Dunstans Church, and not knowing whether he should live or dye, about eleven a clock, told me in Silables the True Matter of the Philosophers Stone : which he bequeathed to me as a Legacy."[36]

A clue to understanding what Ashmole meant when he referred to "silables" may be obtained from consulting an anonymous seventeenth- or early-eighteenth-century manuscript in the Bibliothèque Nationale, Paris.[37] A chapter titled "Sillabes Chimiques" concerns certain syllables derived from seven hieroglyphic signs placed at the start of the chapter to form "un mot significatif ou un caractère universel." And that, dear reader, is about the only clue available; Ashmole never revealed, so far as we know, the Great Secret. Though I should say, if the aim was to transform not the metal but the man, then the secret may be discerned in Ashmole's wonderful life, should one's eyes be opened to it.

A GATHERING REPUTATION

We have had cause to refer to the attention shown by Samuel Hartlib in William Backhouse. Hartlib, a synthesizer of Rosicrucian scientific interest, followed Ashmole's emergence with enthusiasm. Ashmole and Hartlib appear to have first corresponded in about 1656. In reply to an inquiry into his current activities, Ashmole stressed the antiquarian side of his engagements. He informed Hartlib of his plans to execute an

Sir William Dugdale of Blyth Hall, Warwickshire, as depicted on the frontispiece of his *Antiquities of Warwickshire.*

GULIELMUS   DUGDALE
Ætatis. 50.   A. MDCLVI.

antiquarian work on Lichfield and Coventry for a book by his friend William Dugdale (1605–86).

Dugdale, of Blyth Hall, Warwickshire, would eventually produce the classic two-volume *Antiquities* of that county. He would become a close friend of Ashmole and, eventually, his father-in-law. Research notes for the Lichfield and Coventry project abound in Ashmole's papers, but as with a number of his ambitious projects, the task was never completed.

Further evidence of Hartlib's interest both in Ashmole's literary activities and in the Rosicrucians comes from his letter of July 20, 1659, to Dr. John Worthington, DD (1618–71), master of Jesus College, Cambridge: "I hear that Mr Ashmole hath published the orders of the Rosie Crucians & Adepti. Can you tell me what esteem it bears?" Perhaps Hartlib was confusing Ashmole's alchemical work of the previous year, *The Way to Bliss,* with the anonymous 1656 English translation of Michael Maier's *Themis Aurea.* Maier's version of the rules and regulations of the Rose Cross Fraternity, published originally in Frankfurt in 1618, was abstracted from the *Fama* and *Confessio,* the first two so-called Rosicrucian Manifestos.

The translation was probably the work of Nathaniel and Thomas

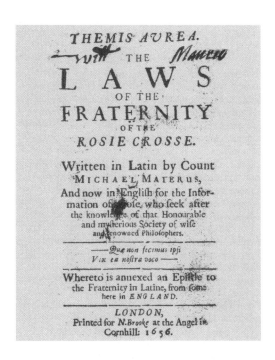

English translation of Michael Maier's *Themis Aurea,* 1656.

Hodges (only initials appear in the text—a common convention in alchemical and particularly Rosicrucian material). *The Laws of the Fraternitie R:C:* was dedicated to Ashmole, described not only as "The onely Philosopher in the present age, but as a Golden Candlestick for the holding forth of that *Lucerna Dei* [lamp of God] to the sons of men by the light whereof the most reclused Mysteries, both naturall and divine, may in some measure . . . be discovered." This is high praise indeed and one wonders whether it had been earned purely on the grounds of his having published the *Theatrum Chemicum Britannicum* in 1652.

One suspects that there was at least one group of Rosicrucian-enthusiasts somewhere who had somehow latched onto Ashmole as a candidate for bringing the Rosicrucian wisdom to light, and that others who had a more *settled* interest in the Rosicrucian Manifestos (such as Hartlib) were wondering what was going on.

Timothy and John Gadbury's *Astronomicall Tables First invented by George Hartgill* was also addressed to Elias Ashmole, commending him in a phrase redolent of Free Masonry "to the safeguard of the Great Architect of Heaven and Earth."[38] It is extremely interesting that John Gadbury takes this opportunity to admonish Ashmole from the "taint" of Rosicrucianism. Clearly *somebody* was attacking Ashmole for his magical pursuits—or getting too close to them.

According to John Gadbury, Anthony Wood, a friendly correspondent with Ashmole in his latter years, said after his death that Ashmole was "accounted a great Rosy Crucian."[39] If this was said, and it probably was during his lifetime, Ashmole would surely have been embarrassed to say the least. He may have put it about his contacts that he was nothing of the sort, attempting to deflect any thought of contact between himself and the fraternity. Gadbury also wrote, "[N]o man was further from fost'ring such Follies." By the time of Ashmole's death, the word had long since acquired connotations of religious anarchy and general subversive battiness. It was used in this sense in Samuel Butler's (1612–80) popular *Hudibras,* written in 1662 after the Restoration, to damn the thinking behind Cromwell's government.

Ashmole never claimed to be a Rosicrucian. Perhaps Gadbury was to keep Ashmole's reputation clear of the kind of exploitative pseudo-Rosicrucianism that had been in vogue in Germany up to the late 1620s.

Furthermore, the Jesuits had consistently held that Rosicrucians were in truth witches out to subvert the planetary order, and this kind of scare may have been prevalent in England at the time.

C. H. Josten makes the point that Ashmole must have been skeptical about the Rosicrucians, and offers a cipher note on Robert Fludd's apology for the Rose Cross, *Summum Bonum* (1629), as evidence for this.[40] All Ashmole says is, "Robt. Flud in his apology for the Brethren of the Rosie Cross hath gone very far herein," which is not particularly conclusive.

The truth seems to be that Ashmole, bemused by the whole subject, could not deny his spiritual identification with the aims of the fraternity as set out in the *Fama* but could find no hard evidence for its actuality— and Ashmole liked his evidence. Nevertheless, he knew that the kind of studies he was pursuing was in tune with the outlook of the *Fama* and in that sense he doubtless felt some kind of inner kinship. He may have asked himself at some stage about his own motivations and wondered if he was not himself guided by an unseen hand. He would also have discerned from the *Fama*'s contents that with regard to membership of the order it was a working principle that "those who know, do not say."

Ashmole may even have thought that the brotherhood's activities had hardly begun, and may have imagined that there was yet a place for him, if indeed he was not already a movement catalyst. In 1652 he had predicted that a "fiery trigon" of Saturn and Jupiter in 1663 would see the appearance of the "more pregnant and famous philosophers"—and in the jargon of the time, philosopher (lover of wisdom) could mean anything in the fields of natural science, theology, alchemy, and magick. It was certainly a designation he was happy to apply to the Fraternity of the Rose Cross in his *Theatrum Chemicum Britannicum*, published in the same year as his prediction. The "famous philosophers" would "Illustrate, Enlarge & Refine the Arts like the tried Gold." [41]

The reference to "tried Gold" finds Ashmole moving in the same prophetic waters as inspired the first Rosicrucian manifestos in the first place—namely, the second book of Esdras: "Then shall they be known, my chosen, and they shall be tried as the gold in the fire."

The real problem at the heart of the issue of Ashmole's relationship to the imaginary Rose Cross Fraternity is that the word Rosicrucian had, by at least the end of the 1650s, come to have two widely divergent meanings. There were inner and outer meanings to the term. There was one meaning for enthusiasts of the esoteric ideal and quite another for those who saw the word as a general adjective for untrammeled popular idealism and fake magick. This situation mirrored to some extent what had already taken place on the Continent some forty years earlier.

For example, in the Restoration comedy *Characters* by Samuel Butler, we hear how "the Brethren of the Rosy Cross" "bring all Things into Confusion, which among them is the greatest Order." Butler identified Cromwell's now defunct government with that of the Brethren, identifying Rosicrucians with Republicanism. Butler used the word in a similar style to that of today when opponents of the government refer to the "loony left." He was saying that the government had been hijacked by a cabal of foolish, devilish, utopian "enthusiasts": wild "new age travellers" squatting in the heart of government, dictating policy. This is all very much in the line of Meric Casaubon's massive attack on John Dee and the "illuminati."

In 1659, Casaubon published juicy details of John Dee's angelic communications that had taken place in the 1580s, during the reign of Queen Elizabeth. His *Strange Relation of what passed for some years between Dr John Dee and some spirits* passed through Britain like a satanic enema. Dr. Dee and his alchemical caravan of magi had uncorked the bottle. The crazy *genii* had been set free. Thus, the Civil War was a result of untrameled "enthusiasm"—a breakdown of order led by those arrogant and quixotic enough to suppose themselves masters of a new one.

In Butler's *Hudibras*, Hudibras (a Presbyterian) and Ralpho (an Independent) set out to reform society. An astrologer, "Sidrophel the Rosy-crucian," is consulted—a possible swipe at Ashmole's friend, the parliamentarian astrologer, William Lilly.

Well, certainly Ashmole was, as Gadbury maintained, as far "from fostr'ing such follies" as could be imagined. Rosicrucian in the 1650s was becoming a philosophical brand name; *fratres R.C.* was perhaps the first occult logo. Witness John Heydon's sometimes ludicrous popularizations, *The Wise Man's Crown*, his *Holy Guide* (based on *New Atlantis*, 1662), *A Rosie Crucian Physick*, and *Voyage to the land of the Rosicrucians*. The word Rosicrucian had become a lick-yer-lips, never-mind-the-quality-feel-the-magic, unique selling point to the quick-on-the-buck publisher. *Real* sympathizers knew better than to parade the name about on cure-all self-healing recipe rags.

THE WAY TO BLISS

By way of contrast, Ashmole finished writing the preface to *The Way to Bliss* on April 16, 1658. He received the text of this anonymous alchemical work from William Backhouse. The publication also included suspected heretic Doctor Everard's transcript and notes. John Everard, DD (1575?–1650?), made the first printed English translation of *The Divine Pymander,* published in 1650. The *Pymander* contained the first four books of the *Corpus Hermeticum,* anciently attributed to Hermes Trismegistus. This was a key text in the 1650s Hermetic book blitz.

The purpose of *The Way to Bliss* was, Ashmole declared, nothing less than "to prove the Possibility of such a thing as the PHILOSOPHER'S STONE." In spite of the evident ambition revealed in its preface, the book landed Ashmole in yet more controversy, as is frequently the case with genuinely occult publications.

John Heydon (b. 1629) was a doctor who claimed to have had unique access to the Rosicrucian Brotherhood, counting himself among its number and publishing popularized versions of what he considered its secrets: a hodgepodge of Paracelsian-style homebrews. Ashmole considered him "an Ignoramus and a Cheate." Heydon called himself, after Vaughan perhaps, Eugenius Theodidactus (the noble or well-born teacher of God).

Ashmole asserted that *The Way to Bliss* was used to make Heydon's two works, *The Wise Man's Crown* and the *Rosie-Crucian Physick,* and that in so doing Heydon had "nefariously robb'd and despoiled" the honor of the anonymous author. Keen to have the last word—sales depended on it—John Heydon replied to Ashmole in the preface to *The Idea of the Law,* alleging that it was *his* "three first books" that were by "Elias Ashmole Esq. made publick, imperfect and rudely Deficient, calling it The way to bliss: In my true copy of which there are four books, all wearing the same title, except the last, which is called, *The Rosie*

Crucian Axiomata . . ." This item appeared shortly after *The Idea of the Law* in London in 1660.

In case anyone missed the point that he was offended by Ashmole's accusation, Heydon warned "all Learned men [was he thinking of men like Wilkins, Petty, and Hartlib, who were considering Ashmole for one of their number?] to take heed of *Theatrum Chemicum Britannicum,* published by Elias Ashmole Esq, and such kind of books as these; for the enemy never resteth, but soweth his weeds till a stronger one doth root it out."[42]

A casual reading of Heydon's works (which were to include in 1660 and 1662, respectively, *The Voyage to the Land of the Rosicrucians—* which linked Bacon's *New Atlantis* to the Fraternity R. C.—and *The Holy Guide*) does nothing to enhance a reputation made by himself.

The 1650s were a sad, mad, bad, and crazy decade—for Ashmole as for many others. Yet they were also a period of intense spiritual searching and profound research in which a number of key figures took divine angler Izaak Walton's advice to their hearts: Resist all temptation to join the clamor and confusion; contemplate the waters, see how they pass and take all before them. Go fishing.

In short: "Study to be quiet."

EIGHT

The 1650s (II)

Study to Be Quiet

ollowing the royalist defeat at Worcester in July 1646, parliamentary officers ordered Elias Ashmole to keep out of London. At about the same time, according to the historian Anthony Wood, Izaak Walton (1594–1684), warden of the Ironmonger's Company Yeomanry, closed his sempster's (seamster's) business on the corner of Chancery Lane and Fleet Street near the Inner Temple and left London, "finding it dangerous for honest men to live there." Like Ashmole, he returned to the area of Shallowford in Staffordshire, near the bishop of Lichfield's palace at Eccleshall, about twenty miles northwest of Lichfield.

Ashmole was a friend of Izaak Walton, but at what date they became friends is unknown. Perhaps they had met around Fleet Street, close to where Ashmole began his legal career in 1638. They were certainly friends by the time of the 1676 edition of Walton's world-famous *The Compleat Angler: The Contemplative Man's Recreation* (first published in 1653), in which Walton referred to their friendship in the context of strange and wondrous marine life.

"I know," wrote Walton, "we islanders are averse to the belief of these wonders; but, there be so many strange creatures to be now seen, many collected by John Tradescant, and others added by my friend Elias

Ashmole, Esq. who now keeps them carefully and methodically at his house near to Lambeth."

To those who are familiar with his references, Walton's work, apparently devoted to the harmless pastime of angling, reads like a covert message to depressed royalists and dispossessed Anglican clergymen throughout the country.

The philosophical roots of *The Compleat Angler* lie in the works of Hermetically influenced Catholic Anglicans and Continental magi. The book's message can be read as "Be calm, contemplate the waters; receive inspiration therefrom: all troubles will pass." Or, as Walton himself recommended, "Study to be quiet." The "troubles" referred to by Walton derived from the puritanical, repressive, anti-ecclesiastical, and generally hot-headed manifestations of Cromwell's government, the Protectorate.

Walton quotes from Albertus Magnus (*On the secrets of Nature,* a favorite work of alchemists and physicists) and from Hieronymus Cardanus's *De Subtilitate* (19th Book: on "raining frogs"). Cardanus was an astrologer (d. 1576) and a favorite author of Johann Valentin Andreae.

Away from the hustle and bustle of city life: stained-glass window from Winchester Cathedral depicting Izaak Walton as the contemplative angler and his excellent advice, "Study to be quiet."

Walton cites Sir Francis Bacon's *Natural History* regarding the mysterious properties of water. When discussing the powers of fish to hear what man cannot, Walton refers to "a mysterious knack, which though it be much easier than the philosopher's stone, yet is not attainable by common capacities, or else lies locked up in the brain or breast of some chemical man, that, like the Rosicrucians, will not yet reveal it."

Walton includes his old friend Sir Henry Wotton (formerly ambassador to the Republic of Venice) as a "chemical man." Walton also uses Du Bartas's *Divine Weekes and Works* (1608, translated by Joshua Sylvester), a book full of Neoplatonic, Hermetic, and Kabbalistic knowledge. The final section of Du Bartas's work deals with Solomon's Temple, with particular reference to those pillars of Jachin and Boaz that appear in masonic lore.

Walton refers with approval to Renaissance Hermetic scholars such as Pico della Mirandola (1463–94) and Franceso Giorgi and his *Harmony of the World*. Indeed, the humble angler's companion reads like a condensation of the spiritual Hermetic reforming philosophy, and would have been understood as such by men of Ashmole's persuasions; it also reads like a book suitable for a Free Mason's vacation. Walton looked to the unity of all things revealed through the deepest contemplation of nature (cf. Ashmole's motto, *Ex Uno Omnia:* both Hermetic-Neoplatonist and monarchist).

Walton was also the biographer of Sir Henry Wotton (1568–1639) and Dr. John Donne (1573–1631). Donne had been a particularly close friend of Walton, a friendship begun when the poet was vicar of St. Dunstan's, Fleet Street. A friendship between a sempster and a famous man might be considered unusual. However, snobs will always fail to see that being special transcends the bounds of class and income. What could possibly have united the sempster and the man who had been chaplain to James I's daughter Elizabeth on her marriage to the elector Frederick of the Palatinate in February 1613? The answer is spiritual insight.

Donne was deeply interested in Pico della Mirandola, Kabbalah, and Hermetism in general. Walton was present when Donne consigned his manuscripts to the care of Dr. Henry King (bishop of Chichester in 1641); at Donne's saintly passing in 1631, Sir Henry Wotton asked Walton to collect material for a life of Donne (published in 1640 with a collection of Donne's sermons). Walton published the biography of Wotton in 1651.

Walton employed a curious seal, given to him by Donne. It shows Christ crucified on an anchor. In his right hand is a set of compasses, compasses being a traditional motif of freemasonry.

SECRET WORK

Two years after the execution of his father, Charles II made a bid to recover the Crown. His Scots army was, however, defeated at the decisive battle of Worcester, following which, after many adventures (such as hiding in an oak tree at Boscobel in Staffordshire), the late king's heir fled to Europe. After the battle, a peculiar correspondence flowed between Izaak Walton (who had been "observing" a "fanaticall meeting" at St. Dunstan's, Fleet Street) and a Mr. George Barlow of Blore Pipe House, near Eccleshall, Staffordshire:

> For Mr Geo. Barlow, att Blowe Pipe House nr. Eccleshalle, in StaffordordeShire, These ffor his owne handes with speede and care.
>
> I praye you Sr to believe this to be a token of my love forr you and a prooffe that I am an honest and loyall man; wh. in these times is a rare character, that it oughte or was wont to be in Englande. Sir 'tis knowne in London that Col. Blague hathe secreted in your house (when you received him after the fatall fighte at Worcester) ye Lesser George of ye Garter, of Gold and Diamonds, belonging to ye King; and there is much talke here of a commission being given to a Troop of horse to searche youre house for it, You may depende on this forr I was tolde it by a Parlimente Captn one Rich: Frankk, whome I mett tonight at a fanaticall meeting called an Evening Lecture held in St Dunstans Churche in Fleete Streete; where a brawling Trooper filled that Pulpit wh. was once occupied by ye learned and heavenly minded Dr Donne. Sr you can devise any meanes of conveying ye Jeuell to me, I praye you to doe so ffor so shall you be discharged, of a dangerous truste and I not suspected, and I will bring it to London where I have some hope of giving it to a gentleman who meanes with all speede to returne unto ye King. I shall follow this letter so

Blore Pipe Farm today—the place where George Barlow hid the Lesser George after the Battle of Worcester.

closely to Stafforde as almost to prevent mine owne messenger, but give him youre commandes and ffear not ffor their coming safe to ye handes of Sr.

Your moste humble servante IZAAC WALTON

From London this second of October 1651.

Elias Ashmole's 1672 antiquarian masterpiece, *The Institution, Laws and Ceremonies of the most Noble Order of the Garter,* tells us what a "Lesser George" is. A George is a medal bearing the image of St. George that hung on a gold chain worn by Knights Companions of the Order of the Garter. Ashmole notes that one such medal was worn by Charles I "at the time of his martyrdom." Ashmole was also clearly aware of the part played by Izaak Walton in the safe transmission of the Lesser George from George Barlow to the exiled Charles II:

> Nor will it be unfitly here remembred, by what good fortune the present Soveraign's lesser George set with fair Diamonds was preserved, after the defeat given to the Scotch forces at Worcester, ann. 4 Car II. Among the rest of his attendants then dispersed, Col. Blague was one; who, taking shelter at Blorepipe house in Staffordshire, where one Mr George Barlow then dwelt, delivered his wife this George, to secure. Within a week after. Mr Barlow himself carried it to Robert Milward, Esq.; he being then a prisoner to the parliament, in the garrison of Stafford; and by his meanes it was happily preserved and restored: for, not long after, he delivered it to Mr Izaac Walton, (a man well known, and as well beloved of all good men; and will be better known to posterity, by his ingenious pen, in the "Lives of Dr Donne, Sir Henry Wotton, Mr Richard Hooker, and Mr George Herbert") to be given to Col. Blague, then a prisoner in the Tower, who, considering it had already passed so many dangers, was yet persuaded it could yet secure one hazardous attempt of his own; and thereupon, leaving the Tower without leave-taking, hasted the presentation of it to the present soveraign's hand.

What an extraordinary business! Here we see Izaak Walton in the role of a trusted agent of the royalist cause, confident that Colonel Blague will be able to escape from the Tower of London and make his way to the rightful monarch, Charles II—and all for the Garter jewel. In his letter to Barlow, Walton notes that he is himself "not suspected," to the extent that he can even attend a "fanaticall meeting" of Puritanical activists, his operation relying on precise knowledge of those individuals with access to the exiled monarch.

We may wonder how it came to be that a tradesman and publisher such as Walton could have had access to such exalted, and risky, circles. In his letter to Barlow he refers to himself as "an honest and loyal man," while in Ashmole's account we are told that Walton was "well beloved of all good men." The adjectives *good* and *honest* seem to bear some special implication in this context. Certainly they are employed with particular reference to those people sympathetic to a traditionalist and sacred commitment to religious and political unity (that in some way, man's place in the cosmic order is dependent upon sacred monarchy: *Ex Uno Omnia*).

It should also be borne in mind that not all those who supported "king & parliament" against Charles I desired either his execution or a cessation of the monarchy. Therefore, Colonel Henry Mainwaring and Ashmole, for example, may have had more in common, politically speaking, than the mere nomenclature of "royalist" and "parliamentarian" might immediately suggest. The issue was essentially one of whether the king could rule without Parliament. Many royalists considered that Parliament had gone too far, infringing more fundamental loyalties. Religious loyalties were also determinative.

A commitment to the principle of unity as both a political and metaphysical principle was not only the hallmark of Walton and his friends, but may well have been an implicit principle and subtending ideal of that "Free Masonry" to which Elias Ashmole was also attached. The hypothesis that Walton was himself a Free Mason—and that this association gave him and others access to a discreet network of operations—cannot be discounted. Such a supposition might well account for Walton's secret part in the affair of the Lesser George. However, Walton's status as agent may also be accounted for on the basis of his privileged friendships with such luminaries as Donne, King, and Wotton: men whose thoughts were characterized by a distinctive Christian spirituality in a monarchical setting.

In fact, there is circumstantial evidence of freemasonic lodge work right in the very heart of that part of Staffordshire where the events surrounding the protection of the Lesser George took place. A few miles on from Eccleshall (in the vicinity of which Walton temporarily retired in 1646) on the Eccleshall-to-Newport road, through Sugnall and Croxton and just before one reaches the magnificent late-Elizabethan hall at Broughton, there is a narrow country lane to a place called Fairoak. A mile down this lane, on the left, one finds Blore Pipe Farm, substantially as it was when George Barlow hid the Lesser George in 1651. Nearby is a sandstone cave where the Duke of Buckingham himself hid after the Battle of Worcester—and just before one reaches Blore Pipe is a country inn called The Freemason's Arms.

While public houses of this name are to be found in towns and cities (notably in London), it is somewhat surprising to find such a place in an isolated country spot like Fairoak. The building dates from the sixteenth century, but no one knows how long it has borne the square and compasses on the outside. There are sandstone quarries at the bottom of the lane, and the area (Bishopswood at the head of the Langot Valley) has revealed evidence of much medieval industry going on in the clearings of the surrounding woods.

Above: The "faery hill" at Fairoak, topped by a grove of oak trees.

Right: George Barlow of Blore Pipe hid the Duke of Buckingham in this cave (overgrown) after the Battle of Worcester (1651).

Masons and freemasons were certainly active in the area in the fourteenth century. A few miles to the east stand the medieval ruins of Ranton Abbey (on lands now owned by Lord Lichfield), while even closer to Fairoak stood Eccleshall Castle, of which Dr. Robert Plot wrote in his *Natural History of Staffordshire:* "And in the reigne of his [Henry III's] Son King *Edw*.I. *Walter de Longton* Bishop of *Lichfield,* and Lord high Treasurer of *England,* some say built, others repaired, *Eccleshall* Castle; and the Manor of *Shoubrough* or *Schuckborough,* which before says *Leland* belong'd to one *Shuckborough* with the long beard, by whom it was given to the Miter [Bishop] of *Lichfield.*"[1]

If associations of like-minded men are simply inevitable, then one does not need to posit the existence of discreet sodalities to explain both Ashmole's and Walton's remarkable connections and activities. Magnetism of mind and inner purpose may be sufficient to account for the great web that bound men like Ashmole and Walton during the 1650s. Royalists, after all, had much in common during this period! Their common cause had been defeated, at least externally. Many suffered and were bound by dependencies.

Nevertheless, it is as natural for like-minded men to form sodalities as it is to be attracted to one another's minds. Something like Free Masonry may have served to ritualize common purposes, like the mathematicians and astrologers feasts to which Ashmole also refers. We cannot say there is *no* evidence for such a conjecture; what we can say is that the evidence does not point inevitably to that conclusion, and for that reason, the question remains open—and the mystery (if there is one) remains.

A JOURNEY TO STAFFORDSHIRE

The destruction wrought by parliamentarian forces did not end with the last shot of the Civil War. A diary note of October 1651 reveals Ashmole's concern for the shelled-out Lichfield Cathedral after two years of the Cromwellian Protectorate: "the stately Cathedrall at Lichfield : set upon to be totally ruined, by Colonel Danvers Governor of Stafford who by authority from the parliament employed workmen to strip off the lead from the roof."[2]

Ashmole kept himself informed of events in Lichfield. A note of July

View of cathedral from the point of view of the artillery at Prince Rupert's Mount.

26, 1653, recorded: "The faire Bell called Jesus Bell at Lichfield knockt in pieces by one Nickins a Pewterer, who was the chief officer for demolishing that Cathedrall."[3]

The violence of the Protectorate extended beyond stones, lead roofs, and church bells. On August 2, 1652, Ashmole "went to Maidston Assizes to heare the Witches tryed, and tooke Mr Tradescant with me."[4] This was John Tradescant the younger, whose private collections at Lambeth so excited Ashmole. In the event, six witches were hanged, accused of bewitching nine children, a man, and a woman, and £500 worth of cattle and corn lost at sea by witchcraft.

Johann Valentin Andreae, the author of the *Fama Fraternitatis*, now an old man in Wolfenbüttel, believed the treatment of witches a stain on mankind. Ashmole did not record his opinion of the sentence. His mind was preoccupied with other things.

Around this time, he and his friend Dr. Thomas Wharton prepared a catalog, published by John Tradescant in 1656: *Amusaeum Tradescantianum: or, A Collection of rarities. Preserved at South Lambeth near London by John Tradescant.* That word *preserved* was very important to Ashmole and he was doubtless worried about what would happen to a collection such as Tradescant's in the future. The making of the catalog was a first step to preserving at least the memory of it. John Evelyn, who visited the Tradescant collection on September 17, 1657, named Ashmole as the sole author of this, "the first English catalogue of a natural history museum."

Soon after the Maidstone trip with Tradescant, Ashmole made an extended journey to Lichfield and Staffordshire. On August 19, 1652, Ashmole "entered Lichfield about sunset."[5] Against the reddish skyline he would have seen the silhouettes of two spires, the third truncated at its base, having crashed through the roof. According to local historian Howard Clayton's *Loyal and Ancient City,* after the parliamentarian destruction of 1646, "Centuries of religious custom disappeared and the Cathedral Close became for 14 years a place of ruin, inhabited by squatters and haunted by owls at night."[6]

Heading north, Ashmole arrived on August 28 at Gawsworth Hall, on the Congleton-to-Macclesfield road, "where my Father in Law Mr Mainwaring then lived."[7] Gawsworth was also the home of Lady Fitton, whom Ashmole had admired six long years before.

"Study to be quiet," advised Izaak Walton, then possibly fishing on the Dove not far away. On September 23, Ashmole himself "took a Journey into the Peake, in search of Plants and other Curiosities."[8] (The river Dove divides the Staffordshire from the Derbyshire Peak District.)

Ashmole's "Noates" of his journey contain short entries of peculiar words, sayings, rhymes, miners' language and customs, cookery recipes, people, inscriptions, and sights. For example, a Staffordshire oatcake was called a "Bannock" consisting of oatmeal and barley, baked on a griddle. "A Spider is called an Aldercrop."[9]

Four miles northwest from Buxton, Ashmole encountered a Mr. Owlerinshaw of Owlerinshaw, who had given "King James [I] greate Satisfaction about the blazing Star. This Owrneshaw [sic] was at Cambridge."[10]

The reference to the "blazing Star" should be of great interest to those concerned with the history of Freemasonry. Ashmole's note is the first reference I have found to this key "ornament" of lodge work.

The "blazing Star" represents the Shekinah, or presence of God. John

Browne's *Master Key*, a book written in cipher in the 1790s, tells us how: "The Blazing Star, the Glory in the Centre, reminds us of that awful period, when the Almighty delivered the two tables of stone containing the ten commandments, to his faithful servant, Moses, on Mount Sinai, when the Rays of His Divine Glory shone so bright, with such refulgent splendour and unparalleled lustre, that none could behold it without fear or trembling."

That King James gained "Satisfaction" on the subject from Mr. Owlerinshaw suggests that His Majesty may himself have been an admitted Free Mason (the word *admitted* refers to Scottish masonic practice where "acceptions" were unknown).

The question-and-answer catechism quoted earlier (Sloane Ms. 3329—the earliest-known English catechism) asks the question: "How many Jewels belong to your Lodge?" To which the answer is given: "There are three. The Square pavement, the blazing Star and the Danty tassley."

There was, at least in the 1720s, a tradition in Free Masonry that

James I as painted by Rubens on the Banqueting Hall ceiling, Whitehall (architects: Inigo Jones and Nicholas Stone). Note the pillars of Solomon's Temple and the figure of Hermes in the foreground. (Photo: Matthew Scanlan)

King James had "revived the English lodges" and was a "Mason King" (Anderson's *Constitutions*, 1723). It is known that he stayed in Staffordshire; hunting expeditions in the vicinity of Hoar Cross in the Needwood (royal) forest occurred in 1619, 1621, and 1624.[11]

The record of Ashmole's meeting characters from the area might also account for his later employee Robert Plot's assertion in his *Natural History of Staffordshire* (1686) that "Free-masons" were "more numerous" in the Staffordshire moorlands than elsewhere. Was Ashmole paying call on brethren?

He mentions a man called "Wagge" from the moorland village of Wetton who "is Staffordshire Astrologus," a fellow astrologer.[12] At Dove Bridge (near Uttoxeter), Ashmole actually participated in a magical "Call," or invocation of spirits. "I came to Mr: Jo: Tompson, who dwells neare Dove Bridge. He used a Call, and had responses in a soft voyce."[13] Ashmole inquired of the spirit concerning the health of his friend Dr. Thomas Wharton, who was poorly. "He told me Dr : Wharton was recovering from his sickness, and so it proved."

On October 2 "I came to Lichfeild."[14] Ashmole's return to his birthplace was to attend to more mundane business than that which occupied him in the moorlands to the north. At 11 a.m. "Mr Anthony Diott offered an agreement between me and my uncle."[15] Anthony Dyott (d. 1662), son of Sir Richard and Dorothy Dyott, was a barrister of the Inner Temple and had been major of a regiment of foot in Charles I's army.

Thomas Ashmole, Elias's uncle, had taken effective possession of the family home in Women's Cheaping (now Breadmarket Street). After negotiations, Ashmole's "Uncle quited his Title to me, which pretended to my home in Lichfeild, and sealed to me a deede of Bargaine and Sale." On the fourteenth, Thomas Ashmole sealed his nephew "a Release and gave me possession."

In 1654, Ashmole was doubtless gratified by the publication of the Oxonian John Webster's *Academiarum Examen, or the Examination of Academies,* wherein Webster advocated that astrology be taught in the universities, which he said, "have not only slighted and neglected it, but also scoffed at it."[16] Webster first eulogizes the exemplary "Mr Ashmole," followed by Mr. William Lilly, Mr. Booker, Mr. Sanders, and Mr. Culpeper. Nicholas Culpeper (1616–54) was an astrologer and physician.

Dr. Seth Ward, one of the core group who would proceed to found the Royal Society, condemned astrology as unsound in his response, *Vindiciae Academiarum* (1654), while admitting that he nonetheless had "a very good respect" for Elias Ashmole. Ashmole himself did not enter the debate and would doubtless have shrugged his shoulders and opined that everyone was entitled to his own opinion. Perhaps he might have added, "Don't knock it until you've tried it." Ashmole never bore grudges and his later relations with Ward were friendly. As usual, he had more interesting things on his mind.

Ashmole had obviously "put it about" that he wanted to know of anything his correspondents could find on the subject of John Dee. In March 1654, Dr. Thomas Browne of Norwich wrote to Ashmole, detailing his meetings and conversation with John Dee's son, Arthur, author of *Fasciculus Chemicus*. Arthur Dee informed Dr. Browne that his father had "small Powder" for projection, which he witnessed.[17]

Dee also informed Dr. Browne that "Kelly dealt not justly with his Father [Dr. John Dee], and that he went away with the greatest part of the powder; and was afterward imprisoned by the Emperor in a Castle from whence attempting an Escape downe the Wall, he fell and broke his Leg, and was imprisoned againe."

This "Kelly" was Sir Edward Kelley, Dee's assistant and subsequently partner in alchemy. Kelley is generally supposed to have led Dee astray, fabricating a number of angelic messages to suit his own purposes or fantasies.

The year 1654 ended sadly. At 6 p.m. on November 24, Ashmole's "good Father in Law Mr Peter Mainwaring died at Gawsworth."[18] One may imagine that the death of his old friend hit him very hard, sending his thoughts back to more innocent times spent joyfully in the bosom of his first Mainwaring home. Peter Mainwaring was buried in the chancel of Gawsworth church.

A fortnight later, "Doctor Pordage [was] put out of Bradfield Living."[19] As the holder of the advowson for Bradfield, Ashmole was to present a successor to the parish. Pordage's ejection had taken some years' effort by the "expurgators" or Commission of Berkshire "for the ejecting of Scandalous, Ignorant and Insufficient Ministers and School-Masters."[20]

The Protectorate had no time for the ancient episcopal order and attempted to rationalize or modernize or reform (whatever the chosen word may be)—or just plain interfere with—religion, as it saw fit.

The Compleat Angler could have been written for John Pordage. However, the mystical doctor did not join Izaak Walton on the Dove or the Ware. Instead, he kept a substantial foot in Bradfield and continued as a fisher of men at a Behemenist "conventicle" in Reading, members of which would go on to form the Philadelphians. Pordage's learned works would inspire the great Non-Juror and mystic William Law (see my book *The Gnostic Philosophy* for an account of Law and Jacob Böhme).

The expurgators, unversed in the profundities of the Silesian shoe manufacturer Jacob Böhme, condemned Dr. John Pordage as "ignorant and very insufficient for the work of the ministry" on sixty-five charges, including blasphemy, heresy, and intercourse with spirits—none of which seems to have caused Elias Ashmole any sleepless nights.

The next year saw the beginnings of Ashmole's consuming interest in the Order of the Garter, perhaps inspired by the story of the fabulous "escape" of the Garter Jewel—the Lesser George—back to Charles II. His manuscript collections for his book *The Institutions, Laws and Ceremonies of the most Noble Order of the Garter* (1672) fill thirty-nine folio volumes. He assembled and reduced most of his material before the Restoration "with ready assistance" from Dr. Christopher Wren, dean of Windsor and register of the Order of the Garter, along with his consulting "other authentick Manuscripts and Autographs." He also made "a painful and chargeable search of our public Records" to produce what would eventually become the greatest work of antiquarian research ever published, a landmark to this day.

Ashmole's instincts for preservation were very marked in the painstaking process that at times must have seemed endless. Furthermore, he chose not to restrict the narrative to the Order of the Garter alone, but to give an account of many other knightly orders (including a watershed account of the Knights Templar—on account of its fairness) and, indeed, a timely exposition of the meaning of nobility and knighthood.

Through all this period, it would appear that not all was well in Ashmole's relationship with his wife. Exacerbated partly by the lawsuits of her own children against her husband, and partly by temperamental conflicts, their mutual affection cooled. One writer has referred to the "slow crucifixion of an unhappy marriage" and something of the kind seems to have been in Ashmole's mind when he secreted the following couplet in his papers on April 27, 1655:

> *How sad's the Lyfe, when cruell Fate*
> *Waste all its Hourse, 'twixt Love and Hate?*

It was probably a deep love that made them hate one another; a love unspoken grows twisted and alien from its root. At the end, a cold heart and a skinny bag of untold memories.

In the following year, Ashmole's wife sued her husband for alimony, having been badgered for years by members of her family. In a chorus led by Sir Humphrey Forster, they had accused her of allowing Ashmole to pressure her into a stance of carelessness toward her own children. This gibe hit home and undermined the couple's relationship. The case came to a final hearing on October 8, 1657.

John Maynard (Ashmole's counsel) asserted that while Mrs. Ashmole's deposition had amounted to 800 sheets of paper, "not one word" had been proved against Mr. Ashmole "of using her ill nor ever giving her a bad or provoking word." The Lords Commissioners denied alimony and delivered Mrs. Ashmole back into her husband's care (they had been living apart). The Ashmoles went to live with William Lilly and his wife.

Lilly recorded that Ashmole never blamed his lady, only her illness and her "Councillors and Abettors." It seems that the couple underwent a genuine reconciliation following the case and that after the storms, fate "pleased to sweeten" Ashmole's "long-Sufferings with a fair and peaceful Issue."[21]

Nevertheless, it would appear that the couple were living apart at the time of Mary's death eleven years later, at which time Ashmole lost all title to the lordship of Bradfield, along with the substantial sum of £602, sixteen shillings per annum.

Happily, there were compensations for the trail of misery walked by the Ashmoles. Ever adept at "locating the talent," Ashmole had become friendly with fellow antiquarian William Dugdale of Blyth Hall, Warwickshire (where a magnificent portrait of Ashmole as Windsor herald still hangs).

CONTEMPLATIVE MEN AND ANTIQUARIAN RECREATION

William Dugdale was Ashmole's senior by twelve years. Perhaps there was a subconscious need for another surrogate father figure after the death of Peter Mainwaring. Happily, the affection Ashmole held for his future father-in-law was reciprocated. They enjoyed the same things: journeying about the byways of England, visiting churches, recording inscriptions, holding up at good taverns, searching through ancient manuscripts, picking up stories and artifacts, and delving deeply into the past. They were the living embodiments of "the Contemplative Man's Recreation." Together, they went a-fishing for England's history.

In Dugdale's *Antiquities of Warwickshire* there is an engraving by Wenceslaus Hollar of "The prospect of Guyes Cliffe from the meadows on the north-east thereof."[22] The engraving bears Ashmole's coat of arms and the inscription *Posteritati Sacrum Per Eliam Ashmole Arm. Mercuriophilum Anglicum.* Perhaps the pair would be pleased to know that a lodge of Free and Accepted Masons now meets at the chapel of St. Mary Magdalene, Guy's Cliff, the lodge dominated by the ancient carving of Guy of Warwick depicted in Dugdale's work. Guy's Cliff's spiritual associations go back to the time of the ancient British saints who emerged from Wales after the Romans departed.

Incidentally, it was Ashmole and Dugdale who initiated the scholarly use of flint instruments for purposes of archaeological dating.

The duo spent May and June 1657 traveling and making extensive observations in Staffordshire, Northamptonshire, Nottinghamshire, Hertfordshire, Devonshire, Lincolnshire, and Yorkshire. They recorded the presence of tumuli, ancient stones, ruined remains of the Roman occupation, churches, and monuments. They measured churches, drew coats of arms, and made copious botanical notes. They were antiquar-

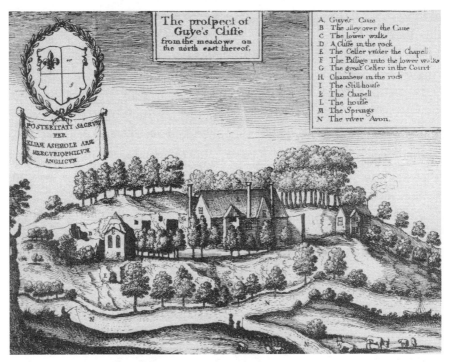

Guy's Cliff, near Warwick, as depicted in Dugdale's *Antiquities of Warwickshire* (1656).

ians, doing what antiquarians are supposed to do. They were easy riders of the wealds, valleys, and plains of England; nothing passed them by.

On January 25, 1658, Sir Thomas Browne of Norwich again put quill to paper on the subject of his conversations with Arthur Dee. According to Dr. Browne, Arthur Dee "was a persevering Student in Hermeticall Philosophy, and had no small encouragement having seene projection made, And with the highest asseverations [*sic*] he confirmed unto his death, that he had occularly undeceavably and frequently beheld it in Bohemia, and to my knowledge, had not accident prevented, he had not many yeares before his death, retired beyond Sea, and fallen upon the solemne process of the great worke."[23]

This letter can only have encouraged Ashmole in completing his preface to *The Way to Bliss* three months later, "to prove the Possibility of such a thing as the PHILOSOPHER'S STONE," as the title has it.

On July 27, 1658, Ashmole was off on his travels again—this time alone. "I went toward Worcestershire and Staffordshire, 4H.P.M. In this Journey I visited Sir Tho : Leigh [August 6]; Sir Harvey Bagot [Bt. 1591–1660; Ashmole visited Blithfield Hall, near Abbots Bromley on August 14], Sir Rich Lewson, the Earle of Denbigh."[24]

Sir Thomas Leigh (c. 1616–62) lived at Hamstall Ridware; his once fine Jacobean mansion is now a set of striking ruins at the back of the fine church, some seven miles north of Lichfield. To stand in the cemetery there and gaze at those ruins, and to imagine Ashmole arriving during a long-lost summer long ago, is to experience what it is to be an antiquarian—to leap across time as the past leaps toward one.

On August 4, Ashmole was in Lichfield, presumably enjoying a not

The ruins of the Jacobean mansion at Hamstall Ridware, visited by Ashmole in 1658. The spire of Hamstall Ridware church rises behind them.

dissimilar experience. He copied lists of streets, places, and tenements mentioned in three registers of Lichfield Cathedral. He also took notes and made drawings of monuments, coats of arms, and inscriptions in the church of St. Michael, Greenhill.

THE TRADESCANT DEED OF GIFT

On December 16, 1659, while England appeared to be slipping out of control after the death of Oliver Cromwell, John Tradescant the younger chose to make an extraordinary gift. He apparently decided that posterity would have a greater chance of viewing his collections intact if he passed them on to Elias Ashmole's charge in the event of his death.

"5H.30' P.M. Mr Tradescant and his wife sealed and delivered to me the deed of Guift of all his Rarities." The Gift included books, coins, pictures, medals, stones, "mechanicks," "Pieces of Antiquity" and "other things and Rarities."[25]

This event has generated some controversy. Since the Tradescant collection became the basis for the first Ashmolean Museum's contents, it has served some writers' evident distaste for Elias Ashmole to regard his achievement as the mere "gifting" to Oxford of Tradescant's achievement, with Ashmole's name cunningly absorbing all the credit.

A recent biography of Sir Christopher Wren by Lisa Jardine sees Ashmole as a somewhat shady character, one who appropriated for himself the credit of another's labor. Taking the (at the time) discredited words of Ashmole's enemy Henry de Vic (c. 1599–1671), chancellor of the Order of the Garter, as ammunition, Ashmole is presented as an overly ambitious fraud who got where he was by grafting himself on to the work of others.

Ms. Jardine writes: "Elias Ashmole is a particularly striking case of someone who did well out of the Restoration through his flair at 'remembering' a largely apocryphal golden Stuart past before the Civil War. His lasting fame and 'name' rest (in the title of the Ashmolean Museum) upon his dubious acquisition of another man's lifetime collection of rarities, and his subsequent gifting of them to the University of Oxford."[26]

This is a serious charge. It is as serious as a supposition that since Ashmole was a Hermetic Philosopher, he stands at the end of a superstitious era (with his back to us), unworthy of little more than quaint footnote status in the era of modern science that succeeded it.

As has been observed, modern science disowned the mother ("natural magick") that bore it. Does it then suffer from an Oedipus complex? Truth will out. Newton practiced alchemy; Ashmole was accounted a fine mathematician. William Dugdale, acknowledged as one of the greatest antiquarians in Britain's history, chose to work in close concert with Ashmole for years. Was he duped?

It is difficult to know on what evidential basis the charge is made that Ashmole had a flair for "remembering" (the use of quotation marks seem to suggest that *fabricating* would be a more appropriate word) an apocryphal Stuart golden age. Nor can the author assess the value of calling Ashmole a "striking case," a phrase redolent of the Bar. However, it is at least possible to disentangle the circumstances that led to Ashmole's temporary possession of the Tradescant rarities. Members of the historical jury will find that there was nothing "dubious" in the transaction.

It is important to recall that Ashmole's personal fame and reputation did not depend upon the restoration of the monarchy. Ashmole was regarded as a leading light in his field—or fields—even while Cromwell ruled. Ashmole's carefulness and powerful preservation drives made him an obvious candidate—in fact, as history shows, a most justified choice—for the care and trust of the Tradescant collections.

The Deed of Gift was first disputed in 1661. John Tradescant's widow, Hester, with motives of her own, said that her husband came home "distempered" and got her to sign the document inadvisedly, as a witness.[27] She maintained that her husband later canceled the deed as he did not want the collections in private hands. Mrs. Tradescant did not know that the deed had legal standing and could not be canceled by one party.

In fact, Ashmole returned the deed to her and said that if she did not like it, he would not "have it for a world"; honesty compelled him to surrender the legal evidence of the advantage he had gained.[28] But the Tradescants must have thought that the return of the deed relinquished its power; it did not. They kept the deed. Tradescant changed his will to leave his collections after his widow's death to the university of either Oxford or Cambridge.

Ashmole did not claim to be the founder of the Tradescant collec-

Elias Ashmole, Windsor herald, by Cornelis de Neve, painted sometime in the 1660s. (Photographed by kind permission of Sir William Dugdale, Bt., Blyth Hall, Warwickshire)

tions, only of the museum that preserved them, among other things. To that museum he entrusted those collections, adding into the bargain his own remarkable collections. The beneficiary of a "dubious transaction" would surely have sold the material for personal profit or attempted to conceal its provenance.

On June 16, 1660, Ashmole "first kissed the King's hand."[29] The madness was over (thought the royalist)—and many an old fool returned to prominence (thought John Milton). The Restoration ended the hard years of Cromwellian rule and the sun kissed the fortunes of Elias Ashmole.

As we shall see in chapter 9, King Charles II regarded Ashmole as a striking case of an honest man; the king was very shrewd.

NINE

The Windsor Herald

M
ay 29, 1660: "For now the nights dire tragedies are done
. . ." King Charles II enters London and Ashmole published a poem, *Sol in Ascendente* . . . to celebrate the
glorious Restoration.[1]

Just over a fortnight later (June 16), precisely at 4 p.m., he "first kissed
the King's hand," having been introduced by the king's page, Thomas
Chiffinch (1600–66).[2] Two days later, the king appointed Elias Ashmole
as Windsor herald. His duties involved keeping accurate records of the
nobility and heraldry of England and establishing rights to coats of arms,
as well as organizing ceremonial occasions and participating in them
as one close to His Majesty. On the same day, Ashmole's good friend
William Dugdale was appointed Norroy King of Arms. Together they
would endeavor to restore nobility to England.

It hardly needs saying, but Ashmole did not ingratiate himself into
the king's favor, having been recommended by those closest to His Majesty. After nine years in exile, Charles II barely had time to see his bags
unpacked before giving an audience to the squire of Bradfield (retd.) and
member of the Inner Temple (since 1657): an astrologer and antiquarian
whose last publication was an obscure text on alchemy. But Ashmole
had a reputation for loyalty.

On what basis, other than having been penalized by Parliament for

Engraving of King Charles II from Elias Ashmole's *Institutions, Laws and Ceremonies of the Most Noble Order of the Garter* (1672).

The most High most Excellent and most Mighty Monarch Charles the Second, by the Grace of God King of Greate Britaine France and Ireland Defender of the Faith and Soveraigne of the most Noble Order of the Garter.

taking up arms for the king, that loyalty was now being rewarded is still something of a mystery. Ashmole had carried out intelligence work for King Charles I's army during the first Civil War. Furthermore, he was approved of by Samuel Hartlib and other scientific advisers to the king's aunt, Elizabeth of Bohemia, and her son Charles Louis (based in the Hague).

In this period, as in our own, science and state intelligence frequently went hand in hand. The first president of the Royal Society was Sir Robert Moray. Moray served on diplomatic missions for King Charles II during the latter's difficult exile. He was an admitted Free Mason (1641, into a Scottish lodge, Mary's Chapel No. 1), astrologer, scientist, accounted a "great patron of the Rosie Crucians" in his chemical enthusiasms, and, at least by the time of his death in 1673, a friend of Ashmole, who remembered him as "learned and ingenious."

On December 1, 1660, Ashmole recorded how the king "gave me [another] gracious audience and among other things told me, he believed I was an Honest man, He lookt upon me as an Honest man, and would take care for me as an Honest man."[3] For a man such as the king, enveloped in intrigue and skulduggery for most of his life, the presence of Elias Ashmole must have made a refreshing change.

On February 9, 1661, the king signed a warrant making Ashmole secretary of Suriname, in the West Indies. Had the story of England's relations with Suriname developed along the lines of some of her other possessions in the region, Ashmole might have found himself extravagantly wealthy after such an appointment. But he always had to make his luck; little material wealth ever simply rolled into his lap.

Disease-ridden and populated with nomadic Arawak Indians, Suriname saw the arrival of Europeans starting in the 1650s. Suriname's first English settlers were dispatched by Lord Willoughby, the governor of Barbados, but after a brief settlement the Zealander Andreas Crijnsen invaded in 1667. The struggle was concluded when the peace of Breda ceded Suriname to the Dutch. England gained New Amsterdam. Now, had Ashmole become secretary to what would later become New York, his life might have been very different.

On February 21 it was decided that Ashmole would be paid forty marks annually for his services as Windsor herald. A mark was worth about two thirds of a pound; he was unlikely to build a palace through such royal favors—but he did get to attend the "big events."

On April 23, 1661—St. George's Day—Charles II was crowned at Westminster. C. H. Josten concluded that as Windsor herald, "[Ashmole] may have been consulted as an authority on doubtful questions of ceremonial and precedence," as well as the practical preparation of the festivities.[4] Josten also emphasizes, "Every detail of the ceremonies was to Ashmole a matter of interest."[5] Ashmole's account of the coronation was authoritative but he was not credited in later accounts of the sumptuous ceremony. In fact, his definitive account received no credit until 1761.

In 1661, Ashmole published *A Catalogue of the Peers of the king-*

doms of England, according to their birth and Creation, and became deputy for Sir Edward Bysshe, Clerenceux king of arms. On May 16 of that year, Ashmole recorded "the Grant of Arms to me from Sir Edward Bysh Clarenceux."[6]

Now holding an important position in the determination of nobility, Ashmole considered that the time had come for some recognition of his tireless work—undergone at his own expense—in preserving, recording, and editing records concerning the Order of the Garter. He hoped the order would grant him the title of historiographer and remembrancer of the Order, not being himself a knight, and grant some recompense for expenses incurred.

Ashmole's legitimate hope was cut cruelly short by Henry de Vic, first baronet of the Isle of Guernsey and chancellor of the order since March 29, 1661. De Vic made a shocking speech to order members, accusing Ashmole of social climbing, big-headedness, and megalomania. Ashmole should be dismissed from consideration as he was, according to de Vic, "unknowne and I am afraid Illiterate" and had "never served the Publick."[7] He was a tiresome money grubber who wanted to run everything and who needed stopping in his tracks.

What, apart from rank snobbery and meanness, drove de Vic to attempt to denigrate Ashmole is unknown. Ashmole had enemies, of course—not least among whom had been his brother-in-law, Sir Humphrey Forster. The king raised his eyebrows and shrugged his shoulders; Ashmole withdrew, not wanting to be the cause of controversy or dissension in the order. Deeply hurt, as one might expect, Ashmole very nearly dropped his long-standing Garter project for good.

On May 29, 1674, Henry de Vic's shameful speech was quietly excised from the Order's written record by Seth Ward, the bishop of Salisbury and chancellor of the Order, lest it stain either the Order's or Ashmole's historic reputation. Had there been any doubt in the king's mind concerning Ashmole's decency where money was concerned, the monarch would certainly not have appointed his herald to the Royal Commission on June 30, 1662, for the recovery of Charles I's belongings, stolen, sold, and scattered under Cromwell's rule.

THE ROYAL SOCIETY

Ashmole's reputation as an invaluable Englishman of learning was reinforced following a meeting held at Gresham College on November 28, 1660. On that date, a preparatory meeting of twelve members of the future Royal Society took place. Four days later, Ashmole's signature appears in the Royal Society's first journal book, among those of 114 specially invited to join the nation's first organization for the furtherance of scientific experiment.

Ashmole, officially proposed on December 12, was duly elected a Fellow on January 2, 1661. "This afternoon [January 9, 1661] I went to take my place among the royall Society [blank left to fill in the final agreed name] at Gresham Colledge."[8] Its declared "designe of Founding a College for the Promoting of Physico-Mathematicall Experimentall Learning" proved too cumbersome to provide its title. The once "Invisible College" of Robert Boyle's dreams became known simply as the Royal Society; its patron, King Charles II.

In 1664, the Royal Society appointed Ashmole to a committee charged with "collecting all the phenomena of nature hitherto observed, and all experiments made and recorded." This somewhat ambitious program (never completed) was very much in tune with the work of the fictional Fraternity of the Rose Cross and certainly consistent with the labors of Sir Francis Bacon's "Merchants of Light" in the latter's influential *New Atlantis* (1627). Sir Francis appeared on the cover of Sprat's official history of the order as a posthumous patron. Ashmole would doubtless have preferred to see John Dee in his place.

Detail from frontispiece of Thomas Sprat's *History of the Royal Society*. To the left (seated) is Robert Boyle and to the right, Sir Francis Bacon.

Ashmole still hoped for a great flowering of alchemical knowledge and cosmic insight (beginning, he predicted, in 1663), led by coming philosophers who would "Illustrate, Enlarge and Refine the Arts like tried Gold." We do not know if the society's confining itself largely to matters of mechanical demonstration would have disappointed him. As a mathematician, he would certainly have been pleased at the society's giving the once suspected discipline of mathematics greater respectability and impetus.

Like many thoughtful mathematicians of the time, Ashmole held Dee's 1570 *Mathematical Preface* (to Euclid) dear. For Dee as well as Ashmole, mathematics was a dimension of the spiritual mind that could be discerned in Nature, but whose source was absolutely immaterial. Dee got bored with mathematics—having been, as Ashmole asserted of him, "a perfect master"—and attempted to communicate with the universe's governing angels directly. I suspect that Ashmole felt similarly; he took scientific method for granted.

Unlike the English population at large—and that of most of the rest of the known and unknown world—he needed no persuasion of the potential of science. He would have found today's continual stream of scientific evangelism tiresome. He knew that experimental methodology was only a means to an end, not a cosmic principle. His feel for evidence and his incredulous common sense are apparent on every page of his antiquarian works. He could relax his guard where medicine was concerned, but many today take their pills in a state bordering on faith.

On May 27, 1663, Royal Society Council Minutes record how it "Ordered that Dr Goddard deliver the Charter of the Society to Mr Elias Ashmole, to enrole the Armes of the Society, and the Claims Concerning the same in the Heralds Office."[9] This person was Dr. Jonathan Goddard (1617?–75). His visit to Ashmole's office might have occasioned a degree of disappointment for Ashmole, who had proposed a beautiful design for the arms.

In Josten's words, "The drawing [of the arms] is of particular interest because of its possibly masonic symbolism, deriving from *Amos* VII, 7–8."[10] Ashmole's design shows the royal standard to the top left while from above condescends a hand, holding a plumb line that is held in suspension in the darker, lower portion of the coat of arms. The motto below is taken from Virgil's *Georgica,* ii, 490: *rerum cognoscere causas* ("to know the causes of things").

Like all human organizations, the Royal Society was always more ready to receive gifts than grant favors. According to Royal Society Classified Papers, on March 29, 1682, it received as a gift from Ashmole a book for its library, *Three Relations concerning ye nature, Effects and Theory of Comets,* written "in High Dutch" (German).

THE ANTIQUARIAN

In the spring of 1675, the secreted bones of the poor "Princes in the Tower" were discovered during renovation work at the Tower of London. On May 9, a letter winged itself from the pen of John Aubrey (1626–97), antiquarian and historian of Wiltshire, to Oxford historian Anthony Wood.

"The bones of Edward V and Brother are found, and the King is making a noble Monument and ISS [inscriptions] for them at Westminster: and Mr Ashmoll (who remembers him to you) assists in the Designe."[11]

We find Ashmole, at the age of fifty-seven, at the center of things: assisting the king in a sensitive memorial project, observed by one of the great antiquarians of the day, writing to the up-and-coming historian Anthony Wood. Ashmole was a news item.

Thirteen years earlier, Ashmole had his busy pen in hand, taking notes in the church and manor house at Blore, near Ilam in the Staffordshire moorlands (August 10, 1662). A priest hole was discovered in the 1990s in one of the bedrooms at Blore. Many of the old genteel families stayed true to the old "Romish" religion. One can only guess as to whether Catholic rites took place in Ashmole's presence. He never seems to have gotten involved with debates about "which religion was better." He was probably loyal to the Anglican Church as the reformed Catholic Church of England but, one suspects, more than tolerant of individual Catholics.

An interesting exchange in this regard was recorded in the autobiography of nonconformist minister (and relative of Ashmole) Henry Newcome, MA. On December 7, 1664, Newcome was reminded of a meeting: "I was thinking of a passage of my brother Ashmole's when we met him at Knutsford, how he discoursed with my wife about my conformity—that nonconformity could be nothing but in expectation of a change. Alas, a thing I never thought of."[12]

This fascinating remark is very telling as to Ashmole's subtlety and originality. If I interpret it correctly, Ashmole seems to have been implying to Newcome that nonconformity, being defined by its *reaction* to something disapproved of, should never be regarded as a stable state by itself. Sects are built on disputes, and are therefore never stable, unless ossified by aggressive oppressiveness. Then brave sparks simply quit. True religion must be rooted in something more than doctrinal disagreement, however sincerely held. Ashmole was always looking for the roots of things. Really, his religion was cosmic, Gnostic, and personal. This was, I believe, his ideal Church for England.

A year after taking notes at Blore, Ashmole was back on the antiquarian peace path, this time in the good company of William Dugdale. Perhaps his mind was more settled than it had been for many years. Ashmole's brother-in-law and enemy, Sir Humphrey Forster, baronet of Aldermaston, Berkshire, had just died. Forster had plagued Ashmole's life with lawsuits and insults for over a decade, destabilizing his marriage and his work. Were it not for Forster, by Ashmole's own account, we should probably have seen a second volume of the *Theatrum Chemicum Britannicum* and who knows what else; Ashmole always had a number of fascinating projects "on the go."

Portrait of Sir William Dugdale, Blyth Hall, Warwickshire. (Photograph taken by kind permission of Sir William Dugdale, Bt.)

Between March 30 and April 10, 1663, Dugdale accompanied Ashmole on a heraldic visitation of Staffordshire. This involved, in part, recording knightly armorial inscriptions and gathering information on ancient families.

On April 1, Ashmole spent the night in the home of Sir Edward Bagot, baronet, at Blithfield. Bagot's descendants abide there to this day; families are the marrow of history. A broken family is as terrible as an ancient tree felled wantonly. Though the mustard seed be smaller than a fingernail, from it comes a home for all the birds of the air. Every home is a nest; every egg has a story.

Above: The entrance to Blithfield Hall, home of the Bagot family.

Left: Blyth Hall (on the river Blyth) as depicted in Dugdale's *Antiquities of Warwickshire.*

From Staffordshire, Ashmole and Dugdale rode on to Shropshire. August 3, 1663: "9 H.A.M. I began my Journey to accompany Mr : Dugdale [Norroy King of Arms] in his Visitation of Shropshire and Cheshire."[13] Visitations were held at inns, where attestations by former Norroy and Clerenceux Kings of Arms were copied. Heads of families were summoned to attest claims of arms and descent. There had been vast despoiling of records during the Reformation and civil wars. Ashmole and Dugdale were endeavoring to play their part in darning the split fabric of English life and history.

For example, Ashmole took notes in the church at Malpas, Cheshire, recording inscriptions to "Judith, wife of Thomas Dod of Shoklach" (d. January 21, 1651); Dr. Thomas Dod (d. March 10, 1647)—the Dods had been at Edge since Saxon times; "Thomas Bulkley of Bikerton" (d. October 24, 1624); "Owen Clutton of Chorlton" (d. November 18, 1648); " . . . a coat of arms . . . of Mr Dod of Edge."[14]

Ashmole made notes on the church at Gawsworth, where his late father-in-law Peter Mainwaring lay beneath the chancel. Ashmole described a portrait in the east window of the chancel and an inscription

Left: Blithfield church.

Right: Malpas church, Cheshire, visited by Ashmole and Dugdale in the summer of 1663.

beneath, commemorating Sir Richard Sutton, co-founder of "Brazen-nose Colledge in Oxford : and benefactor to this Church. Anno Domini 1505."[15] Brasenose was, of course, Ashmole's college. The other founder of that excellent college (and founder of Lichfield's Grammar School) was Bishop Smyth of Lincoln.

On June 3, 1668, William Dugdale addressed a letter "from Mr Ashmoles Chamber in ye Middle Temple Lane" to Thomas Yate, Principal of Brasenose College, Oxford.[16] According to C. H. Josten (another Brasenose man): "This letter, which deals with the restoration of the tomb of Bishop William Smyth in Lincoln Cathedral, is preserved among the muniments of Brasenose College; it has been printed in R. Churton, *The Lives of William Smyth Bishop of Lincoln and Sir Richard Sutton Knight, Founders of Brasen Nose College*, Oxford, 1800, pp. 532–3."[17] The author, Archdeacon Ralph Churton (1754–1831), was himself a Fellow of the Royal Society of Antiquaries, an institution that owed much of its founding impetus to the pioneering works of Ashmole, Dugdale, and Aubrey.

Two months after Dugdale visited Ashmole in Middle Temple Lane, Ashmole himself visited Dugdale at Blyth Hall, Warwickshire. The purpose was probably to propose marriage to Dugdale's third and second surviving daughter, Elizabeth. Shortly before they were married at the chapel of Lincoln's Inn on November 3, 1668 (Ashmole's second wife having died on April 1), William Lilly "predicted" the nature of Ashmole's third wife; he had probably met her already.

The chapel at Lincoln's Inn, London, where Ashmole married Elizabeth Dugdale.

Blyth Hall today. (Photographs taken by kind permission of Sir William Dugdale, Bt.)

Note the date on this chimney on the side of Blyth Hall.

" . . . (O)f a middle stature, round visage, having a mole on her cheek . . . of a lovely feature indifferent fleshy or Corpulent, or inclining thereunto, loving hospitality or to live handsomely.

". . . (I)t is very probable, a third wife shall bury him, yet will shee bee very flegmatiq, and accidentally inclined to the spleen and griefe." Ashmole would find her "instabliem in venerijs et amoribus."[18] Josten summed up the picture of a woman "amorous, unstable, charming and probably rather foolish."

It is impossible to know what Elizabeth brought to the marriage, apart from a father-in-law who had first been Ashmole's true friend. Elizabeth admired her husband and, according to Anthony Wood, was wont to embrace him in public—something the author suspects would have induced pleasantly raised eyebrows—and perhaps a twinkle from Elias Ashmole. Now fifty-one, the Windsor herald had known matrimonial and social coldness for over a decade.

Some signal recognition of Ashmole's skills did come in his lifetime: "I received the honor of being made Doctor of Phisick at Oxford" (August 19, 1669).[19] While Ashmole was mentioned by Anthony Wood as one of Oxford's famous authors who were members of Brasenose College, Wood failed to mention some of Ashmole's most important antiquarian work.[20]

This omission was brought to Wood's attention in a letter from John Aubrey on the publication of Wood's work: "(H)e [Ashmole] is a mighty good man : and very obliging : . . . Mr Ashmoll is troubled that you have omitted in his *Life* what he most valued, *viz*. His Catalogue of the Collection of Rarities of the University which he did with his owne hand, and was a very laborious worke . . ."[21] There are references to Ashmole's manuscript catalog in the three-volume register of consular and imperial Roman coins in the Bodleian Library. Great achievements of antiquarians rarely rise farther than the footnotes of unloved works; posterity has little time for gratitude.

THE MASTERPIECE

There was, however, one antiquarian work accomplished in his lifetime that did garner the recognition Ashmole justly deserved. On May 8, 1672, he recorded how at "2H 40' I presented my Book of the Garter to the King."[22] The mighty work was "very graciously" received. He also dispatched a copy to the Dean and Chapter of Lichfield, where it still resides in the Cathedral Library. Nathaniel Greenwood, *Custos Jocalium* of Brasenose College in 1675, inscribed the flyleaf of that college's presentation copy of the book as follows: *Liber Aulae Regiae et Collegii de Brasenose ex Dono Authoris, huius Collgij olim Alumni.* John Wilkins formally presented a copy of the masterpiece to the Royal Society.

According to Dame Frances Yates, "The book is a landmark in antiquarian scholarship and still unsurpassed as the main authority on its subject. In the preface Ashmole tells of his distress at seeing the honour

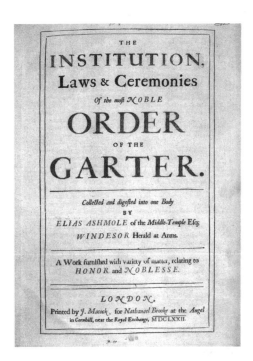

Title page of Elias Ashmole's
antiquarian masterpiece.

of the Garter trampled on in 'the late unhappy times' of the civil wars. His purpose was to restore the image of the Order as a step toward the Restoration. When his great book was published, copies were sent abroad, almost like embassies to foreign potentates."[23]

On October 25, 1673, Ashmole received a letter from the court of Charles Louis, elector of the Palatinate and Samuel Hartlib's patron. Even while the French army was marching through the Palatinate to further Louis XIV's imperial ambitions, R. Rockwood, "Counsellor to his Electorall Highness and Governor of Oppenheim and Heidelberg," found time to write to Ashmole to thank him for the Garter book.[24] Charles Louis' heir, Prince Charles, a great admirer of Ashmole, would seek conversation with the old man on a visit to London in 1690.

The German Palatinate was not the only court to express its gratitude for Ashmole's work. The antiquarian recorded how on June 17, 1674, "The King of Denmarke has sent me a gold Chaine and Medal worth 80l. [pounds]."[25] Ashmole was justifiably proud of the gold medal and chain.

At Epiphany 1675, for example, a procession to St. George's Chapel, Windsor, to honor the Magi's adoration of the infant Christ occasioned this gleeful diary entry: "I wore the Chaine of Gold (sent me from the King of Denmarke) before the King in his proceeding to the Chapell to Offer, Gold Frankencense and Mirh."[26] One would like to know whether Ashmole played the part of a late magus at this royal magian offering; Ashmole was well suited for the part. One can at least imagine his attendance inducing some appropriate quip from the king!

Ashmole's famous portrait (now in the new Ashmolean) of himself as a thoroughly established figure, slim in crimson dress, bewigged with hand on hip, reveals his affection for the medal. It is draped by his great Garter book, on which rests his right hand. The befittingly elaborate frame for this portrait, incidentally, was the work of the "Excellent Carver" Grinling Gibbons (1648–1720), who wrote to Ashmole on October 12, 1682, to ascertain whether the stars would favor the enterprise outlined in a previous letter.[27]

This astrological inquiry was not unique in Ashmole's later life. Whereas once his astrological skills had served the lovelorn wishes of suitors and ladies—as well as himself, of course—his astral abilities were now in demand for serious matters of state from officials of government, and from the king himself.

ASTRO-POLITICS

Ashmole was approached on January 15, 1672, by Lord Treasurer Clifford, of the governing "Cabal." The question to which he sought a horary solution was as follows: "Whether his Majesty's Declaration of Indulgence [to religious dissenters] of the 15 of March 1671/2 will not occasion such a contest in the House of Commons at their next meeting as to hinder the King's supplies of moneys, unless it be set aside."[28]

According to Josten, this is "a typical example of the far reaching conclusions which were derived, by those who believed in astrology, from such horary figures, the text also affords evidence of Ashmole's grasp of the possibilities of a complex political situation. Ashmole's notes convey the impression that he favoured developments towards a greater measure of toleration, but we do not know whether he shared the King's and Lord Clifford's opinion that full toleration should be granted to the Roman Catholics."[29]

Likewise, Sir Robert Howard sought astral guidance from Ashmole on October 13, 1673: "Whether the house of Commons shall have good Success in these proceedings to settle the protestant Religion and the Interest and prosperity of the nation; and whether they and theyre King shall unite in a good correspondency."[30]

Ashmole gave a full answer to the question, concluding that "About Christmas [now happily restored] the Eyes of many of the House of Commons wilbe opend, and seeing further into the present designes then now they doe, will withdraw themselves and cleave to the King."[31]

Between January 7 and 15, 1674, Ashmole recorded parliamentary proceedings, along with the current disposition of the constellations. Josten considered, "It is not unlikely that Ashmole had been asked by Charles II to interpret the course of the planets during this period."[32]

Ashmole was probably aware of the happy circumstance by which he was now fulfilling the role that his hero John Dee, following the thirteenth-century genius Roger Bacon, had outlined as suitable for a magus: acting as privileged adviser to the monarch, for the greatest good of the country. Unlike Dee, he had not sought the role; it had been thrust upon him. Loyalty and discretion were rewarded.

However, the responsibilities that went with earlier rewards were becoming onerous to him. A month after making the aforementioned parliamentary reports, while residing at the upper end of Sheere-lane in Lincoln's Inn Fields, Ashmole wrote a letter to the Earl Marshall's secretary, Mr. Hayes. "I desired Mr : Hayes to move his Lord, to give me leave to resign my Heralds place."[33] Ashmole was planning a retirement.

On January 29, 1675, nearly a year after making his request, Ashmole recorded that "This afternoone I obteyned the Earle Marshall's leave to resigne my Heralds place."[34] On April 17, Ashmole's brother-in-law John Dugdale took his place, while on that same morning Ashmole agreed with his carpenters on building a home at South Lambeth. He and his wife Elizabeth (daughter of William Dugdale) moved into their new home at South Lambeth on October 2, 1674.

Those involved were loath to lose his expertise and there were several attempts in later years to get him to reverse his original decision; Ashmole had set a high standard and none could match it, not even his wife's brother.

Portrait of Sir John Dugdale (1628–
1700), Blyth Hall, Warwickshire.
(Photograph by kind permission of Sir
William Dugdale, Bt.)

Ashmole had also set an exemplary standard in his other main appointment, that of comptroller of excise in London. This service was a latter-day development of his first royal appointment, as Commissioner for Excise for Staffordshire during the Civil War. Here his mathematical skills found pecuniary outlet. The comptroller's task was not to raise taxes, but rather to oversee the accounts of monies raised to see that there was proper accounting with no embezzlement.

Officially, Ashmole had been comptroller of excise for England and Wales since 1661, but in fact his share of the task had been confined to London, whose range was bounded by "the Bill of Mortalitie" to be about ten miles radius of the City.

On December 17, 1674, the Lord High Treasurer resolved, "At Midsummer next Mr Ashmole [was] to enlarge his comptrol throughout England and Wales and send his Deputies into ye Respective Countyes."[35] Four days later, the Lord High Treasurer warranted £500 per annum from the Excise to be paid to Ashmole—an increase of £100 to cover additional labors in going beyond the bounds of the capital. This compensated Ashmole for the loss of his Windsor herald income.

On February 14, 1685, Ashmole's duties to Charles II ceased; the king was buried. Just a little less than a year later (January 20, 1686), Ashmole undertook a task for the new monarch, James II. It was not quite the kind of thing he was used to: "The Commissioners of Sewers met, and I (with some of the other Commissioners) tooke my Oath."[36] It is hard to say whether this would have been an entirely positive oath.

TEN

Lichfield—The Reconstruction

Spring 1685: Lichfield was all in a hubbub. Why? An election had been called and a meeting arranged at Captain Orme's home of Hanch Hall, three miles north of Lichfield. Present were Captain Orme, the candidate Sir Francis Lawley of Canwell, and Lawley's election agent, John Lamb. Temperatures ran high; intemperate things were said.

Lawley had wanted to be the sole candidate, but on February 28, Simon Marten, junior bailiff of Lichfield, made contact with Elias Ashmole in

Hanch Hall today, some three miles north of Lichfield.

London. Marten invited him (and Sir Francis Lawley), in the name of the bailiffs and the majority of the twenty-one brethren of the City's Corporation, to be their candidate. The letter to Ashmole further alluded to the latter's merits as signal benefactor to the City. Lancelot Addison, dean of Lichfield, made the same point in his letter to Ashmole. The dean and chapter also urged Ashmole to become the City of Lichfield's Member of Parliament.

In the capital, meanwhile, King Charles II had only recently been buried, and Ashmole was required to assist with plans for the coronation of James II. However, honored by the junior bailiff's request, he accepted the candidature, noting in his diary: "I sent them word I would stand, whereupon they set about getting votes for me, and I found the citizens very affectionate and hearty."

Not all of the citizens were so affectionate. At Hanch Hall, John Lamb protested vehemently against Ashmole's inclusion. In the excessive language familiar to observers of elections, Lamb declared Ashmole to be nothing more than a "Pittifull Exciseman," a gibe intended to make the citizens of Lichfield look to their pockets—the election smear that usually works.

Ashmole calmly responded to the serious accusation in a letter to his election agent, Robert Wright, "next the Swan in Lichfield": "There is little reason why I should be called Pitifull Exciseman, for I am not one in the usuall sense; but am set over the whole Revenue of the Excise by the King, to Controll and Check the Accounts thereof, and see that the Officers imployed in that affaire, doe not deceive the King of what they receive from the People: Soe that my Office (if rightly considered) should rather gaine me the good esteeme of the People, then calumnious reproach."

While Ashmole was busy preparing the Coronation, Lawley and Captain Orme spent great sums on "treating." However, what neither side in the election knew was that the king himself had already favored another candidate, Richard Leveson. The king innocently informed an anxious Ashmole that had he himself known of His Majesty's comptroller of excise's candidacy, he would not have hindered him. The new king asked Ashmole to stand down.

This was a hard blow for a man with such great affection for his birthplace and who deeply desired to serve her people. Republicans and cynics might suggest this to be an ironic commentary on the one-sided loyalty existing between royalists and their monarch. Observers of the career of James II might note this incident as a first sign of the hopeless ineptitude that would lose him the crown in 1688.

In spite of Ashmole's resignation, the majority of voters still clung to him. He informed the king of this development, only to be told that the business had now "gone too far." He must stand down. Somewhat humiliated, Ashmole then had to confirm his resignation and request that his supporters switch their vote to the king's favorite. Nevertheless, many still voted for Ashmole, believing with all the naïvety on which democracy thrives that their will would give them the candidate they desired.

High-handedly, the sheriff gave all the Ashmole votes to Leveson, who thus won the seat. On March 28, 1685, the Lichfield City Muniments Hall Book recorded that the bailiffs and mayor had agreed that Richard Leveson Esq. "beinge Recommended by many of the Noble persons of the Nation" was elected Member of Parliament for Lichfield. Ashmole generously paid all his agents' expenses and gave them an extra ten pounds (a considerable sum) with which to enjoy themselves.

The bailiffs and justices wrote to Ashmole on April 29, 1685, to say that his interest had been "the strongest of all the competitors."[1] This would hardly have mollified his feelings. The letter continued to say how they had now spent his ten pounds on a coronation party where they drank to Ashmole's health—and, presumably, to that of King James II as well—from his "owne noble Bowl." That "noble Bowl" (of which we shall hear more presently) had been a gift to the Corporation, sent by Ashmole nearly two decades previously. This letter must have brought a slightly bitter, if ironic, smile to Ashmole's ruddy face.

Ashmole nevertheless replied to the bailiffs and justices with all due grace, indicating his sorrow at the outcome of the election. He knew that this had probably been his last opportunity to sit for the City and County of Lichfield.

Serving the City and County would have meant a very great deal to him: "You cannot but imagine I looke upon my selfe as a very unfortunate man, that finde the love of my country men (almost without parallel) so great, and yet cannot accept of their Votes."[2] A bitter cup to drink.

Contrary to the jibe of John Lamb the election agent, Ashmole had, in the previous decades, done greater service for Lichfield than toting up the excise returns, but what has truth got to do with elections?

RESTAURATOR

At Ashmole's first meeting with King Charles II on June 16, 1660, he informed the king of the regrettable condition of the cathedral of Lichfield. He told of how the central spire had been toppled by cannon shell, how only the chapter house and vestry were now roofed, and how beneath these tiles, prayers were being said for the king. The king "much lamented" the sorry picture and encouraged Ashmole to accomplish all things necessary that he could to reverse the situation.[3] The king would himself contribute timber to the project in the tradition of King Hiram of Tyre, who gave timber for Solomon's temple.

Ashmole spoke to his friend William Dugdale about what would need to be done. Within two days of meeting the king, Ashmole noted that "Mr Dugdale moved Dr Sheldon [Gilbert Sheldon, 1598–1677, bishop of London] to become an Instrument for the repaire of Lichfield Cathedral, and proposed that the Prebends &c. that were to be admitted shoulde parte with one half of the profits of their living towards the repaire of the Fabricke, which would be no great burden to them, considering their livings are all improved to a treble value at least, and by this example the Gentry might be invited to join with them in some considerable contribution."[4]

Thanks to the urging of Ashmole, Dugdale, and Sheldon, John Hacket (1592–1670) was consecrated bishop of Lichfield in 1661. Hacket was a royalist hero, and the kind of man who would—and did—put his hand in his own pocket to oversee the restoration of the cathedral. His architect was William Wilson from Sutton Coldfield, of whom more will be said in due course.

Dr. Hacket was a natural choice for the bishopric. Under the Protectorate, he had been rector of St. Andrews Holborn, London. While serving there, his observation of traditional Anglican liturgy had been opposed by Puritans. According to Harwood's introduction to Sampson Erdeswick's *Survey of Staffordshire* of 1598, in order to enforce the Puritans' prohibition, a soldier entered the church and put a pistol to Hacket's head, ordering him to cease. Hacket continued, indifferent to the threat of death, saying, in a calm and grave voice, "Soldier, I am doing my duty; do you do yours." The soldier, abashed, fled the field.[5] Hacket was the right man for Lichfield.

Fourteen years earlier, when Ashmole had arrived in Lichfield from the siege of Worcester in 1646, he had to stand by as parliamentarians ransacked and vandalized the cathedral. Nevertheless, he managed to enter the shattered precincts and save precious music books of the cathedral library from the flames. (These works have since proved invaluable for our knowledge of sixteenth-century English church music.) Once library space was available, Ashmole returned the books along with others he had bought to the cathedral. On May 3, 1662, he wrote to Mr. Zachary Turnepenny, subchanter of the cathedral:

> Mr : Subchantor
>
> I have now sent down by Mr : Rixam your Lichf : Courier the Sett of Church Services and Anthems for the use of your Quire, with two Bookes of ruled paper wherein to Prick the Organ parte for both : in all 12 : Bookes [seven of them preserved today in the cathedral library] and well bound having the Episcopall Armes of your See imprest on the foreside, and my owne upon the other [Ashmole paid sixteen pounds for these books]. This is my first free-will Offring, which with a cheerfull and willing mind I dedicate to the Service of your Temple, and may as Pious a use be made of them in sounding forth the praises of the Almighty, as the donation hath sincerity of heart from your reall friend and humble servant E : A : Middle Temple 3 : May 1662[6]

Ashmole's reference to the "Service of your Temple" might suggest a conception of the cathedral touched by his Free Masonry. Perhaps he recalled the words spoken at his initiation back in the dark days of 1646:

> And there was a King of an other Region yt men called Hyram and hee loved well Kinge Solomon; and gave him timber for his worke;

And hee had a sonne that was named Aynon & he was Mr of Geometry; and hee was chiefe Mr of all his Masons; and Mr of all his
graved works; and of all other Masons that belonged to ye Temple;
& this Witnesseth the Bible in libro 2 Solo capite 5.

From the vantage point of Ashmole's inner life, it would be hard to avoid
the conclusion that the restoration of the cathedral was understood to
be an unmistakable analogy both for the alchemical renewal of the spirit
that underpinned his life and, possibly, for the practical application of
Temple symbolism.

Ashmole was certainly interested in the Temple of Jerusalem. There are
among his papers extracts in his own hand taken from John Lightfoot's
*The Temple: Especially as it stood in the dayes of our Saviour. With
measurements of the second Temple of Jerusalem* (London, 1650). Dr.
John Lightfoot, learned divine and one of the editors of the *Polyglot
Bible*, was born in Stoke, Staffordshire, in 1602.

In 1663, Gilbert Sheldon became archbishop of Canterbury. He would
initiate the rebuilding of St. Paul's Cathedral after the Great Fire (1666)
and as chancellor of the University of Oxford would at his own expense
employ Christopher Wren to build the extraordinary Sheldonian Theatre, Oxford, in 1665.

In the same year as his friend Sheldon's consecration as archbishop,
Ashmole contributed twenty pounds and again ten pounds toward the
restoration of the cathedral. Praised for this act in a Latin poem by
Thomas Smith, the cathedral sacrist, Ashmole did not confine his benefactions to the Cathedral Close.

On January 19, 1660, before the Restoration, Ashmole received a
letter addressed to his chambers in the Middle Temple from the church-
wardens of St. Michael's, Greenhill, Lichfield, thanking him for "freely
giv[ing] £5 towards the building of St. Michael's Church in Lichfield."[7]
Ashmole never gave anything less than five pounds a year for the city's
poor. The City and Corporation also received a share of Ashmole's love
for Lichfield.

THE LOVING CUP

On the evening of Thursday, January 17, 1666, the Lichfield Corporation held its Epiphany Feast at the George Inn, Bird Street. A party of about thirty gentlemen, including two bailiffs, the sheriff, members of the Corporation and the Grand Jury, the steward of the City, and the Earl of Southampton, gathered to witness the handing over of a gift.

"I bestowed on the Bailiffs of Lichfield a large chased silver bowl and cover, cost me £23 8/6d,"[8] Ashmole recorded. Was this presentation, made by Zachary Turnepenny, the cathedral sacrist, a way of somehow "paying his dues" to his uncle and grandfather, both bailiffs, a loving nod and smile in the direction of his humble origins?

Ashmole's commitment to Lichfield was not a matter of the past. He carried his interest in Lichfield with him all his life. Furthermore, he had property interests—apart from the family house—in and about the city. On November 9, 1667, for example, he took a lease of the Moggs in Lichfield "from the Bailifs, and then d[ul]y paid 20*l* : in part of 40, Fine."[9]

The chased silver bowl and cover presented as a gift to the bailiffs of Lichfield by Elias Ashmole in 1666. (Photographs taken with the kind permission of the staff of St. Mary's Heritage Centre, Lichfield.)

This may have been a way of contributing to the income of Lichfield's Conduit Lands Trust, which leased various properties (including part of the Moggs, or marshy places, around Stowe and Minster Pools) to raise money for provision of water to the citizens of Lichfield and to support the poor.

At the discretion of the trustees of the Conduit Lands Trust, Lichfield underwent some major structural improvements after the Restoration, particularly as regards the probable addition of three conduits in the city; money had to be raised to pay for the work.

In 1666, for example, new conduit work and repairs had reached the stage where a permanent plumber was required. According to Trust records, "William Hollis . . . Common Plummer for the Common Conduits of the City" was the first to hold the job.[10] He was to be paid six pounds annually. It is possible that part of his income derived from Ashmole's generosity. The "Courier Mr Rixam" mentioned by Ashmole as the one who carried the cathedral service books from London to Lichfield may have been the William Wrixam (or a relative of the same) who was named warden of the Conduit Lands Trust in 1676.

On September 29, 1674, Ashmole paid thirteen shillings, four pence rent for waste ground on Bacon Street. On August 1 of the same year, Ashmole had "lent Mr Edw : Hopkins 400*l* : upon a Mortgage of his Lands in Little Pipe neere Lichfeild."[11]

Ashmole's continuing contribution to Lichfield life was recognized in the extraordinary letter of thanks sent to him in gratitude for that stunning bowl inscribed "The Gift of Elias Ashmole Esq., Windsor Herald at Arms, 1666," now on display at St. Mary's Heritage Centre, Lichfield.

OUR MAGUS

The letter from the bailiffs John Burnes and Henry Baker on January 26, 1666, is highly revealing both of the way they saw Ashmole and of the way they thought he saw the cathedral—and, doubtless, himself. The letter presents us with the glittering picture of Ashmole, a trusted servant of the king, an astrologer and profound scholar, being hailed by a group of Staffordshire *bourgeois* as nothing less than a Magus:

For the truly honoured Elias Ashmole Esq., at his chamber in the Middle Temple, over Serjeant Maynard's Chamber. In his absence, to be left with the Butler or Porter of the Middle Temple, London . . .

. . . It is the gift of an *Elias,* a herald, not only proclaiming, but actually contributing good things to our city; and that by the hand of a Zacharias [Zachary Turnepenny], a faithful messenger, who with the gift did emphatically communicate the sense and good affection of the giver . . . as if some propitious stars arising in the East had, (at this time) gone before our *Magus* [Ashmole], steering its course to this our city of Lichfield, (the *Sarepta* of our *Elias*) and stood over the new-erected pyramids of our cathedral, (where as yet a star appears) darting its benign influence on this poor and loyal city, inviting the *Magi* from afar, to offer some tribute to it : a city that hath nothing to glory in but its ancient and modern Loyalty to God and Caesar . . . like one of those true Magi that offered to Christ in his poorest condition, you have largely offered to the repaire of his Church our ruined Cathedral. But you have likewise Annually and liberally offered, relieved, and refreshed Christ in his members, the poor of our City.[12]

The constant references to Ashmole as a magus and the description of the restored spires as "pyramids" suggest strong Hermetic (Egyptian) implications and in-references. His reputation in such matters was now public knowledge—and was approved of, at least by these loyal bailiffs.

In 1673, the bailiffs and Corporation entertained Ashmole and his wife at "a dinner and a great Banquet" to honor their benefactor.[13] Four years later, the Ashmophile bailiffs had another opportunity to demonstrate their appreciation of "our Magus." On November 4, 1677, Ashmole recorded how "Mr Rawlins Towne Clarke of Lichf : said Richard Dyott MP had died" and that Rawlins and his friends would therefore like Ashmole to be returned member for the City and County of Lichfield.[14]

"I answered," he noted, that "I had noe inclination to accept of that Honour, and therefore desired him to give my thanks to all that were so well affected to me."[15] Support for him was so great, however, that on New Year's Day 1678, after much hesitation, Ashmole changed his mind and declared his willingness to be "Burgess" of Lichfield: "I am still very willing to stand and serve my County, if my well-wishers there be not too much weakened by this my unwilling delay."[16]

ASHMOLE'S POLITICS

What were Ashmole's politics? An intriguing question, for which we have little evidence to assist us in finding an answer, save his loyalty to the king and deep love of tried and trusted tradition. He had no bees in his bonnet about religion, and he was friendly with men who thought differently from himself.

In a letter of April 15, 1675, his friend William Lilly signed off, "no Tory—but your old friend William."[17] Lilly, of course, had been a supporter of Parliament during the civil wars. The use of the word "Tory" is fascinating and is, according to Josten, "a remarkably early occurrence of the word in a connotation which could not be other than political. William Lilly appears to imply that Ashmole favored the opinions of the court party and perhaps the interests of the Duke of York [the king's brother in favor of Catholic toleration]." This may in fact be the first ever use of the word "Tory" in a political context, and it is most amusing to find it in relation to Elias Ashmole. Indeed, the phenomenon should give us pause for thought.

According to the *Oxford English Dictionary* (1926), "Tory" is a nickname first used by Exclusioners in 1679–80 for those who opposed the exclusion from the throne of the Roman Catholic Duke of York. If Ashmole might have been "the first Jacobite" (!) the world had no chance of finding out for sure. On January 4, 1678, the bailiffs of Lichfield called a Common Hall and gave their votes to Sir Henry Litleton, believing Ashmole was not committed to stand. His aforementioned letter asserting his willingness to stand arrived later and caused fresh debate. However, the matter was settled in Litleton's favor in February.

Neither Lichfield nor Ashmole could leave the other alone for long. Even after his sad resignation in favor of the king's candidate, Richard Leveson, in 1685 (which might make one wonder how attached Ashmole *really* was to the court party after the death of Charles II), he could always rely on being called upon when Lichfield lacked funds for renovation.

Three years later, James II fled the country in the "Glorious Revolution" that ousted him in favor of William and Mary. While King James dropped his lions' seal into the Thames, Dean Lancelot Addison begged Ashmole to pay for the completion of the cathedral's ten-bell peal (October 15, 1688).

"Whatever interest this City and Church have in your Birth and Education," wrote Addison, "hath already redounded, insomuch honour thereby, and in your continual bounty, to both . . . nor in truth have we any other Argument, but your Charity and our necessity."[18]

Ashmole played such an important and nowadays unrecognized role in the renovation and restoration of Lichfield (especially her cathedral) after the disaster of the civil wars that it is worth looking in more depth at just exactly what that renovation involved.

That is to say, if we were to take our own time's shiny, colorful guidebooks as a guide, we might well infer that the renovation of the cathedral was simply an ecclesiastical matter, overseen by good Bishop Hacket in a glorious declaration of faith. The Church itself apparently knew its duty and did all it could to set things in order and strive forward in willing readiness for that deeply solemn service held on Christmas Eve 1669, when Bishop Hacket at long last reconsecrated the cathedral as Lichfield's children dreamed of Boxing Day.

My own recent researches into the matter reveal a somewhat different picture from this triumphalist if nonetheless inspiring image. The aim is to locate where the true inspiration came from.

BILLS, BILLS, AND MORE BILLS

Ten years after the reconsecration of the cathedral, vital work was still going on. William Gorton's rough bills for mason work and for drawing stone in 1677–78 give us some idea of where Ashmole's and others' benefactions were going.

Stone Load, payd for Carridge of 21 Loads . . . £3-16-10d
[there follows William Gorton's Mark—two interlocking V's, like a "W']
A Bill for ye Deane and chapter 2nd March 1677

For 12 loade of stone att 2 shilling 6 pence A loade and six ode foote
att three half pence a foot and one penny carridge £1 10 10d
For Ralph Nicklin 2 days att ten pence a day 1/8d.
For one Peac 1/6
For one Burkett 0/0/8
For one Riddle 0/0/4
For William Kiss 2 days att 1 shilling, one penny a day 0-2-2
Mr Nichols of Atlow of this Bill and would get it payd by you
A friend A Hen : Greswold.

9 Mar 1677 £1-11-9 of which
for William Kiss ten days being ye 4 day and ye 5 days of masonry
0-2-2
for Ralph Nicklin ye 5 days of masonry
for working of Low masonry . . .[19]

Details of restoration
work on the pinnacles
above the west front of
Lichfield Cathedral.

Bills, receipts, letters, and the contract for the altarpiece of the cathedral, 1677–1680, tell a sorry story of unwillingness on behalf of the dean and chapter to pay properly for work undertaken by the finest carvers and joiners in the land.

A (draft) letter "To the Reverend the Dean of Lichfield [Dr Small-wood] Tho : Kinward Hen : Philips":

> Price paid for his work on Chapell Royal—93*l* "as was approved under Sr. Chris : Wrens hand in ye office of his works, and your altar is full as great as that : only the 2 sydes of your Church is not carved which is about 1/3d your work less than that. I dare submitt those whole to you when it is done, but sure I am that 50*l* is the least I can afford it fore, . . . so craving your Speedy anser, knowing our materials already—Your most humble servants. Robert Streeter London the 13 October 1677.[20]

Letters passed to and fro on the subject of the money owed. Finally, on November 14, the dean and chapter paid fifty pounds. In July 1678 there arrived in Lichfield another bill, "for painting and gilding the great Altar of Lichfield," also from Robert Streeter.

> Gilding and moulding £93/15/0
> For gilding and painting the Kinge's Armes on the top of the altar £3-15-0
> An allowance to be made for the time that my son and servant spent going up and down to Lichfield
> For 3 tyme colouring in oyle all the main cross and carvings 03:15:0[21]

This bill, along with others, was not paid. Still waiting for the money to feed his family, Robert Streeter died, leaving his son Robert Jr. to pick up the pieces. He wrote a letter of complaint to the dean and chapter, informing them of his father's death and the debts unpaid, along with outstanding travel expenses. The dean had little comfort to offer, giving his opinion that Robert's father would have settled for a hundred pounds in full "had he survived."[22]

Young Robert was having none of it and invoked a powerful precedent:

> I do affirm that my father was so far from doubting of being well paid counting to the said and Modest Amount He rendered to you that he was not without hope that you would consider with extraordinary care . . . on his part so far as to . . . in some further reward as was done for his work at the [Sheldonian] Theatre of Oxford when he had a [indecipherable] made him of 100£ more than his modest demand.
>
> We have asked Surveyor Generall Sr Christopher Wren to examine the Bookes of the offices and under his hand what payment was mad[e] . . . and you make the better judgement of what I offer to you. That for the painting and guilding of the whole Altarpiece with the 2 sides (which in length are . . . rounds to £157-13-0 . . .
>
> . . . humbly submitted to your Charity and goodness toward a disturbed widow . . . [23]

While his father had had better treatment from Ashmole's friends Gilbert Sheldon and Christopher Wren, Streeter was still trying to wring the money out of the stingy dean and chapter in June 1679. However, while no record survives of a payment to him and his widowed mother, the younger Streeter was again working for the dean and chapter in September of that year, along with his brother Charles and Nathaniel Pollard, both painters. A bill survives:

> Charles and Pollard went to Lichfield and they were out 22 working days.
> Charles at 3/4d a day. Pollard at 3/- a day—Bill £6:19:04
> For both these going down in the Coach and 5d each towards these Charges, and for roaming up again—£6.[24]

Twenty years later, important work was still going on at the cathedral. Eleven years after Dean Lancelot Addison begged Ashmole for money for the ten-bell peal, the same Dean Addison and his Canon Residentiary John Willes drew up Articles of Agreement with Henry Vernon, freemason.

Articles of Agreement made and agreed by our beloved John Willes Dr. in Divinity one of the Canons Residentiary of the Cathedral Church of Lichfield . . . Lancelot Addison Dean of Lichfield" and "Henry Vernon of the City and County of Lichfield freemason" 4 May 1699. "to finish by 1st day of September. . . . Making Globes . . . Steeples . . . £66/10s over and above £5 already paid him.—in instalments £300—£36/10- . . . that the said Henry Vernon shall towards the carrying on . . . the work of the said Steeples have all ye rough unhewn stone lying in the churchyard of the said cathedrall Church, belonging to the said Dean and Chapter, first for his use therein, that also the Iron, Lead, Globe . . . and all of ye . . . the old materialls of the said Steeples . . . or taken down and which did belong thereto.

W. Walmisley Public Notary—Henry Vernon [very rough signature] John Willes.[25]

One can see from all of this that money for the dean and chapter was in very short supply. Old and used materials were being recycled and debts were avoided where possible. Dean Addison did not overstate his position when he referred in his begging letter to Elias Ashmole of the dean and chapter's "necessity."

It may be recalled that when Charles II first encouraged Ashmole to render service to the cathedral's restoration at the time of the monarch's own restoration, he spoke to William Dugdale. Dugdale and Ashmole established the principle that the cathedral's prebendaries should pay a portion of their income toward the repair of the cathedral fabric. It may not come as a complete surprise that this recommendation was blankly ignored by a number of the prebendaries.

Less than two years after Hacket's reconsecration ceremony, the dean and chapter were forced to petition the Court of Exchequer for the submission of John Manwaring, Alexander Featherstone, and several other prebendaries with regard to their refusal to pay fees due to the Fabric Fund. The case was complicated by the fact that the dean and chapter asserted the precedent that such a requirement existed before the civil wars, but that the documentation appertaining thereto had been lost at the hands of parliamentarian vandals.

However, it appeared in the course of investigations in 1671 that relevant documents were being witheld deliberately by the prebendaries themselves!

> Prebends . . . have severally and responsibly paid and ought to pay unto the said dean and chapter for the time being the yearly rent or sum of 20 shillings or some such like sum for and towards the repairs fabrics or other uses of the said Cathedrall church and the prebendary of the prebend of high Offly [near Lapley, to the east of Lichfield] not having his [?] residence as aforesaid hath paid and ought to pay . . . yearly sums of forty shillings which said severall and respective payments have for many hundreds of years . . . before the yeare one thousand six hundred and 40 boons paid by the several and respective prebendaries . . .
>
> . . . the payment thereof until the late troublesome times when the lands and Revinues of the said Church were sequestered and exposed to sale and all the deeds writings evidences booke notes and Records of and belonging to ye Orators . . . and Interests of the said Church were taken away lost and imbezilled . . . being part of the 26 prebends that is to say John Manwaring Doctor of Divinitie now is and for the space of 4 yeares ended at Michaelmas last past hath been prebendary of the prebend of Weeford within or belonging to the said Cathedrall Church and Samuel Gardner Doctor of Divinitie now is for the space of nyne yeares ended at Michaelmas last past hath been prebendary of the prebend of high Offly within or belonging to the said Cathedrall Church. And John Boylston Doctor of Divinitie now is and for the space of ten yeares ended at Michaelmas last past hath been prebendary of the prebend of Sandacres [?] . . . and John Cornelius, prebendary of Hansacre. And Hugh Humfryes Clarke . . . prebend of Skipton Deveraux Sparrow Clarke . . . prebend of Gay Minor Thomas Indman Clerke . . . prebend of Whittington and Alexander Featherstone, Clerke . . . prebend of Colwich. Samuel Bold, Clerke . . . prebend of Curdborough.[26]

The prebendaries' defense was that without the deeds and books taken in the troublesome times, the orators could not make sufficient title to "the said severall yearly sums of 20 shilings and 40 shillings." There was no testimony from the Vicars Resident before 1640, as all from before that time were now dead. The dean and chapter took the legal path of Equity, especially as the dean and chapter knew that the prebendaries:

> [h]aving in their hands some deeds writings or other evidences notes or Memorandums touching or concerning their said several prebends which doe manifest the original ground reason cause or uses of our . . . for the said annual payments of the said sums of money and do refuse to search . . . or discover the same . . . the said confederates do now . . . and give out in speeches that these are not now such annual sums of money as aforesaid nor any other whatsoever due or payable from the same confederates as any of them unto ye Orators to or for the uses and purposes aforesaid or to or for any other use or purpose whatsoever and therefore the said confederates do refuse to pay the said several and respective sums of money as aforesaid.
>
> Which in Justice and Equity they ought to do although the said confederates very well know and have heard that the same is justly by them due and payable to ye Orators as aforesaid—all the other prebends with or belonging to the said Cathedrall Church have paid and do pay unto ye Orators the like sums . . . and that the said Cathedrall Church at Lichfield is very much decayed and out of repair.[27]

The message was simple. "We know you've got the documentary evidence; it belongs to the cathedral. The reason you won't surrender it is that it proves you owe the money. Pay up!"

I hope the above examples from the very slender quantity of surviving documents from the restoration process serve to emphasize the dire need of the Church for men such as Ashmole and his friends. Contrary to popular belief, the Church could not—and on occasion *would not*—provide wholly for itself.

It is touching, then, to note that the visitor to Lichfield Cathedral today will find many carvings of whole figures on the cathedral's exterior, most of them the work of eighteenth- and nineteenth-century operative freemasons. Of these the vast majority depict English kings, biblical figures, saints or Fathers, and officers of the Church. The only figures that do not fit into these categories are as follows: Godfroi de Bouillon, who took Jerusalem for Christ in 1099; Elias Ashmole, holding his museum; Christopher Wren, carrying dividers and clutching St. Paul's; Izaak Walton, holding a book; and King Charles II, wearing the "Lesser George" that Walton helped redeem for the king by secret means in 1651. Except for the mighty Crusader, the representatives of the laity all accomplished their works during the maturity of Elias Ashmole. The sculpture of Ashmole is the only one depicting him in the world.

The oldest of these sculptures is by far the largest. Standing some eight feet high, the statue of Charles II used to rest on a plinth inscribed RESTAURATOR, itself poised high above the west end of the cathedral. Perhaps biting the hand that fed it, the dean and chapter removed the statue to make way for a statue of Christ in the nineteenth century. One would care to know why: The statue of Christ was predictable; that of Charles, unique.

Sculptures on the exterior of the Lady Chapel, Lichfield Cathedral, depicting (left to right) Elias Ashmole (holding his museum), Izaak Walton, and Sir Christopher Wren (holding St. Paul's and a pair of dividers).

Statue of King Charles II, Restaurator, carved by Sir William Wilson for the west front of Lichfield Cathedral. The king is wearing the Lesser George (Garter jewel) worn by his father at his martyrdom in 1649 and rescued by Izaak Walton in 1651.

The Restaurator now stands alone, governing no one and nothing, by the south door of Lichfield Cathedral. A small inscription from the 1990s says that Charles provided timber for the restoration of the cathedral. What it does not tell the visitor is that this great sculpture was the work of Sir William Wilson, architect and Accepted Free Mason.

ASHMOLE AND THE MASON'S COMPANY

Whatever else the statue of King Charles II may be thought to represent, it certainly serves as a remarkable objective correlative to the timely coming together of a set of persons and principles of great historic significance. These principles must seem practically invisible, and certainly hostile, to today's Tupperware-deep "political correctness," a new name for an old disease.

When the Church of England was spiritually revived in the midnineteenth century, the Oxford Movement that galvanized the revival looked back to the restored Caroline Church as a marker of church and state in a dynamic, even harmonious spiritual relationship. They believed that King Charles I had been "martyred": that is, he had borne witness to this cause and been prepared to suffer death for it, if need be. The monarch needed the Church and the Church, the monarch.

Left to freewheeling, "free-thinking" Republicans and assorted radical interest lobbies, the Church had, under Cromwell's rule, been laid waste. The people did not, by and large, like the new regime either— not that Cromwell cared much for the people. He had a personal "hot line" to God's will. So the people, were they not so wicked, should have *understood* why they lost Christmas, Maypoles, theaters, sport, some sexual innocence. They also lost favorite buildings, traditional loyalties, historic continuity, and the vital spirit of mystery that gives a people infinite depth.

A modern *res publica* is quick to give the folks back their jollies (in the name of personal liberty, or votes), but cannot for the life of it supply the mystique, having intrinsically denied "infinite depth" to anything. Most "modernizers" are either atheists by conviction, agnostics by the lack of it, or purveyors of their own versions of religious idealism that they choose to call "Christian" or the name of some other religious tradition. From these traditions they cherry-pick the bits that suit their purposes and those "deepest convictions" that are deep only to superficial minds.

Lichfield's fate was, to the thinking part of the royalist cause, a patent object lesson of the Cromwellian disaster; its restoration was therefore vital. It has seemed to this author that the spiritual, intellectual, and psychological mortar that bound the deeper needs of this country into a coherent program of restoration found much of its substance in a spiritual conception of Free Masonry.

The statue of Charles II is like a mason's mark made flesh, so to speak: a union of a divine monarchic principle, the Church as the repository of the nation's highest spiritual inheritance, and the lay spiritual traditions of freemasons' labor and inspirational Accepted Free Masonry. This invisible union lasted surprisingly well and can be shown to have served the country through the gravest of crises.

The detaching of the king and the Free Masons' work from the main body of the cathedral may then appear to be a parable of a greater rift in English society. A tree may think itself strong by virtue of its pretty flowers, until a strong wind whisks it away with a chuckle.

Men of Ashmole's caliber know how deep the roots of lasting human endeavor must be. Those roots must grow in both directions, he asserts in *Fasciculus Chemicus* (and all his works): to the highest—to heaven—and to earth and nature, bound and wed within the operator, or *artifex*. This image he understood in the esoteric principle of the "alchemical wedding," which Blake later described cheekily (following the language of Jacob Böhme) as "the Marriage of Heaven and Hell." Mathematics is glimpsed first in the material, then stretches forth to the immaterial, which principle *in ourselves* enables us to see the mathematical laws in the material in the first place. The alchemical serpent swallows its own tail: *Know thyself.*

The traditions of the freemasons, given additional symbolic emphasis in Accepted Free Masonry, served to assert the truth that whatever man conceives from the infinite ocean of imagination, its outer representation must *work;* it must stand, must last. That is to say, the work must be in harmonic concordance with cosmic, natural law that is a universal principle for all things; man is a participant. The work must be *true.*

For a person to grasp the deeper truth underlying both the theological commonplaces of conventional religious education and the wide practical traditions of geometry and construction, he must be "reborn." The Master must die to his old self and be raised in conscious awareness to an ego-defying sodality with high-minded individuals dedicated to perfection, the greater Good, the revelation, and practical service of the greater Architect.

That "Architect" may be understood as the "lost word" of Free Masonry: the implicate principle of mind, or *logos,* in the universe, detectable as a "divine signature" in any part of the creation, however small. Each part contains the whole, Hermeticists believed, and the whole is in each part. A world is in a grain of sand.

History demonstrates that those ignorant of these simple rules of life are agents of or dupes in the destruction of all that is good. Good intentions are frequently the mask of devastating ignorance and stupidity, like the fool who in digging a well sticks his spade through his own power supply and electrocutes himself. "Whomsoever shall fall upon that stone shall be crushed; but on whomsoever it shall fall, he shall be winnowed" (Luke 20:17–18).

So when one looks at the simple word *restaurator* applied to the majesty of King Charles II, one can with a little effort see a greater principle of restoration and spiritual resurrection that is as valid today as it was three and a half centuries ago. Ashmole's life was in its highest phase in the service of that principle; this is what makes him great. He truly was the Mercuriophilus Anglicus, and like all great mercurial characters, he had the power to attract dynamic people to his purposes.

In Sir William Dugdale's *Antiquities of Warwickshire* we learn that in the church of Holy Trinity, Sutton Coldfield, was once the following inscription:

> Near this Place lieth the Body of Sr WILLIAM WILSON Knight, interred here by his own desire. He was born at Leicester; but after his Marriage with his well beloved Lady JANE, Relict of HENRY PUDSY Esq; he lived many years in this Parish, where he also died the 3d Day of June 1710 in the 70th year of his age, and generally beloved, and very much & no less deservedly lamented : being a Person of great Ingenuity, singular Integrity, unaffected Piety, and very fruitful in good Works, the only issue he left behind him.
>
> Aut tumulis flamma, aut imber subducet honores,
> Annorum aut Ictu pondera victa ruent.
> At non ingenio quaesitum nomen ab aevo
> Excidet Artifici : stat fine morte decus.
>
> Mr. John Barns set up this Marble Table in Pious and Grateful Memory of his Honoured Uncle.[28]

In March 1682, William Wilson (1641–1710) was knighted for his services to architecture. He worked on the restoration of Lichfield Cathedral, and on the rebuilding of Nottingham Castle, where King Charles I first flew the royal standard of resistance to Parliament.

A few days after having been knighted by King Charles II, Sir William Wilson joined a group of five other men, most of whom were closely involved with the freemasons' governing body, to become an accepted Free Mason. In attendance as the "senior Fellow" present was Elias

Ashmole's record of the Acception of Sir William Wilson and others at Mason's Hall, London, in March 1682 (Bodleian Library, Ashmole MS. collection)

Ashmole, presumably summonsed by the Master. Ashmole left the sole record of this occasion.

March 10. 1682 :

About 5pm I received a summons, to appear at a Lodge to be held the next day at Masons Hall London.

Accordingly I went, and about Noone were admitted into the Fellowship of Free Masons,

Sir William Wilson Knight, Capt. Rich: Borthwick, Mr Will: Woodman, Mr Wm Grey, Mr Samuell Taylour & Mr William Wise.

I was the Senior Fellow among them (it being 35 years since I was admitted). There were present beside my selfe the Fellowes after named. Mr Tho: Wise Mr: of the Masons Company this present year. Mr: Thomas Shorthose, Mr: Thomas Shadbolt, Waindsford Esqr Mr: Nich: Young. Mr: John Shorthose, Mr: William Hamon, Mr: John Thompson, & Mr: Will: Stanton.

We all dyned at the halfe Moone Taverne in Cheapside, at a Noble Dinner prepared at the charge of the New: accepted Masons.[29]

Mason's Hall used to stand in Masons Avenue, Basinghall Street, in the City of London. The hall had been the headquarters of the London Company of Masons (formerly the Company of Freemasons) since 1463. The company was awarded its arms in 1472, its main feature being the outstretched compasses so familiar to students of the Craft. By the time of the Stuarts, the London Company of "ffreemasons" consisted of a master, two wardens, a court of assistants (the ruling body), a livery, and a body of freemen, or yeomen.

THE ORIGINS OF FREEMASONRY

Some readers may be aware that there has been a long-standing debate over the origins of Freemasonry. The English order that thrives today—the oldest organized body—tends to date its creation from 1717 when, it is commonly held, the use of the expression "Grand Lodge" was first associated with a midsummer activity organized by four London lodges.

MASON'S COMPANY
LONDON

Left: The site of Mason's Hall, Masons Avenue, off Basinghall Street, City of London.

Above: The arms of the London Mason's Company (seventeenth century), formerly the Freemasons Company. (Photo: Matthew Scanlan)

After that date, Freemasonry as a body distinct from the trade of freemasonry begins to emerge. That is to say, by 1730 the order could technically function as an order even if the trade of masonry and architecture hypothetically vanished.

However, the two accounts that Ashmole made, together with other evidence, make it clear that there was a body *within* the freemasons' governing trade body that practiced *Accepted* Free Masonry. The survival of Accepted Free Masonry did not require severance from the trade.

Fellowship in this body did not require an operative apprenticeship, but we may sensibly suppose its ceremonies and symbols to be at one with the trade at its highest level. While it might appear at first sight that Ashmole's 1646 account of his initiation had no necessary connection with the trade, most initiates in the 1682 acceptation were members of the trade body. Ashmole's extraordinarily revealing record, including the "acception" (acceptation) of Sir William Wilson, proves that Accepted Free Masonry was an infra-trade practice.

Let us look at the men with whom Ashmole enjoyed fellowship—and a fine dinner—on that late afternoon in the City in the spring of 1682.

William Wilson was, according to Josten (who researched the Fellowship), originally a freemason from Sutton Coldfield; he was not a member of the Mason's Company of the City of London.

William Woodman, on the other hand, took the Freedom of the London Mason's Company on July 21, 1678 ("probably aged 21").[30] He was to be master of the Mason's Company in 1708 and is mentioned in Grand Lodge lists in 1723 and 1725.

William Grey was "probably the youngest candidate," a member of the Mason's Company who became master of the company in 1703.[31] Thomas Wilson (c.1618–85) was elected master of the Mason's Company on January 1, 1682. Thomas Shorthose was renter warden of the Mason's Company in 1656 and master in 1664. Thomas Shadbolt (or Shotboult) was master of the Mason's Company in 1668.

Regarding "[blank] Waindsford Esq," the man was probably Rowland Rainsford (described in the records of the Mason's Company as "late apprentice to Robert Beadles"), who was "admitted a freeman" of the company on January 15, 1668. Nicholas Young was master of the Mason's Company in 1682 and 1683. John Shorthose was warden of the Mason's Company for the same period, along with William Stanton (1639–1705).

William Hamon was, according to Josten, "doubtless identical" with the William Hammond who was present at a meeting of the Mason's Company on April 11, 1682.[32]

John Thompson was a member of the Mason's Company. One can only speculate as to whether this fellow Accepted Free Mason was the John Tompson whom Ashmole visited in September 1652 at Dove Bridge, Staffordshire, and who used a magical Call to ascertain the health of Ashmole's friend Dr. Wharton. He may also have been the same John Thompson recorded by Ashmole as having been present at the evocation of a spirit by a "speculator" using a magick circle in Buckinghamshire in 1667.

In 1682, Ashmole is specific about the events that took place on March 11—the "new *accepted*" masons paid for the noble dinner at the Half-Moon Tavern. What was this acception that had apparently grown up within the London Company? Masonic historian Matthew Scanlan has expressed the view that from the scant records, "it appears to have involved some kind of a meeting, followed by a dinner paid for by those who had been 'accepted.'"

Scanlan considers it likely that the *acception* dealt with the symbolic, allegorical, or so-called speculative side of architecture. However, if one had suggested to Ashmole himself that Free Masonry was "speculative," he might well have thought you were referring to the activities of the "speculator" in Buckinghamshire who tried to evoke a spirit, a suggestion that would doubtless have given him pause for thought.[33]

The adjective *speculative* generally referred to an occult activity, or one that involved mathematics or imaginative projection: that is, conjuring. We have all at some time or another "conjured up an image." The earliest English masonic catechism, in answer to the question "How high is your Lodge?" gives the answer "It reaches to the heavens." The lodge was an imaginative projection, "conjured up" by its members to embody a center of the universe.

There were to be other visitants to the center of the freemasons' universe. Some of them were known personally to Elias Ashmole.

A note in the hand of Ashmole's friend the antiquarian John Aubrey was found attached to a manuscript copy of his *Natural History of Wilt-shire* (1685):

> This day (May 18th Being Munday 1691 after Rogation Sunday) is a great Convention at St Paul's Church of the Fraternity of the Adopted Masons where Sr. Christopher Wren is to be adopted as a Brother.

This convention is also reported in a manuscript of John Evelyn, another acquaintance of Elias Ashmole:

> Sir Christopher Wren (architect of S.Paules) was at a convention (at S.Paules 18 May 1691), of Free-masone adopted a Brother of that Society; shore have ben kings of this sodality.[34]

Wren, most famous as the architect of St. Paul's Cathedral, had been president of the Royal Society (1680–82), and at his death in 1723, several newspapers referred to him as that "worthy Free Mason."[35]

Christopher Wren Jr. belonged to the Old St. Paul's Lodge, serving as master in 1729. Since 1691 (the date in Aubrey's account of Wren's "adoption" at St. Paul's church), that lodge had met at the Goose and Gridiron tavern in St. Paul's churchyard. The first "Grand Lodge" (openly discussed in 1716 to organize a midsummer shindig) was formed, according to Anderson's *Constitutions of Freemasonry* (1738), at the Goose and Gridiron.

In the same year as Wren's "Adoption," John Thompson was the master of the Mason's Company. His workshop supplied work for Wren. Thompson, a Free and Accepted Mason, was, as we have seen, present at the acception of several brethren that took place with Elias Ashmole as Senior Fellow at Masons Hall, Basinghall Street, in March 1682.

High on the south side of St. Paul's Cathedral sits a huge carving of a phoenix, symbolizing the rebirth of the cathedral after the Great Fire of 1666. The phoenix was of course an alchemical image. In Ashmole's transcription of alchemist Norton's *Ordinal of Alchemy*, 1477 (*Theatrum Chemicum Britannicum*, 1652), it is recorded that a number

Phoenix carved high on St. Paul's Cathedral by Caius Gabriel Cibber. The inscription below reads *Resurgam* (I will rise again). (Photo: Matthew Scanlan)

of professions, including the Free Masons, "love this profound philosophy." The phoenix carved on St. Paul's was the work of Wren's expert carver, Caius Gabriel Cibber. Cibber's son was a Free and Accepted Mason. The latter's father had inherited his workshop from *ffreemason* and king's master mason Nicholas Stone, who had joined the *Accepcion* [*sic*] at Mason's Hall in 1638.

It is now perfectly clear that a vivid world of Free and Accepted Masonry existed within the world of stone masonry craftsmanship before the establishment of the Grand Lodge. As Masonic historian Matthew Scanlan has written in his fascinating essay, "New Light on Sir Christopher Wren": "Indeed, if we remember that the earliest known masonic ceremonies date from as early as Wren's alleged initiation and that these rites centerd upon veiled notions of death and rebirth, then we are a step clearer to understanding the origins and meaning of the Craft."[36]

We are also a step nearer to understanding Elias Ashmole, the Magus of Lichfield.

ELEVEN

The Museum

By the 1670s, Ashmole had enjoyed a long acquaintance with the key figures of the Royal Society. He would have been familiar with what Joseph Glanville in 1665 declared to be "a Prophetick Scheam" of that Society: namely, the dream of establishing "Saloman's House."[1] The potent image of Saloman's House was derived from Sir Francis Bacon's allegorical fable *New Atlantis*, which first appeared as an addendum to his *Sylva Sylvarum, or Naturall History, In ten Centuries*, published a year after Bacon's death in 1627. It was a popular work and was republished several times throughout the century.

New Atlantis tells an allegorical tale of a ship that arrives at a mysterious island called Bensalem. The voyagers are greeted cautiously by a people of enviable educational and psychological endowments. The narrator is informed of how they came to be such a peculiar people of advanced attainments. An ancient patriarch had established an order on the island, and the islanders had proved faithful to his inspiration. The patriarch's name was Solamona.

The author of *New Atlantis* seems to have been acquainted with Johann Valentin Andreae's *Christianopolis* (1618), as well as the *Fama Fraternitatis* (ms. c. 1610). In Andreae's utopian classic, *Christianopolis*, a traveler is washed ashore on an island that likewise demonstrates every

237

aspect of contemporary scientific and mystical idealism in its organization and physical structure.

Furthermore, inhabitants of Bensalem (the "New Atlantis") somewhere in the Pacific (the Solomon Islands?) seem familiar with Rosicrucian imagery. A scroll first delivered to the travelers before they are permitted to land is "signed with a stamp of cherubin's wings, not spread, but hanging downwards; and by them a cross." This image is reminiscent of those under the protective eye of the Rose Cross Brothers: *Sub umbra alarum tuarum Jehova* ("under the shadow of Jehovah's wings") in the so-called Rosicrucian Manifestos.

Bacon seems to have taken Andreae's ideas and recast them for his own, not dissimilar purposes. Those purposes seem to have involved the realization that there was advantage to be gained not only in *arguing* a case for a reform of learning, but also in *showing* an attractive and intriguing image of a place where the reform has already occurred. Hence, Bacon looks forward to a *New* Atlantis that might stem from the reform of natural philosophy detailed in his earlier works.

This new philosophy is embodied in the concept of Saloman's House, which suggests, among other things, the Temple of Solomon familiar to the scripture-read people of his own day.

Bacon's aim was to get people from the known to the unknown: from *worshipping* God in his "House" (church) to *examining* God's creation in his "other" house: the universe, or Temple of Nature. This idea goes back to Hermetic and natural philosophic sources that Bacon shared with Elias Ashmole, though Bacon gives his reform program a slightly more worldly flavor than some other followers of the Hermetic tradition such as, in Bacon's own time, Dr. Robert Fludd.

To return to Bacon's story: Having been permitted to land on the island, the travelers to Bensalem are informed of a king, the island's lawgiver Solamona, who had established the island's distinctive organization 1,900 years earlier:

> Ye shall understand, my dear friends, that amongst the excellent acts of that king, one above all hath the pre-eminence. It was the erection and institution of an order, or society, which we call Saloman's House; the noblest foundation, as we think, that ever was

upon the earth, and the lantern of this kingdom. It is dedicated to the study of the works and creatures of God. Some think it beareth the founder's name a little corrupted, as if it should be Solamona's House. But the records write it as it is spoken. . . . I find in ancient records, this order or society is sometimes called Saloman's House, and sometimes the College of the Six Days' Works; whereby I am satisfied that our excellent king had learned from the Hebrews that God had created the world, and all that therein is, within six days: and therefore he instituting that house, for the finding out of the true nature of all things (whereby God mought have the more glory in the workmanship of them, and men the more fruit in the use of them), did give it also that second name.[2]

A number of scholars today believe that it was the idea of Sir Francis Bacon's Saloman's House that provided the mainspring of inspiration for the Musaeum Ashmoleanum.[3]

The first Ashmolean Museum was constructed at Ashmole's behest on Broad Street, Oxford, between 1679 and 1683. As far as we know, he never referred to his brainchild as Saloman's House, though he might, being an Accepted Free Mason, have been flattered by such an allusion. Flattered or not, he would have doubted whether the design of the building had risen to such an exalted conception.

There is no doubt that several core members of the Royal Society (such as John Wilkins) were inspired by Bacon's call for a revised program of "Natural History." The *Sylva Sylvarum* ("The Forest of Materials") was intended as part 3 of Bacon's *Great Instauration*. His Instauration (or reform of learning) was intended to both usher in and form a sound basis for a new era of experimental learning, orderly exploration of nature, and careful classification of evidence—that scheme familiar to science today as the Baconian Method. However, it appears that Ashmole was not personally moved by the Baconian bandwagon, at least under the Baconian name, though he was clever enough to take it into account.

It is understandable why Bacon's New Atlantis imagery was employed to make Bacon and his method look like the true father of what is now the Museum of the History of Science. The thesis has logic

The Old Ashmolean Museum, Broad Street, Oxford, now the Museum of the History of Science.

and is doubtless tempting, since Bacon is often credited with being a father of modern science, a John the Baptist to Isaac Newton's scientific messiah.

However, it is clear from the quotation in "New Atlantis" above that the "House" referred to as being "Saloman's" was an order or society. To superficial observation this image might appear to have been most clearly and exoterically expressed in the establishment of the Royal Society, of which Ashmole was of course a founding fellow. However, the "order or society" established on Bensalem was plainly an allegory for a hoped-for assembly or association of talent, not a blueprint for an institution in stone. Indeed, if one were to seek a historical precedent for an allegorical "house" that is also an order or society, the nearest analog in England would be a "lodge," which, while suggesting place, is part assembly and part concept or symbolic *locus*. The symbolic "lodge" is an imaginative projection.

The second, Continental, precedent that would undoubtedly spring to Ashmole's mind when faced with Bacon's story would be the "virtual fraternity" of the Rose Cross Brothers. The *Fama* tells us that the Brothers of Christian C.R., the order's founder, met in the "House of the Holy Spirit." That is to say, those considering themselves the followers of Christian C.R. met *in* a holy spirit; they did not need to gather physically, for they were united in spiritual communication "under Jehovah's wings." But they needed to communicate their discoveries; in that sense, the "house" traveled. This concept seems to have informed the story told in *New Atlantis*. Bensalem sends out "Merchants of Light" to gather knowledge for the House as a whole.

However, it is not Bacon's ideas so much as Ashmole's own esoteric—and practical—mode of thinking that we need to understand when attempting to grasp his intentions when he established his museum in Oxford. The museum was not simply an Oxford foundation; it was the result of cooperation between the university and a private person, a benefactor who was respected for his learning and his closeness to the king—and of course for what he could give to Oxford.

Oxford absorbs gifts and returns kudos; Ashmole knew that. Furthermore, he had studied at Brasenose College and fought for the royalist cause in royalist Oxford; he was a luminary of the Restoration, on close terms with the stars of that era. The museum, while akin to the Royal Society's ambitions, was not a project of the Royal Society as an institution, though it may be seen as an expression of the stream of inspiration that led to that fellowship. That stream was as much spiritual as it was practical.

In recent times there has been an uncontested tendency to sweep Ashmole's achievement into an undifferentiated state as part of a wider and inevitable movement, Oxford born. This view shares characteristics with that discussed earlier wherein Ashmole somehow stole John Tradescant's credit for the collection. This tendency appears so negative toward Ashmole at times that one wonders if the proponents of these views would prefer to go back to the seventeenth century and rename Ashmole's achievement the Bacon-Tradescant Museum of Modern Science.

A fascinating recent guide to the discovery of seventeenth- and eighteenth-century chemical instruments, ephemera, and anatomical remains (human and canine) at the rear of the Old Ashmolean expresses the essence of what is practically an obliteration of Ashmole's significance:

> Recent historical accounts of the Ashmolean Museum have recognized that Elias Ashmole's offer to present the rarities he had acquired from John Tradescant, and the need for a "large Roome" to contain them, came at a time when these could be incorporated into broader ambitions to make provision for experimental natural philosophy in the University. In July 1677 the orientalist Humphrey Prideaux of Christ Church traced the progression of this initiative from the publication in the same year of Robert Plot's *Natural History of Oxfordshire,* whose title continues in a Baconian vein, *Being an Essay Towards the Natural History of England.* According to Prideaux, "we are now on a design of erecting a Lecture for Philosophical History to be read by the author of that booke," and the incorporation of the Tradescant-Ashmole collection fell within this wider project:
>
> > . . . as soon as we have agreed on the ground, we shall build a school on purpose for it with a laboratory annext and severall other rooms for other uses, whereof on[e] is to hold John Tredeskins raritys . . .[4]

The author doubts whether this modern account may be taken wholly at face value. First, Ashmole's contribution is diminished to the offering of a collection "acquired" from Tradescant; this offering is grammatically separate from the need of a large room to "contain" it. The use of the word *offer* is also somewhat light.

Ashmole's active donation of what was his own property included his own collections, which he had acquired. Indeed, he had the decency to maintain the integrity of the Tradescant collection, rather than, as other collectors have done, simply absorbing it as part of his own collections.

Ashmole was magisterially involved in the establishment, detailed regulation, and underlying philosophy of the museum. According to the quotation above, the rarities could be "incorporated into broader ambitions." *Broader ambitions?* It has not been established that Ashmole's ambitions were not as broad as the university's own.

Humphrey Prideaux is cited as an authority to support the paragraph's rather sweeping judgment. Prideaux, an orientalist "of Christ Church" in July 1677, traces the progression of "this initiative" from Plot's *Natural History of Oxfordshire*—whose subtitle in the "Baconian vein" makes it very acceptable to the thesis.

By 1677, Prideaux had held his master's degree for only two years, and was not to receive his doctorate of divinity until nine years later. His literary reputation as an orientalist (such as it is) rests on a "Life of Mahomet," published in *1697*, "written," according to the Oxford *Concise Dictionary of National Biography*, "as a polemical tract against the deists, and worthless as a biography." The title "the orientalist . . . of Christ Church" hardly applies to the young man of July 1677; what is the value of what he writes concerning Dr. Plot? It is merely his opinion. Furthermore, it has been placed in a context where such an opinion might lead one to suppose an encounter with an authority.

At any rate, the first reference to the founding of a "publique musaeum" comes not in 1677, but in a letter written by Ashmole to His Excellence Count Griffinfeld, Lord High Chancellor of Denmark, dated September 18, 1674, three years before Dr. Plot's book on Oxfordshire.

On July 3, 1675, Ashmole wrote a letter to Mr. Thomas Hyde, library keeper of the Publique Library in Oxford. In it Ashmole describes his wish to "propose the building of some large Room, which may have Chimnies, to keepe those things [his collections] aired that will stand in neede of it."[5]

It is reasonable, then, to assert that Prideaux is speaking from hearsay about activities already in motion. His use of "we" simply means

"Oxford is planning." The reference has little to no bearing on the true part played by Elias Ashmole in the foundation of his museum.

Let us then trace Ashmole's own involvement with his museum project.

THE TRADESCANT RARITIES

On December 16, 1659, John and Hester Tradescant sealed and delivered to Ashmole the Deed of Gift of all John Tradescant's rarities, including books, coins, pictures, medals, stones, "mechanicks," "pieces of antiquity," and strange and wondrous things brought back from sea voyages—such as a mermaid's hand.

Ashmole noted on April 4, 1661, how Tradescant left "my closett of rarities" to his wife Hester in his will.[6] Hester claimed that her husband never wanted his collection to go into private hands, but should instead go to the University of Oxford or Cambridge. John Tradescant the younger was buried on April 25, 1662.

On May 18, 1664, Ashmole's "Case came to hearing in the Chancery against Mrs : Tradescant [sic]."[7] The validity of the Deed of Gift was upheld; Ashmole's possession of the Tradescant rarities was established.

In the year that Ashmole obtained a fragment "of the True Cross" and obtained a term of 500 years in a moiety (portion) of a house, garden, and orchard at South Lambeth (by assignment of Rebecca Blackamore, a widow of Lambeth), he wrote a letter to His Excellence Count

The tomb of John Tradescant the younger, who was buried at St. Mary's, Lambeth, on April 25, 1662.

Griffinfeld. Based in Copenhagen, the count was Lord High Chancellor of Denmark.

The year was 1674. The fragment of the True Cross disappeared from the museum after 1697. The house at South Lambeth was situated next to Hester Tradescant's house, and Ashmole's letter to Count Griffinfeld marks his first mention of his plan for a "publique musaeum." The museum would be the first open to the public in the nation's history; very few people in Britain had ever heard the word *museum*, let alone had the remotest idea of what one was for. The public museum was a remarkable and historic innovation; it was the first purpose-built museum in the world.

On June 17 of that year, Ashmole had received his gold medal and chain (worth eighty pounds) from the king of Denmark in grateful recognition of the magnitude of scholarship evinced in Ashmole's History of the Order of the Garter. Ashmole informed His Excellency that "when

The Ashmolean Museum, Oxford, in its current magnificent home on Beaumont Street, Oxford.

I dye, [I will] bequeath it to a publique Musaeum, that Posterity may take notice of the largeness of his [the king of Denmark's] Bounty to an English Gentleman."[8]

The motive here for the bequest is absolutely true to Ashmolean form. It is in order that *posterity may take notice.* This is in tune with his whole life's feeling and conviction for the need for preservation, "lest we forget." This is the antiquarian motive, not the Baconian, scientific one. The history of science shows a perpetual discarding of yesterday's theories and practices, even, in some important cases, the attempted obliteration of memory. Isaac Newton's destruction of Robert Hooke's reputation while president of the Royal Society, for example, is something Ashmole could never have countenanced.

Ashmole desired to bring the best of the past to the attention of the present for the betterment of the future. Ever poised between earth and heaven, matter and spirit, the past is his heaven that must be joined to the earth of the future, and his future is his heaven that must be joined to the earth of the past. The present is incidental, mercurial, mysterious: the past in the making. The future is made in the past; it has its owner's stamp upon it. What is Time? According to Ashmole, time is that which reveals meaning in the universe.

As stated before, Ashmole took the importance of knowledge of nature for granted; it was an obvious aspect of "natural magick" (physics) and of common practical sense (the how-to-do of the born Midlander). Ashmole would be the very last person on earth to denigrate the importance of learning, or of the benefits of a reform of learning, as long as that reform was properly and comprehensively rooted.

It is to be doubted whether Ashmole would have regarded Bacon's "Great Instauration" as all that great; he would have regarded Bacon's program as rather weak on the spiritual side: a little too clever by half, sometimes simplistic and frequently rhetorical.

A true "revolution" was, for Ashmole, the culmination of an astronomical cycle with astrological meaning, based on the past and tested by experience. To ordinary eyes, such a revolution could appear wholly novel, as a revelation. To Ashmole, the Book of Nature had many more tricks up her sleeve. He should have known; he was the Mercuriophilus Anglicus, not entirely confined (in his own mind) to history.

On October 2, 1674, Mr. and Mrs. Ashmole (Ashmole having been married to Elizabeth, daughter of Sir William Dugdale, since 1668) moved into their house at South Lambeth. On November 26, their neighbor "Mrs Tredescant[,] being willing to deliver up the Rarities to me," enabled Ashmole to carry "several of them to my House."[9]

It would be hard to imagine that Ashmole moved into his house to spare himself removal costs. Whatever his reasons, he appears to have done so in innocence, perhaps to provide some comfort for Mrs. Tradescant; the rarities, after all, were not going to go very far. This innocence may later have given him cause for regret.

On August 6, 1676, Ashmole was robbed during the night of thirty-two cocks and hens. It is likely that the thieves climbed into Ashmole's garden over a great heap of earth and refuse laid against his garden wall by Hester Tradescant.[10] Widow Tradescant seems to have entered a state of mind we should now call, with no great accuracy, "paranoid."

Something of this affliction seems to have gripped Ashmole himself. Until the heap was removed, he lay in abject fear night after night lest his house be broken into. His fears were justified, however. His neighbor does indeed seem to have "lost her marbles" over Ashmole.

On September 1, Hester Tradescant was forced to make a legal Submission, confessing that she had made defamatory statements about Ashmole's rights, intentions, acts, and character.[11] Pitifully, the widow Tradescant had even falsely accused Ashmole of making a hole in her wall so that he might pass through it to steal her goods once she was dead. Freudians could doubtless make something of that.

THE ASHMOLEAN

An engraving by Michael Burghers on the east front of the museum in about 1685 bears an inscription reading "T. Wood Arch.t." Thomas Wood, architect, was the master mason in charge of the building operations from 1679. He received a weekly wage of ten shillings and occasional payments of ten pounds for stone carving. This is revealed in the university archives, *Computus Vice-Cancellarii*, 1666–97. However, there is reason to consider that the design on which Wood based his elegant work derived from a plan Christopher Wren had made for a new home for the Royal Society a decade earlier.

Wren wrote a letter to fellow Royal Society member Henry Oldenburg on June 7, 1668, describing a plan for new premises at Arundel Gardens, London. Though never executed, it, like the first Ashmolean, had a laboratory in the basement. It also had a large room on the ground floor linked by a principal staircase to another large room on the first floor for a collection of rarities. It may be that Wren provided Wood—or Ashmole—with the design, or at least some ideas.

It would have been natural for Ashmole, seeing Gilbert Sheldon's "Theatre" next door to his museum, to think Wren was the man for the job. On the other hand, Wren may have found the project less than challenging in the 1670s; he disliked architecture, considering himself first and foremost a physicist. The Sheldonian had involved unique architectural challenges answered with brilliance—the single roof over the main chamber was a masterpiece. Wren was older now, and the most challenging aspect of the Ashmolean was resolved by his ingenious method for getting smoke from the basement laboratory out into the main chimneys.

The Ashmolean is not disharmonious to the overall effect of the Sheldonian and the towering Bodelian Library close by. However, it is not as

Left: Michael Burghers's engraving of the east front of the museum (c. 1685).

Right: Morphological relationship between the east door of the museum and the title page of Dee's *Monas Hieroglyphica* (1564). Was Ashmole involved in the design?

Wren's magnificent Sheldonian Theatre, adjacent to the Musaeum Ashmoleanum on Broad Street, Oxford.

striking as the Sheldonian, and one might think that Wren would have come up with something more remarkable to stand next to his youthful masterpiece. Furthermore, this author cannot help but observe a great similarity between the magnificent east door of the Old Ashmolean and the frontispiece to Ashmole's great inspiration, the *Monas Hieroglyphica* by John Dee (1564). Perhaps Ashmole suggested something of the kind to freemason Thomas Wood. In the light of the evidence, Wood properly deserves all the credit for his stately, lasting work.

The requirements of the Ashmolean were simple enough and would have appeared so to Ashmole. But to a British university, the museum was epoch-making by virtue of its basement laboratory, stocked with "state-of-the-art" chemical instruments. One might object that the state of the art of chemistry in 1683, when the museum opened its doors to the public, was pretty low. But it had to start somewhere, and the Ashmolean provided impetus.

In fact, it provided a great deal. For more than 150 years after its foundation, the museum remained the center for scientific studies (which included anatomy) in Oxford—a great tribute to the powerful spiritual impulse that drove Ashmole's great energies into such a life-enhancing and generous direction. The inclusion of the laboratory was farsighted and clear-sighted.

The remainder of the building required a large hall to accommodate the displays of rarities and a lecture hall so that natural science might gain the image of being a school. It was competing with Oxford's established tradition, those great schools celebrated with their names above the doors of the Bodleian quadrangle: logic, metaphysics, divinity.

Ashmole no doubt harbored hopes that some day the laboratory would produce great advances in alchemical achievement. However, in his prolegomena to the regulations that he devised for the strict running of the establishment, he was content to use the utilitarian, even prosaic, language favored by the Royal Society in its commitment to public experiments of a useful nature.

> Because the knowledge of Nature is very necessarie to humaine life, health, & the conveniences thereof, & because that knowledge cannot be soe well & usefully attain'd, except the history of Nature be knowne and considered; and to this, is requisite the inspection of Particulars, especially those as are extraordinary in their Fabrick, or useful in Medicine, or applied to manufacture or Trade . . .[12]

Today it is very hard for us to fully understand what was extraordinary about the activities of leading members of the Royal Society. As we have seen, the effort of natural philosophers such as Bacon was to get people to consider the leap between worshipping the Creator and respecting (or "worshipping") the wisdom inherent in His Creation.

There existed an ancient ecclesiastical and religious prejudice against finding this life too interesting in its details; you might become a pagan (by worshipping the creation) or sorcerer (by knowing too much for everyone's own good). Either way, you could end up dead, even damned for eternity; an herbalist could be suspected of witchcraft.

Most people had not been raised in such a way that they would or should find Nature interesting. The human body was largely a closed book. Most theological teaching was concerned exclusively with morals and salvation; the earth was as God made it and that was that. Farming was farming; milk was milk; war was war; and we should all strive to be good and to be saved. From hell and—yes—from this world that was corrupted by the Devil. Fallen man was in no state to come to grips with its secret construction. Similar anxieties prevail in today's era of genetic and nuclear research.

Therefore, to ask people to be open to the idea that Nature had something to teach required a hook: that what they looked at in a museum (the place of the Muse) would be striking, intriguing, rare. Ashmole expressed this requirement when he demanded that "the Particulars" to be inspected be "extraordinary in their Fabrick." Things seen should be "useful in Medicine" (curing disease) or applicable to "Trade" (making money).

The "rarities" therefore had to look as surprising as the performances seen at a fair. There was *joy* in knowledge. The museum was *open*. This was something that, if not entirely new (the theater could be an educational force), then certainly gave a fresh focus and a new, magical twist. Learning could be—and had to be—*entertaining*. It would have been no good exhibiting coal or grass or a stuffed cow. A museum must *amuse*.

One needed extraordinary rarities. The Tradescant collection contained these in abundance. Ashmole wanted to provide contrast and balance between the stranger things of nature with the stimulating survivals of the past and the finds of antiquarian research, preserved for the enlightenment of those who would otherwise either forget or not know at all. These, Ashmole also possessed in abundance. He had acquired them through years of dedicated and precise, systematic collecting.

But then a tragedy happened for Elias Ashmole—and for knowledge.

"THOSE FATALL FLAMES"

On January 26, 1679, at 10 p.m., a careless fire began in Pump Court, the Middle Temple, in a room next to Ashmole's chambers. It destroyed Ashmole's library—thirty-three years of collected books. Nearly 9,000 coins and medals ancient and modern—the product of thirty-two years of collecting—melted in the flames. Carbonized beyond recognition and scattered about the embers that Ashmole trudged through on the following morning, was a large collection of ancient manuscripts and seals pertaining to the English nobility and gentry.

Pump Court, Middle Temple,
London.

Ashmole had collected examples of all the Great Seals of England from the time of the Norman Conquest, as well as many from the religious houses of England and Scotland. His observations on history, coins, medals, heraldry—the studies of three decades—all went up in smoke. Valuable pieces of antiquity, sundry curiosities of art and nature: "All these, and many other things of worth, perished in those fatall Flames."[13]

For Ashmole the preserver, the event came as a hammer blow, a wasting of the soul. As if feeling his pain, friends and well-wishers sent letter after letter of commiseration. It was, in fact, a national cultural disaster. There was no British Museum or British Library then: only people, and only a few like Ashmole.

It must have been with particularly mixed feelings, then, that Ashmole noted on May 15 that year that the first stone of the Ashmolean Museum was laid, on the west side of the Sheldonian Theatre.[14] Inexplicably, half of his eventual gift had already gone forever.

Possibly as a result of the anxieties engendered by the destruction of so much of his collections, Ashmole's health became impaired. Attacks of gout increased. In 1681, the vain application of poultices to his right foot weakened the tendons. The result was pain so acute that attempts to walk became a nightmare. It must have been a great disappointment to Ashmole that the growth of his most public enterprise was accompanied by pains that only fellow gout sufferers could understand for their debilitating, frustrating intensity.

August 17, 1682, saw the completion of "the building prepared to receive my Rarities. . . . Between 8 and 9, I first saw the said Building. I was invited by the Vicechancellor & dyned with him at Queenes Colledge."[15] The arms of Vice Chancellor Timothy Halton, DD (1632?–1704), provost of Queen's, still hang over the east entrance of the Old Ashmolean. The vice chancellor had served as comptroller of works.

Following Ashmole's approval, the antiquarian Dr. Robert Plot was appointed first keeper of the Ashmolean and professor of chemistry. It may be argued that Ashmole's ambition was somewhat greater than that of the university's powers that be, for an attempt to establish an Ashmolean Professorship in chemical and natural history was prevented by ecclesiastical influence. The proposed chair was regarded as too alarming an innovation to be countenanced by its opponents. Times have changed.

Dr. Plot was with Ashmole at South Lambeth when on March 24, 1683, as Ashmole records it, "I began to put my Rarities into Cases, to send to Oxford."[16] A contemporary letter from the Rev. Thomas Dixon to Sir Daniel Fleming follows up the story: ". . . John Tredeskins Rarities are come down from London by water. The Elaboratory (which some call the Knick-knackatory) is almost finish'd and ready to receive them. Doctor Plot who is to be Superviser of ye Elaboratory brought them downe."[17] If they had TV news in those days, the event would doubtless make the six o'clock bulletin.

Two months later, on May 21, the Duke and Duchess of York, the Princess Anne (the Duke's second daughter—and future Queen—by his first wife, Anne Hyde), and a throng of earls and lords arrived at the Ashmolean Museum looking for entertainment and perhaps a little magick. A set speech by Dr. Plot served to welcome them to the museum. He then presented the rarities, accompanied by the bishop of

Oxford, the vice chancellor, and the doctors of all the faculties. According to Anthony Wood, "Then they went donne to the Elaboratory, where the[y] saw some experiments to their great satisfaction."[18]

This was of course the gala opening. The whiff of regal patronage was in the air and everyone was on best behavior. There had been dreams of such an event but it had taken someone special to turn them into reality. Sadly, the man without whom it would never have happened was unable to attend.

Elias was now sixty-six years old. The dreadful affliction of gout prevented him both from directly overseeing the movement of his collections into the museum itself and from attending the grand opening—a sad double blow. Throughout the spring and early summer, the gout to his feet was so agonizing that he was unable to leave his house; he could not walk without an intense, depressing, psychologically aging pain. Magicians are not immune to the worst that Mother Nature has to offer.

Sir Francis Bacon's "cure" for the ailment, given in his *Sylva Sylvarum,* gave no relief. Not for many years would the world of science, which had offered the universal law of gravitation, discover—perhaps belatedly—that gout could not be cured by external poultices.

On May 24, the university gained entry to its new house on Broad Street, as recorded by Ashmole's man-in-Oxford, Anthony Wood: "Those Doctors and masters that pleased retired to ye Musaeum which is ye upper room, where they viewed from one till 5 of ye clock what they pleased. . . . Many that are delighted with new phil[osophy] are taken with them; but some for ye old—look upon them as ba[u]bles—Ch.Ch. [Christchurch] men not there."[19] One can imagine the Common Room banter on that particular day.

Ashmole kept a careful eye on events at the museum, but from a distance. He rarely made the journey to damp old Oxford, having to rely on the mail. Oxford doubtless lost something in not having the genius on the doorstep, so to speak. His emphatic speech and humorous manner would certainly have inspired those involved with the museum and set its work in a fuller perspective than bookish dons would have been able to do. Ashmole would have been popular with undergraduates, who, when suitably impressed, have been known to warm to their elders.

The Oxford historian Anthony Wood, or Anthony à Wood, as he styled himself. Wood was a keen observer of Ashmole's life.

Not all of his days were darkened by ill health, however. On July 17, 1690, the warm air brought Elias to the doors of his creation at the grand old age of seventy-three. The event was again recorded by Anthony Wood: "Thursday [the] Vi[ce]ch[ancellor]—Heads of Houses and others to the numb[er] of 30 or thereabouts dined in the upp[er] house of the Musaeum where the rarities lay—Mr Ashmole was carried in a chaire or sedan[;] was placed at ye end of that place and the Doctor standinge about him, Mr Ed Hanner of Ch. Ch. [Christchurch] chymical professor spoke a speech to him—afterwards they went to dinner—Mrs Ashmole Jack Cross and Mr Sheldon [not the archbishop] dined together in Doctor Plots Study."[20]

Mr. Ashmole's body was, sadly, not as sharp as his mind, "being then much out of order and brought very low by divers indispositions" (Wood).

Still in Oxford, two days later, Ashmole spent Saturday evening dining with his wife "at the provi[ce] ch[ancellor's] Doctor Meer at Brasn. Coll."[21] John Meare, DD (c. 1659–1710), principal of Brasenose College, had the privilege of being the last man to entertain Elias Ashmole at Oxford, forty-five years after the young captain Ashmole had commanded the grim artillery post of Dover Pier in the defense of that great city from her enemies.

TWELVE

Coming Home

It is not less absurd, then strange, to see how some Men
. . . wil not forebeare to ranke True Magicians with
Conjurors Necromancers, and Witches . . . who insolently
intrude themselves into Magick, as if Swine should enter
into a faire and delicate Garden, and, (being in League
with the Devill) make use of his assistance in their
workes, to counterfeit and corrupt the admirall wisdome
of the Magi betweene whom there is as large a difference
as between Angels and Devils.
ELIAS ASHMOLE: *THEATRUM CHEMICUM BRITANNICUM*[1]

O n May 30, 1662, Ashmole had to record that "My father
Bachus died this Evening at Swallowfield."[2] As usual in the
notes he made on his life, there is no betrayal of emotion. To
find that emotion one must again refer to a poem he wrote eleven years
earlier. In 1651, he had first celebrated his being made spiritual son to
William Backhouse of Swallowfield, his Hermetic adoption:

From this blest Minute I'le begin to date
My Yeares and Happines . . . & vow I be're perceiv'd
what Being was till now.[3]

This is powerful testimony to the effect of the older man on his mercury-loving son; Elias experienced a profound rebirth. Backhouse had expanded his mind, opened his eyes, had brought him into contact with a greater sense of Being: the infinite canvas of spiritual, magical life. Backhouse's coming into his life was providential, marvelous—a key moment in life's initiation.

Even Ashmole's nickname for his adoptive father, "Bachus," is revealing. He is a divine figure of fun and intoxication, even of danger. To share the wine of Bacchus may entail the rending of the soul. Bacchus is master at the table of the finer feast and, in Renaissance iconography, an equivalent figure (as was Hermes) to John the Baptist: he who anoints the son and acquaints him with his destiny.

Ashmole must have experienced a feeling of having been cut adrift when Backhouse died, of having to take the reins. He was, in spiritual terms, Backhouse's alchemical heir, privy to his greatest secret—the philosopher's stone itself—and might risk failure in life should he not live up to the responsibilities of his adoption.

When *The Way to Bliss* appeared in 1658, Ashmole informed his readers that protracted lawsuits had prevented him from producing a projected second volume of the *Theatrum Chemicum Britannicum*. He also knew that he had not fully enjoyed the intense solitary conditions (or peace of mind) necessary to explore the practical side of alchemy. This cannot be said of "the alchemist recluse" Backhouse, however. A man who would take on Ashmole as spiritual son would hardly restrain him from attendance to his alchemical work. This work, Ashmole knew, had more significance than all the world could offer him. As a twentieth-century magus observed, a master yogi derives more joy from moving his leg than a millionaire gets from a week in New York.

An obscure note of February 2, 1683, is the sole item in Ashmole's papers that implies "Manuall Practise" of alchemy. He acquainted a "Mr : Woolrich (in part) with the secret of raising flowers from a Virgin Earth."[4] According to C. H. Josten, "Virgin earth" is a *substantia arcana* frequenting alchemical texts.[5] The term may also denote earth dug up from great depths. When sealed in glass, it was supposed to generate flowers spontaneously.

However much Ashmole tried to balance the active and the contemplative pillars of life, he generally seems to have felt a painful tugging between the two. He was ambitious, but he could kill his ambition temporarily. He could immerse himself in abstruse spiritual studies, but the world's clamor would soon be at his door. Working on royal business must have provided a mighty tide to draw him from his soul's quest. Besides, he had proved over the years that he was truly useful in the world; he could accomplish where others fretted. He had to admit that for a mystic, he was a hell of a man of action. He was determined, powerful in law, and forceful in nature, and he possessed long-term willpower.

Compare, if you will, these characteristics with Ashmole's epitome of John Dee's system of religious magick, taken from the Elizabethan magus's Spiritual Diaries: The operator must "3 days before abstaine from Coitus, & Gluttony &c." He must "wash hands, face, cut nailes, shave the beard, wash all." When all this is done, he must intone his "invocations seven times." These actions ought to be practiced in the sunshine and for a fourteen-day limit each time. It was necessary to work on even days and only in the "increasing hours"—from sunrise to noon and from sunset to midnight. To add to this itinerary, the sun must "be well placed with a beneficent planet reigning." Furthermore, the importance of prayer, even unto "enflaming oneself with prayer," was a vital key to opening the inner worlds and receiving guidance and knowledge.[6]

Ashmole always had a great deal on his mind and probably suffered, like his lusty contemporary Samuel Pepys, from some degree of sexual guilt. This might have made the purification of prayer, of removing his mask before God, a difficult prospect. His spirit was most willing, but his flesh was frequently elsewhere.

Nevertheless, Magick still provided the golden thread in the velvet of his life after the Restoration. In December 1667, William Lilly made notes for an autobiography and asked for Ashmole's help. Ashmole wrote down some questions that Lilly answered on the same sheets; the sheets have survived.

Ashmole asked his fellow astrologer who had been with him, "When he invoked the queen of faeries in the Hurst Wood [a wood belonging to Mr. Lilly], and upon her appearance was so frightened that he was glad to desist." Lilly replied: "Mr Thompson and a speculator in Buckinghamshire, who tried presently after in Mr Lilly['s] closet the circular way but the spirit would not appear."[7]

The evocation of a spirit in a magick circle was an activity that could lead to the most dire punishment, but Ashmole was not abashed by the activity. "If you can be stout enough to endure the stirrings and winds before the first appearance (which perhaps may be after 3 or 4 [magickal] calls)," wrote Lilly, "they will after appear without disturbance. If you hold them longer than the sign ascending at your call, they will grow unruly and troublesome, perhaps dangerous, and not stay neither."[8]

In seventeenth-century usage, a *speculator* was an observer of spirits or one engaged in occult pursuits. Was Ashmole a "speculator"? It does not appear that he was one in the sense of evoking and banishing spirits—ceremonial magick—but he was not averse to making sigils and, as we shall see, he may have experimented with John Dee's system and magickal "Calls." There is evidence of Ashmole's interest in fairy calls and the fairies' appearance in "christalls."[9] The texts include two Calls where Ashmole himself was the magician, for the initials of the operator's name are given as E. A.

A cipher note records Ashmole's interest in the governing angels of the cosmos: "Michael is the angel of the sun/is to be called for general accidents of the world / The inferior spirits can do little and answer but to few things but they will commonly direct a man to those spirits that will / The queen of the fairies, is one of those that give but little satisfaction."[10]

If one can speak of a slight change of emphasis in Ashmole's spiritual direction, especially after the death of Backhouse, it is toward his heart's desire, namely, Magick. In this movement, he rather mirrors his great hero, the mathematician and magus John Dee, in whose works Ashmole became deeply embroiled. Dee grew frustrated with the state of science in his time and attempted a more profound acquaintance with what he believed were the deeper and higher springs of cosmic activity. According to the "three worlds" theory of the universe prevalent at the time (sublunary, celestial, supercelestial), this entailed making contact with angels of the supercelestial sphere that governed terrestrial life.

This perilous activity was considered legitimate because it was widely held among magi that before the final wrapping up of the world's destiny, there would be a great outpouring of heavenly knowledge of the deeper facets of nature.

As we learned in chapter 1, this expectation was linked to the return of "Elias the Artist." Isaac Newton himself shared the principle of this belief; it was a widespread gnostic and apocalyptic hope and expectation; it persists to this day. Therefore, to be chosen—that is, to be the recipient of special gifts of perception—was to be given a special divine pass for operating on levels forbidden to the uninitiated.

Ashmole had long considered himself to be in the line of the trusted magi, but he was wary in this as in most other things. There would be no books on magick or antiquarian works reflecting his magickal concerns. He had seen the crazy furor engendered when Meric Casaubon published a selection of Dee's spiritual diaries in 1659; Dee's reputation suffered most severely as a result. However, Ashmole made a concerted attempt to rescue Dee's reputation. He did this in the sober spirit of the antiquarian inquirer.

SAVING DEE

On August 20, 1672, by an extraordinary set of coincidences, "My good friend Mr : Wale sent me [Ashmole] Doctor Dees originall Bookes and Papers."[11] These covered the period from December 22, 1581, to May 1583, a period preceding the extracts given in Casaubon's *A True and Faithful Relation of what passed for some years between Dr John Dee and some Spirits* (1659).

On the flyleaf to John Dee's *Liber Mysteriorum 1-V,* Ashmole recorded the story of how he was brought the valuable cache of John Dee's "spiritual diaries."[12] These included that magical system restored by Robert Turner in 1983, the *Heptarchia Mystica:* a guide to the seven orders of angels and their operations in the governance of the universe:

> Be it remembered, that the 20th August 1672, I received by the hands of my servant Samuell Story, a part of Dr. Dee's manuscripts all written with his own hand; *viz* : his conference with Angello, which first began the 22nd December *Ano* 1581, and continued to the end of May Ano 1583, where the printed Booke of the remaining

The "Illuminati" paraded on the frontispiece of Meric Casaubon's *A True and Faithful Relation of What Passed for Many Years between Dr John Dee and Some Spirits* (London, 1659). The accused are (*left to right from the top*), "Mahomet," Apollonius of Tyana, Edward Kelley, Roger Bacon, Paracelsus, John Dee. Conspiracy theory in action, seventeenth-century style.

conferences (published by Dr. Casaubon) begins, and are bound up in this volume.

. . . The Booke entitled *De Heptarchia Mystica—Collectanorum Lib : Primus,* and a Booke of (Invocations or Calls beginning with the Squares, filled with letters about the Black Cross). These four Books I have bound up in another volume.

All of which were a few daies before delivered to my said servant for my perusall (I being then at Mr Lillies house, at Hershaw in Surry) by my good friend Mr Thomas wale, one of his Majesties Wardens in the Tower of London.[13]

Ashmole must have been overjoyed. The most intimate records—unseen by any but Dee and his assistants—had arrived in his lap, so to speak. It must have seemed like magick. Also in the collection were *The 48 Claves Angelicae* (Angelic Keys) of which Ashmole wrote: "This booke is written in the Angelick Language Interlined with an English translation. *Cracoviae, ab Apilis* 13.ad July 13 (*diversis temporibus*) *Receptae Anno 1584.* At the bottom of the title page—*Liber 18.*[14]

The "Angelick Language" was that tongue called Enochian, an extraordinary language with its own syntax and grammar revealed to, or devised by, Dee's assistant, Edward Kelley, depending on your point of view. This language was communicated through the use of specially constructed magick tables that Dee had made. One of them is on display today at the Museum of the History of Science (Old Ashmolean), either a relic of antique superstition or a promise of a science of which we as yet know little, again depending on your point of view.

On September 10, 1672, Mr. and Mrs. Wale came to see Ashmole at the Excise office on Broad Street, London, to explain to him how Dees's priceless manuscripts had come into their possession. Ashmole was keen to obtain and preserve the details of the discovery in the strict interests of provenance—and, doubtless, with some very natural and proper excitement.

Mr. and Mrs. Wale explained to Ashmole that Mrs. Wale had formerly been married to a Mr. Jones, a confectioner of Lombard Street, London. Shortly after the latter marriage the couple had gone to look at some furniture put up for sale by a joiner. Among the household items was a chest of fine workmanship, formerly belonging to a Mr. John Woodall, who had very probably bought the chest when Dee's goods were sold after his death in 1608.

About four years before the Great Fire of London (1666), the Joneses heard rustlings inside the chest when they moved it, and on inspection (and with the help of a piece of iron) discovered a secret drawer full of books, together with a rosary. A maid burned about half of the collection, but the then Mrs. Jones put the rest safely away. It even survived the Great Fire while the chest itself was destroyed. The manuscripts were taken out with the rest of the savable goods to Moon Fields and then, after the Fire, finally returned home.

On marrying Mr. Wale, Mrs. Wale informed her husband about the books and he, on hearing that Ashmole had lately passed through London, brought them to him; Ashmole's reputation was pervasive. Mr. Wale agreed to exchange the manuscripts for a gilt copy of Mr. Ashmole's Garter book. This was one of Ashmole's better deals.

On October 10, 1672, Ashmole recorded: "This night I began to consider of the 12 Names of God being the first in the Book (which I suppose Doctor Dee called *Liber Enoch*) & found them in the middle lynes of each of the 4 great Squares in the first Table on either side about the black Cross."[15]

The Magus of Lichfield was becoming seriously involved with decrypting the communication methods of Kelley's angels. This was something he was well equipped to do; ciphers had been a specialty of his, as they were of Dr. John Dee, and, like Dee, of no small interest to members of the nation's intelligence services.

On October 26, Ashmole commenced a transcription of John Dee's manuscript, beginning: *Anno 1581 : 1582. Mysteriorum Liber primus Mortlaci*—Mortlake being Dee's home.[16] One must presume that at this time, his accounting work at the Excise office must have paled somewhat in interest. One can imagine him itching for a return to nighttime forays into the magical universe of his hero.

By the end of the year, he was considering writing a biography of Dee or, rather, one suspects, a vindication of the man he had described twenty years earlier in his *Theatrum Chemicum Britannicum* as one deserving of "the commendation of all Learned and ingenious Schollers, and to be remembered for his remarkable abilities"—not the least of which lay in mathematics, of which Dee was "in all parts . . . an absolute and perfect master."

On December 30 it looked like he was going to hand over the project to the younger Oxford historian Anthony Wood. He had heard that Wood was writing a biographical work of remarkable men that would include Dee (and Ashmole himself). Ashmole explained his reasons to Wood for wanting to provide the country with a greater knowledge of the magus. Dee was "a very Learned and truly pious man, but deserves much better esteem of our Nation than yet he hath obtein'd. . . . I have had it in my thoughts to write his lyfe, but now you are about it, shall rather contribute what I have for your use."[17]

This was modest of Ashmole, though perhaps he preferred the research to the finishing. It also appears to this author that Ashmole favored the role of *éminence grise,* the hidden hand that makes things happen. He liked to get others to back into the limelight he had created; this is the way of the magus, who must always suffer incomprehension to the extent where his white is always perceived as black by the uninitiated.

Within six months of obtaining the *Heptarchia Mystica,* Ashmole had asked the antiquary John Aubrey (in whose *Lives* Ashmole features) to inquire after contemporary accounts of Dee in Mortlake and received a report from Aubrey on January 27, 1673: "Mr Aubreys Account of Doctor Dee which he received from Goodwife Faldo of Mortlack the beginning of January 1673 and delivered to me the 27 of the same month."[18]

Aubrey had made contact with the eighty-two-year-old widow Faldo. He informed Ashmole that "the children dreaded him [Dee] because he was counted a Conjurer."[19] The local grown-ups valued his presence, however. Aubrey, perhaps using Widow Faldo's words, insisted that Dee was "a mighty good man : a great Peacemaker. If any of the neighbors fell out, he would never let them alone till he had made them friends."[20] He would later use the phrase "A mighty good man" with reference to Ashmole. It is interesting that the two men had become so identified in his subconscious.

Ashmole was not wholly satisfied with Aubrey's interview and decided to go to Mortlake himself as soon as he was able. If a job needs doing well, do it yourself.

In the interim, Ashmole had to record the death of his old friend Sir Robert Moray: "The learned and ingenious Sir Rob: Murrey died" on July 4, 1673.[21] "Learned and ingenious" is a phrase reserved by Ashmole for those versed in the Hermetic Art, and that is certainly true of Robert Moray, first president of the Royal Society, patron of Rosicrucian enthusiast Thomas Vaughan, alchemist, and admitted Free Mason (Newcastle, 1641).

On August 11, a month after Moray's death, Ashmole went to interview the widow Faldo. One wonders what his thoughts were as he approached Mortlake, last home of his Hermetic hero. Widow Faldo told Ashmole that she had known Dee well and had been inside his house, four or five rooms of which had been "filled with bookes." He kept a "plentifull Table and a good Howse" and once permitted Faldo and her mother the vision of "the Ecclips of the Sun in one of his Roomes, which he had made darke."[22]

The sight of the sun's eclipse was afforded chiefly for the benefit of "the Polonian Embassador."[23] This was Lord Laski, Count Palatine of Siradz, who visited England in 1583, and with whom Dee and Edward Kelley returned to the Continent.

Ashmole carefully described the site at Mortlake where Dee had once lived three quarters of a century earlier.

> The buildings which Sir Fr : Crane erected for working of Tapestry hangings (& are still employed to that use) were built upon the Ground whereon Doctor Dees laboratory (& other homes for that use) stood. Upon the West is a square Court, and next to the home wherein Doctor Dee dwelt (now inhabited by one Mr Selbury) and further west his Garden.
>
> He lyes buried in the Chancell of Mortlack Church about the middle yet neerer the South side, betweene the graves of Mr : Holt & Mr : Myles who have Grave stones with Inscriptions upon them.
>
> When Doctor Dee lay sick of the sickness whereof he dyed, his maiden daughter Katherine conveyed away his Bookes unknowne to him about a fortnight before he dyed which when he came to understand, it broke his heart.
>
> Barne Elms was the house of Secretary Walsingham, there afterwards lived Rob : E of Essex [1566–1601] who married his Daughter [the widow of Sir Philip Sydney], and there was borne Robert his Son, the Parliaments Generall. [This was Robert Devereux, third Earl of Essex, 1591–1646, who appeared in chapter 1 as desirous of income from the lease of the manor of Lichfield.] "Doctor Dee being after there : and wellbeloved and respected of all persons of quality thereabouts, who very often invited him to their houses, or came to his.[24]

Ashmole was still engrossed in gathering material for a biographical treatment of John Dee in the new year of 1674, but whether for himself or for Anthony Wood is not clear. On February 17 of that year, Ashmole drew up "[a]n Account [pedigree] of the family of Dr John Dee taken from the relation of his Grandchild Mr : Rowland Dee."[25] Ashmole was attempting to obtain as much direct testimony of Dee as he could. Unprepared to rely wholly on secondhand accounts, Ashmole will always have the advantage over any subsequent biographer of Dee.

Rowland Dee, a merchant in London, was born c. 1613, the fourth son of John Dee's son Arthur. He had a rare portrait of his grandfather, now exhibited at the new Ashmolean in Beaumont Street, Oxford. He told Ashmole of how on June 4, 1594, Doctor Dee, his wife, and seven children presented themselves to Queen Elizabeth I at Thistleworth. Dee's wife kissed the Queen's hand.

Rowland Dee told Ashmole more about his father: "Doctor Arthur Dee was the Emperor of Russia's Phisitian, he dwelt in Muscovy 18 yeares, and upon his retourne into England he was sworne Phisitian in ordinary to King Charles the first, afterward he went to dwell at Norwich and then dyed about the year 1650 & lyes buried in Saint Georges Church, at Norwich."[26]

Further information was obtained from Sir Thomas Browne (knighted September 29, 1671), who had interviewed Arthur Dee in Norwich before his death. In a letter received from Dr. Browne on March 29, 1674, Ashmole learned how

> (H)ee [Arthur] sayd also Kelly delt not justly by his father and that hee went away with the greatest part of the powder [of projection—for transmutation] . . . That his father . . . presented Queen Elizabeth with a litle of the powder. Who having made triall thereof attempted to get Kelly out of prison, and sent some to that purpose who giving opium in drink unto the Keepers, layd them so fast asleepe that Kelly found opportunity to attempt an escape & there were horses readie to carry him away butt the business unhappily succeeded as is before declared. Hee sayd that his father was in good credit with the emperor Rodolphus.[27]

According to Arthur Dee, Kelley broke his leg while attempting the escape and was returned to captivity and eventual death. Arthur Dee's reminiscence of how Sir Edward Kelley, formerly knighted by the

Emperor Rudolf, tried to escape by the walls of a castle has recently been confirmed by the Polish scholar Rafal T. Princk. In a superb study of the "hidden" Polish alchemist, Michael Sendivogius (1566–1636), Princk uncovered the truth about Kelley.[28] Ashmole would have been most grateful for the information.

SENDIVOGIUS, KELLEY, AND DEE

It should be borne in mind that the secret of alchemical tramsmutation was regarded by the state in the late sixteenth and seventeenth centuries as nations today regard nuclear secrets—as issues of nonproliferation. The difference in the past was that most alchemists did not sell themselves or their secrets to the state. Kelley was something of an exception to the rule. He promised Rudolf II, the Holy Roman Emperor, that he could perform transmutation—something Arthur Dee himself told Dr. Browne he observed—but, unable to make the "powder of projection," he struggled. The emperor thought it best to keep him under house arrest and, in the event of failure, imprisonment. Kelley had enjoyed the gold and the favors; now he would pay the price.

Arthur Dee's story, which enthralled Ashmole, has the ring of truth about it. If Kelley had the secret, it was best that the government bring him back to England for the good of the nation. This was an intelligence operation and after its failure, what could have been a national scandal—the Kelley scandal—was hushed up. Dee's career declined in its wake.

Dr. Princk, in his study *The Twelfth Adept,* relates how in 1596 Sendivogius established a new laboratory at a rented apartment on St. Stephen's Street, Prague New Town. The alchemist also leased a house from Edward Kelley on the latter's estate in Jílové. Sendivogius, who envisioned a "Society of Unknown Philosophers," was an admirer of John Dee's *Monas Hieroglyphica.*

Meanwhile, as the Polish alchemist organized his laboratory, Edward Kelley, laboring on alchemical treatises, was arrested at his cottage in Novy Liben. In November 1596, Kelley was incarcerated in the state prison at Most. Lady Joan Kelley was offered 900 thalers and sanctuary at a Prague monastery; she refused the offer and moved to Most to be close to her husband.

Left: The "Unknown Philosopher" Michael Sendivogius (1566–1636) in his late years from a manuscript in the University Library of Warsaw. Right: Portrait of Sendivogius engraved from an oil painting: frontispiece of *Michaelis Sendivogii, Novum lumen chemicum aus dem Brunnen der Natur dürch handangelegte Erfahrung beweisen . . .*, Nuremberg, 1766.

On November 1, 1597, Kelley's aforementioned attempted escape was foiled by a poignant moment of bad luck. Returned to prison, he died in the presence of his wife and stepdaughter, the poet Elizabeth Jane Weston. In a manuscript containing news of events relating to alchemy at Rudolf II's court, Šimon Tadeáš of Falkenberk described Kelley's death.

Ludvik Korálek of Těšín, a wealthy merchant and great lover of alchemy, who had rented the apartment in Prague New Town to Sendivogius, now lent the latter 5,695 Meissen marks with which Michael Sendivogius bought the Fumberk estate in Jílové from Joan Kelley.

Sendivogius was the author of the highly influential work *Concerning the Philosopher's Stone in 12 chapters*. He always wanted to remain unknown—a reserve I suspect may have impressed Ashmole. Most alchemists in Sendivogius's lifetime granted the Polish aristocrat's wish; one such was Arthur Dee.

In a work published in Paris in 1631, John Dee's clever son made it clear that he knew the author of the work on the philosopher's stone.

The work first published in Paris was *Fasciculus Chemicus,* whose only English translation was by one Elias Ashmole, obscured under the anagram, James Hasolle. This is Ashmole's 1650 translation of Arthur Dee's work concerning Sendivogius:

As for that clear water sought for by many found by few, yet obvious and profitable to all, which is the base of the philosopher's work, a noble Polonian not more famous for his learning then subtlety of wit (not named, whose name notwithstanding a double Anagram hath betraied). In his *Novum Lumen Chymicum, Parabola and Aenigma*, and also in his tract on Sulphur, he hath spoken largely and freely enough; yea he hath expressed all things concerning it so plainly, that nothing could be more satisfactory to him that desireth more.

The circle of alchemists is a closed one.

On August 13, 1674, Ashmole completed his transcription of the five *libri mysteriorium* by John Dee, which he had begun on October 26, 1672. Ashmole was haunted by the story of Dee and Kelley. C. H. Josten speculates (in the modern sense) that Ashmole may have tried to reactivate Dee and Kelley's angel-summoning system. We do not know.

Is it only coincidence that in February 1674, Ashmole begged leave to resign from his post as Windsor herald? He appears to have had enough of the position. Its social obligations must have tired him, but one cannot avoid proposing a deeper underlying motive for this partial withdrawal from the world. What had happened, he must have asked himself, to the Mercuriophilus Anglicus? Had he been buried beneath all the pomp and circumstance? Was his true Being—shown him by his "father Bachus"—not embedded in the society of unknown philosophers? Had his rise not been bought at a price?

He must have looked at Kelley's demise and Arthur Dee's quiet anonymity with deep consideration. In 1685 he wrote an account of how the angels found Kelley distasteful, favoring John Dee's son Arthur, but that Kelley insinuated himself with Dee and his family. Misguided, Kelley proposed the bad spiritual doctrine of sharing wives and the vision of the little angel Madimi appearing naked. Kelley was ambitious beyond the needs of truth and, quite literally, fell.

Ashmole knew well the injunction of alchemist Heinrich Khunrath: "Be cleansed of the world!" Had he, Elias, the coming one, the *herald*, picked up a staining portion of the world? He had tried to keep the pillars of the active and the contemplative sides of existence apart and in proportion. Had the relationship between them become somewhat unbalanced?

His Garter book had brought him international fame; he had the gold chain from Denmark to prove it. He wanted to give it all away to a museum along with the lawsuits and jealousy, the attempted murder, the slander and suspicion. He had fought the good fight. He needed to separate his being, part his soul, from worldly entanglements.

The collector—the being that had brought so much pain and loss—could be left in Oxford. The royal servant at the beck and call of inferior men could be left at Windsor. The country squire? Leave him in Berkshire. What was left? The antiquarian—he would always be that. The Hermetic brother; the Magus of Lichfield? Too grand, one surmises. The quiet life of the gentleman: the English spiritual ideal—our greatest gift to the vain world.

Ashmole's South Lambeth house would be his Mortlake, to be visited by inquirers. This is where Izaak Walton would visit him, preparing a new edition of "the Contemplative Man's Recreation." This would be the style of the true English gentleman, not seeking fame, not pushing and shoving for glories made of paper—or videotape.

South Lambeth was where Flower, the Countess of Clarendon, the only daughter and heir of William Backhouse of Swallowfield, paid a

The aging herald—Ashmole in a detail from an engraving by Wenceslas Hollar from *The Institutions, Laws and Ceremonies of the Most Noble Order of the Garter* (1672).

visit to Ashmole and his wife on June 28, 1680, many years after her father's death. This was where he pondered the miraculous universe about him. He never doubted the existence of the universe, its physicality, its reality, but he was not a materialist.

The word *magic* today suggests illusion, and *Magick*—the art of the Magi—is today regarded by many as illusory. It is worth considering that the quality that Buddhists perceive as illusion in the universe is the very thing that makes it possible.

Associated with the "falsity" of impermanence, this quality of illusion is rather the dragon of change and the serpent of flexibility. Properly handled (magick), this perceptual phenomenon makes impermanence into permanence and dreams into reality. Will and Imagination are intangible things, but focused together, they make all things possible. This is (never let it be forgotten) the optimistic sub-creed of the Western world, but its current materialistic emphasis requires a belated spiritual balance, lest the *techno-magi* disappear (with the rest of us) in a puff of smoke.

A quieter, chastened Ashmole emerges in the 1670s; he seems to be seeking his own spiritual balance. He has seen the world. And the world has seen him—or thinks it has. But he has no heir. "Fail not of an heir," says the Rosicrucian adage.

On September 19, 1681, his "wife [Elizabeth] miscarried, having gone about three months."[29] He was married three times but had no children, and, as far as we know, had no Hermetic adoptive children either. His heirs may yet come; to them he would pass on his secret, should they prove worthy of that "found by few, yet obvious and profitable to all. . . . A soul so deep buried further than history, for what they sought was the spirit of mystery."

Mystery. From the time of his first christening, mystery was never far from Elias Ashmole. In October 1679 or later, Ashmole received an alchemical manuscript. Attached to it was an undated, anonymous letter, signed only "J: W:":

> It is not unknown to you that the generalty of Mankind are content with an externall and superficiall [?]on and enjoyment of things created, standing on the Circumference, Few in the Centre, where the

discovery of [. . . page torn off] causes of the great variety of Naturall productions is to bee found . . . A man newly awaked although in the midst of the darkest Night may immagine an approaching day, But hee that sees the Morning Starre arise knows the Sun is not farr distant. Such a State putts Life into a Searcher of Natures Secretts and leads him by the hand til (if adapted unto it) hee attains to the Sunshine of true Knowledge. There are many Starrs but which is the true morning Starre The Magi only are Judges, wherefore I have here given you a Short hint of it, according to my weake Apprehension, and subjected it to your Correction, which (if you please to undertake it) will much add to the true Felicity of Sir,

Your most obliged servant J: W:

Ashmole would have recognized a communication from a Brother.

TOWARD HOME

It has been irresistible for modern commentators on Ashmole to make mention of certain "superstitious" and—to us—amusing practices that he observed. Superstition means an outmoded belief, superseded in later times by greater knowledge. Ashmole's actions to be related here were not superstitious in his time but rather based on available knowledge. We should recall that the circulation of the blood was a relatively recent discovery (1619).

On July 3, 1678, Ashmole "cut out the livers of forty Froggs, and set them to drying."[30] The reason for this mysterious activity was to be found not among the witches of *Macbeth*, but rather in the *Pharmacopoeia Londiniensis*, by the astrologer Nicholas Culpeper (London, 1654): "The liver of a Frog, being dried and eaten, helps quantane agues, or as the vulgar calls them third-day agues."

On April 11, 1681, again suffering from an ague, possibly of the throat, "I tooke early in the Morning [a] good dose of Elixer, & hung 3 Spiders about my Neck and they drove my Ague away, *Deo gratias*."[31]

This successful cure for which Ashmole thanks God appears to have been derived from Robert Burton's *The Anatomy of Melancholy*.[32] Therein it is recommended that a live spider, worn around the neck in a nutshell, causes "the ague to decline and depart in sympathy with the life of the spider." The ague sufferer may presumably have undergone frustration in seeking the text of the cure similar to what we today might experience in finding a way though the thorns of modern packaging.

There is a charming note from Samuel Pepys's famous diary (May 23, 1661) that might be employed to suggest some eccentricity in Ashmole's makeup. Pepys recorded how he "had very good discourse with Mr Ashmole, wherein he did assure me that froggs and many other insects do often fall from the sky ready-formed."

If the author may hazard a guess on how this attested phenomenon crept into the conversation between Pepys and Ashmole, the subject may have arisen thus. Looking for common ground, Pepys (possibly knowing that Ashmole and Walton were friendly) brought the subject of Walton's popular Compleat Angler to Ashmole's attention, wherein the occurrence of raining frogs is memorably discussed. Ashmole, knowing the reference, may have indicated that Walton's source for the raining frogs was the nineteenth book of Hieronymus Cardanus's De Subtilitate, Cardanus being an authority on astrology and other matters of natural philosophy.

If only we knew the remainder of Pepys's and Ashmole's "very good discourse"! In point of fact, fish were reported falling from the sky in Britain in August 2004 and nobody seemed surprised.

Such subjects would doubtless have made for equally merry and satisfying discourse at the Astrologers Feast, held on July 13, 1682, attended by Ashmole at the ripe old age of sixty-five.

The Astrologers had clearly not feasted together for a considerable time, for Ashmole noted that it had been "restored by Mr : Moxon."[33] This was probably Joseph Moxon (1627–1700), Fellow of the Royal Society, mathematician, maker of mathematical instruments, hydrographer to Charles II, and the first writer on the mechanics of typography.

The event would probably have been an emotional occasion, carrying back the old man's memory to the late 1640s, when he had returned from his sojourn with Peter and Colonel Henry Mainwaring in Cheshire to London, where, very soon, he was to meet William Lilly.

The subject of his dear friend William Lilly would probably have added a somber pall to conversation at the Astrologers Feast, especially when the time came to toast "absent friends." William Lilly had died at 3 a.m. on June 9, 1681. Ashmole had taken charge of the funeral at Walton in Surrey. Lilly's widow, Ruth, sent Ashmole a cape "as a relique."[34] Ashmole put the black marble stone on Lilly's grave.

Another "absent friend" never again to be seen in the flesh was Sir George Wharton, the cavalier who had introduced Ashmole to military service in Oxford in 1644. He had died two months after his old rival Lilly, on August 12, 1681, at Enfield, "betweene one and two in the Morning."[35]

Ashmole returned to the fellowship of another Astrologers Feast "held at the 3 Cranes in Chancery Lane" on January 29, 1683.[36] Sir Edward Deering and the town clerk of London were the stewards.

On the morning of February 10, 1686, Ashmole, lying in his bed at his house in South Lambeth, "dreamed that being at my old house in Sheere Lane, the side of the Garret seemed to totter and fall, insoemuch that I thought the house it selfe would presently fall downe."[37] That afternoon, "about one a Clock Sir William Dugdale my wives Father dyed."[38] Again, no emotion is expressed; the clock keeps ticking.

It was not only Ashmole himself who suffered from persistent and painful attacks of gout and other agues. One severe attack left Mrs. Ashmole unable to leave her bed for two months. Desperate for a cure, Ashmole even asked visiting ambassadors from Morocco if there was a cure known to the physicians of that distant country. They offered one (it involved the binding of the shells of snails about the afflicted foot); it did not work.

Gout still has the power to rob the joy from many sufferers' lives. We now know how it is caused (uric acid), but cures are not always effective. Ashmole's last years might have been far more productive if he had known of certain dietary considerations and the provision of alopurinol, the common palliative prescribed by today's medical practitioners. *The Anatomy of Melancholy* gave no joy.

At the beginning of May 1690, Mr. and Mrs. Ashmole embarked on what was then a very substantial journey, to Bath. They must have gained at least some respite at the famous waters, for they resided at the Spa for ten weeks. Had they drunk more water than usual, and taken more exercise, they would have enjoyed some relief from the symptoms of arthralgia. The air would probably have been an improvement on Lambeth as well.

From Bath, Mr. and Mrs. Ashmole headed for Oxford, where Anthony Wood observed them. According to Wood, Ashmole arrived "in a week [weak] condition so feeble that he could not goe without leading."[39] This was the occasion when Ashmole was brought to a banquet in his museum in a sedan chair.

Elsewhere there was war. Limerick, the headquarters of the exiled James II's supporters in Ireland, fell to the forces of William III in 1691. The peace of Limerick gave Catholics a measure of religious toleration, while Jacobites remaining in Ireland were granted security of life and property.

No property is ever entirely secure. In the autumn of that year, there was a theft from the museum at Oxford. This was the kind of occurrence Ashmole most feared; he had left strict instructions for the keeper of the Musaeum Ashmoleanum to prevent it.

In a letter (March 2, 1692) to the keeper's assistant (the very able Edward Lhuyd), Dr. Martin Lister appended a postscript: "I have been three times with Mr Ashmole latelie; and find all things well, and not a word of the matter more."[40] Ashmole's condition was not to be disturbed by hearing about the theft; he would certainly have been extremely angry. His whole adult life had been dedicated to preservation. He had seen so much lost through anger, stupidity, carelessness, folly, arrogance, blindness—and war.

When he died two months later, Elias Ashmole took most of himself with him, but not all. He left parts behind, not to be lost.

Many years before, in 1656, when he was hardly known, Timothy and John Gadbury had addressed their *Astronomical Tables* to Ashmole, commending him "to the safeguard of the Great Architect of Heaven and Earth." Indeed, the Great Architect had kept him safe to the end.

Gadbury did not forget Ashmole. In his *[Ephemeris], or A Diary Astronomical, Astrological, Meteorological, For the Year of Our Lord, 1694* (London, 1694), Gadbury wrote in his "Observations" for May 1694:

Upon the 19th day of May, 1692 Dyed that Learned Vertuoso, and Encyclopaedia, ELIAS ASHMOLE Esq. In the 75th year of his Age.

St. Mary's, Lambeth, burial place of Elias Ashmole.

He was a great ANTIQUARY, and Singular Herald, & Historian. It was this worthy Person that first gave a Public Credit to ASTROLOGIE, [and] CHYMISTRIE, in these Nations, by his generous encouraging THE Students in both Professions.

He was also my most Honour'd FRIEND and PATRON, and I had the Happiness of an Intimate Acquaintance with him near Forty Years, which commands, in Gratitude, from me, this short remembrance of him. That Envious Man, Mr ANTHONY WOOD hath falsly calleed him A ROSICRUCIAN, whereas no man was further from fost'ring such Follies.

His nobler BEQUEATHMENTS of many Choice rarities, and Manuscripts to the University of Oxford and his own Admirable Works in Print, will give him a Fame little less than IMMORTAL.

Anthony Wood may have confused elements of Ashmole's thought with a debased, popularized image of the "Rosicrucian" that has always been a distracting feature of that spiritual movement. However, while Wood had had some painful "run-ins" with Elias Ashmole (particularly over Wood's mystifying intransigence in refusing to deposit John Aubrey's manuscripts in the museum in the 1680s), he nonetheless echoed Aubrey's own description of Ashmole.

While Aubrey had described Ashmole as "a mighty good man," Wood recorded his view of the famous writer of Brasenose College, Oxford, as being "the greatest virtuoso and curioso that ever was known or read of in England before his time."

Elias Ashmole was buried at the east end of the south aisle of St. Mary's Lambeth on Corpus Christi Day (May 26) 1692. His grave is currently obscured by the Museum of the History of Gardening's offices now occupying the church. The irony might have amused Ashmole.

Within the museum at Lambeth stands an intriguing little memorial to Tradescant and Ashmole: "These famous antiquarians—that had been, both gardeners to the rose and lily queen—transplanted now themselves sleep here. And when Angels shall with their trumpets waken men, and fire shall purge the world; these hence shall rise, and change their gardens for a Paradise."

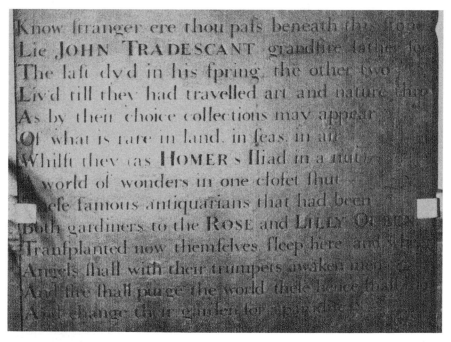

Memorial inscription to the Tradescant family's genius for collecting (St. Mary's, Lambeth).

POSTSCRIPT

On March 15, 1694, John Aubrey wrote a letter to Edward Lhuyd "at the Laboratory in Oxford," informing him that "Mrs Ashmole is married to a Stonecutter of Lambeth [John Reynolds] . . . so I hope she will now at last put a memoriall for her first Husband."[41]

She did: a tombstone of black marble inscribed in Latin and translated as follows:

> *Here lies the famous and most erudite*
> *Elias Ashmole, of Lichfield, Gentleman,*
> *Holder, among other public offices, of the*
> *   Comptrollership of the Excise:*
> *And also honoured for many years with the title of*
> *   Windsor Herald,*
> *Who, after two marriages, married, as his third wife,*
> *   Elizabeth*
> *Daughter of Sir William Dugdale, Knight, Garter*
> *   Principal King of Arms,*
> *He passed through death 18 May 1692, in the 76th year*
> *   of his age,*
> *But so long as the Ashmolean Museum of Oxford endures*
> *   he will never die.*

Notes

CHAPTER ONE: THE COMING ONE

1. Howard Clayton, *Loyal and Ancient City—The Civil War in Lichfield* (Lichfield, 1987), 4, quoting from Rev. Thomas Harwood, *The History and Antiquities of the City of Lichfield* (Gloucester: Cadell and Davies, 1806), 340.
2. C. H. Josten, *Elias Ashmole (1617–1692)* (Oxford: Oxford University Press, 1966), v. 2, 310, n. 7.
3. Ibid., 1.
4. Ibid., 12.
5. Ibid.
6. C. G. Jung, *The Spirit in Man, Art and Literature* (London: Ark, 1984), 4.
7. Josten, *Elias Ashmole*, 12.
8. Ibid., 12–13.
9. Ibid., 2.
10. Ibid.

CHAPTER TWO: LICHFIELD—THE HIDDEN LIGHT OF ENGLAND

1. Howard Clayton, *Loyal and Ancient City*, 145–46.
2. Public Record Office, POB 11/83, Staffs. F.154.v.
3. Josten, *Elias Ashmole*, 14.

CHAPTER THREE: LONDON CALLING

1. Josten, *Elias Ashmole*, 15.
2. Ibid., 17.
3. MS. Ashm. 1136, f.7.
4. Ibid., 16.
5. MS. Ashm. 1136, f.10.
6. Sequestration Records, Stafford Record Office.

7. Raymond Richards, "Upper Peover," in *Old Cheshire Churches* (London: B. T. Batsford, 1948), 268.

CHAPTER FOUR: WAR

1. Howard Clayton, *Loyal and Ancient City* (Lichfield, 1987), 4ff.
2. Josten, *Elias Ashmole,* 20.
3. MS. Wood, F.39, f.63.
4. Josten, *Elias Ashmole,* 21.
5. Ibid., 23.
6. Ibid., 1.
7. Elias Ashmole, *Theatrum Chemicum Britannicum* (London: J. Grismond for Nathaniel Brooke, 1652), 451.
8. Ibid., 26.
9. MS. Ashm. 1459, 469–71.
10. MS. Ashm. 1819, art. 15.
11. Josten, *Elias Ashmole,* 23; 56, n. 3.
12. From the Introductory poem "To S.A." in T. E. Lawrence, *Seven Pillars of Wisdom* (London: Jonathan Cape, 1926).
13. Josten, *Elias Ashmole,* ii, 313; MS. Rawl. D864, f.199–199.v.
14. MS. Ashm. 1136, f.211.
15. Josten, *Elias Ashmole,* 31.
16. MS. Ashm. 1136, f.212.
17. Josten, *Elias Ashmole,* 32.

CHAPTER FIVE: DEFEAT AND REBIRTH

1. MS. Ashm. 1136, f.214.
2. MS. Ashm. 1136, f.215.v.
3. MS. Ashm. 1136, f.214.
4. MS. Ashm. 1136, f.214.
5. MS. Ashm. 1136, f.214.v.
6. MS. Ashm. 430, f.71.v.
7. MS. Ashm. 1136, f.214.v.
8. MS. Ashm. 1136, f. 214.v.
9. MS. Ashm. 430, f.70.
10. MS. Ashm. 1136, f.214.
11. MS. Ashm. 1136, f.19.v.
12. *Biographia Britannica,* vol. i, 224 and footnotes (London: W. Innys), 1747.
13. Robert Plot, LLD, *The Natural History of Staffordshire* (Oxford: The Theatre, 1686), ch. 8.

14. Jean Gimpel, *The Cathedral Builders* (Salisbury: Michael Russell, 1983), 68ff.

15. Sloane Ms. 3848, British Library.

16. Rev. Joe Speakman, *Church of Saint Lawrence Over Peover—A History and Guide* (St. Lawrence Church, 1989).

17. Douglas Knoop, Gwilym Peredur Jones, and Douglas Hamer, *Early Masonic Catechisms* (Manchester: Manchester University Press, 1963).

18. Ibid.

19. John Sleigh, *A History of the ancient Parish of Leek* (London: R. Nall, 1862).

20. See *Mainwaring* (of Whitmore, Staffs.) Mss. Collection, "Deeds of Confraternity," Stafford Record Office.

21. William Beamont, *The Chapelry of Sankey* (Warrington: Guardian Office, 1882).

22. Record Society of Lancs. and Cheshire, Lancashire funeral certificates, vol. vi, 207.

23. Raymond Richards, *Old Cheshire Churches* (London: B.T. Batsford, 1947), 874.

24. R. N. Dore, *The Civil Wars in Cheshire* (Chester: Cheshire Community Council, 1966), 72.

CHAPTER SIX: RETURN TO LONDON

1. MS. Ashm. 1136, f.215.v.

2. Josten, *Elias Ashmole*, 36.

3. Ibid.

4. MS. Ashm. 1136, f.191.

5. MS. Ashm. 1136, f.20.

6. MS. Ashm. 1136, f.19.v.

7. Ibid.

8. MS. Ashm. 1136, f.219.

9. Ibid.

10. Ibid.

11. Ibid.

12. Ibid.

13. Ibid.

14. MS. Ashm. 1136, f.219.

15. MS. Ashm. 1136, f.20.

16. Josten, *Elias Ashmole*, 44.

17. MS. Ashm. 1136, f.191.v.

18. Ibid.

19. Ibid.

20. Ibid.

21. MS. Ashm. 1136, f.207.v.

22. MS. Ashm. 1136, f.192.

23. From the song "Serve Yourself" by John Lennon, © 1985 Lenono Music.

24. MS. Ashm. 1136, f.192.

25. MS. Ashm. 1136, f.193.

26. MS. Ashm. 1136, f.191.v.

27. MS. Ashm. 1136, f.199.

28. MS. Ashm. 1136, f.20.v.

29. MS. Ashm. 1136, f.199.

30. MS. Ashm. 1136, f.20.v.

31. Ibid.

32. MS. Ashm. 1136, f.188.

33. MS. Ashm. 374, f.37.v.

34. MS. Ashm. 374, f.37.v.

CHAPTER SEVEN: THE 1650s (I)

1. See C. G. Jung's great book *Psychology and Alchemy* (London: Routledge and Kegan Paul, 1968).

2. Josten, *Elias Ashmole,* 304.

3. MS. Ashm. 374, f.37.v.

4. Elias Ashmole, *Prolegomena, Theatrum Chemicum Britannicum* (London: J. Grismond for Nathaniel Brooke, 1652), 10–11.

5. Josten, *Elias Ashmole,* 59.

6. MS. Ashm. 1136, f.22.

7. MS. Ashm. 374, f. 39.

8. *A Most faithful relation of two wonderful passages which happened very lately . . . in the Parish of Bradfield in Berk-shire* (London: James Cottrel, 1650).

9. Desirée Hirst, *Hidden Riches* (London: Eyre & Spottiswoode, 1964), 105.

10. MS. Ashm. 1136, f.22.

11. Josten, *Elias Ashmole,* 525.

12. C. H. Josten, "Introduction and translation to Dee's *Monas Hieroglyphica* (The Hieroglyphic Monad)" in *Ambix,* vol. 12, no. 2/3, 1964, 100–01.

13. MS. Ashm. 374, f.48.v.

14. Ibid.

15. Ashmole, *Theatrum Chemicum Britannicum*, 445

16. MS. Ashm. 374, f.48.v.

17. Ibid.

18. Dedicatory poem, Heinrich Cornelius Agrippa, *Three Books of Occult Philosophy* (London: G. Moule, 1651).

19. MS. Ashm. 1136, f.24.v.

20. Ashmole, *Theatrum*, 440–41.

21. MS. Ashm. 36–37, ff. 241.v.–2.

22. Samuel Hartlib, *Ephemerides* 1660, sect. 61, 3–4.

23. From John Evelyn's diaries, quoted in *Swallowfield Park, A Brief History* (Banbury: The Country Houses Association, 2003).

24. Hartlib, *Ephemerides* 1650, sect. 4, 6.

25. MS. Ashm. 1417, 41.

26. Ashmole MSS, 1459; ff. 280–82; ff. 284)

27. Ashmole MSS., 1478, ff. 125–29.

28. Frances Yates, *Rosicrucian Enlightenment* (London: Routledge and Kegan Paul, 1986), 195.

29. MS. Ashm. 1136, f.25.v.

30. Yates, *The Rosicrucian Enlightenment*, 196.

31. MS. Ashm. 1446, fol. 237v.

32. MS. Ashm. 1136, f.25.

33. MS. Ashm. 1136, f.27.

34. Ibid.

35. MS. Ashm. 36–37, f.241–42.v.

36. MS. Ashm. 1136, f.29.

37. MS. Français 12335.

38. Timothy and John Gadbury, *Astronomicall Tables First invented by George Hartgill* (London, 1656).

39. John Gadbury, *Ephemeris, or, A Diary Astronomical, Astrological, Meteorological, For the Year of Our Lord, 1694* (London, 1694).

40. MS. Rawl. D864, f.209.

41. Ashmole, *Theatrum Chemicum Britannicum*.

42. John Heydon, *The Idea of the Law* (London, 1660).

CHAPTER EIGHT: THE 1650s (II)

1. Robert Plot, *Natural History of Staffordshire* (Oxford: The Theatre, 1686), Ch. 10, 83.

2. MS. Ashm. 826, f.125.

3. Ibid.

4. MS. Ashm. 1136, f.27.

5. MS. Ashm. 374, f.152.

6. Howard Clayton, *Loyal and Ancient City*, i.

7. MS. Ashm. 374, f.152.v.

8. MS. Ashm. 1137, ff.145–47.v.

9. Ibid.

10. Ibid.

11. See "Needwood Forest" in *Victoria County History of Staffordshire*, vol. 2 (Oxford: Oxford University Press, 1967), 349–58.

12. MS. Ashm. 1137, ff.145–47.v.

13. MS. Ashm. 1137, f.146.

14. MS. Ashm. 1136, f.27.v.

15. MS. Ashm. 374, f.156.v.

16. John Webster, *Academiarum Examen, or the Examination of Academies* (London, 1654), 51.

17. Josten, *Elias Ashmole*, 662.

18. MS. Ashm. 1136, f.30.v.

19. Ibid.

20. Josten, *Elias Ashmole*, 667.

21. Josten, *Elias Ashmole*, 665, n. 3; 678, 685.

22. William Dugdale, *Antiquities of Warwickshire* (1656), 184.

23. Josten, *Elias Ashmole*, 730; MS. Wood. f.39, f.93.

24. MS. Ashm. 1136, f.34.

25. MS. Ashm. 1136, f.34.v.

26. Lisa Jardine, *On a Grander Scale* (London: HarperCollins), 207.

27. Josten, *Elias Ashmole*, 771.

28. Ibid.

29. MS. Ashm. 1136, f.35.

CHAPTER NINE: THE WINDSOR HERALD

1. MS. Ashm. 36–37, ff.17–20. Ashmole's poem *Sol in Ascendente* . . . was printed "for N.Brook, at the Angel in Cornhill, 1660."

2. MS. Ashm. 1136, f.35.

3. MS. Ashm. 826, f.78.

4. Josten, *Elias Ashmole*, 822.

5. Ibid., 823.

6. MS. Ashm. 1136, f.36.

7. Josten, *Elias Ashmole,* 142.

8. MS. Ashm. 826, f.80.v.

9. Royal Society Council Minutes Copy, vol. i, 1663–82.

10. Josten, *Elias Ashmole,* 925; MS. Ashm. 836, 723.

11. MS. Ballard 14, f.115; MS. Ashm. 1136, f.52.

12. *Autobiography of Henry Newcome, MA,* ed. R. Parkinson, vol. i. (Chatham Society, vol. xxvi, 1852), 145.

13. MS. Ashm. 1136, f.39.

14. MS. Ashm. 854, 300–304.

15. MS. Ashm. 854, 338–39.

16. Josten, *Elias Ashmole,* 1122.

17. Ibid., n. 4.

18. MS. Ashm. 421, ff.53.v.–79.

19. MS. Ashm. 1136, f.44.

20. Anthony Wood, *Historia et Antiquitates Universitatis Oxoniensis* (Oxford: Theatro Sheldoniano, 1674), vol. ii, 224.

21. MS. Ballard 14, f.111.v.

22. MS. Ashm. 1136, f.47.v.

23. Yates, *The Rosicrucian Enlightenment,* 198.

24. MS. Ashm. 1131, ff. 297–98.v.

25. MS. Ashm. 1136, f. 50.v.

26. MS. Ashm. 1136, f.52.

27. MS. Ashm. 243, ff.331–32.v.

28. MS. Ashm. 436, f.17.

29. Josten, *Elias Ashmole,* 1296.

30. MS. Ashm. 436, f.14–14.v.

31. Ibid.

32. Josten, *Elias Ashmole,* 1364; MS. Ashm. 436, ff.24.v., 24.

33. MS. Ashm. 1788, ff.161.v.–162.

34. MS. Ashm. 1136, f.52.

35. BM Add. MS. 28077, 179.

36. MS. Ashm. 1136, f.88.

CHAPTER TEN: LICHFIELD—THE RECONSTRUCTION

1. MS. Rawl. D.864, ff.145–46.v.

2. MS. Rawl. D. 864.f.7–7.v.

3. MS. Ashm. 1521, VI, 161.

4. Ibid.

5. Sampson Erdeswick, *Survey of Staffordshire of 1598* (London: J. B. Nichols, 1844).

6. MS. Ashm. 1521, III, f.123.

7. MS. Ashm. 1521, III, 115–16.

8. MS. Ashm. 1136, f.41.

9. Josten, *Elias Ashmole,* 1113.

10. Percy Laithwaite, *The History of the Lichfield Conduit Lands Trust* (Lichfield: Lomax's Successors, 1947), 22.

11. T. Harwood, *The History and Antiquities of the Church and City of Lichfield* (Gloucester: Cadell and Davies, 1806), 391.

12. Harwood, *The History and Antiquities of the City of Lichfield,* 347, in Clayton, *Loyal and Ancient City,* 145–46.

13. Clayton, *Loyal and Ancient City,* 147.

14. MS. Ashm. 1136, f.57.v.

15. Ibid.

16. MS. Ashm. 1731, ff.76–77.

17. MS. Rawl. D. 864, ff.97–98.v.

18. MS. Rawl. D. 864, ff.169–170.v.

19. Lichfield Record Office, D.30/6/1/3, *William Gorton's Bills for drawing stone/masons' work 1677–1678.*

20. Lichfield Record Office, D.30/6/1/1, *Altarpiece, contract, letters, bills, receipts 1677–1680.*

21. Ibid.

22. Ibid.

23. Ibid.

24. Ibid.

25. Lichfield Record Office, D.30/0/1/8/1–3, *Article of Agreement with Henry Vernon, freemason.*

26. Lichfield Record Office, D.30/5/37, *Petition of the Dean and Chapter to the Court of Exchequer and to the non-payment by John Manwaring, Alex, Featherstone, and several other prebendaries of fees due to the Fabric Fund. 1671.*

27. Ibid.

28. Dugdale, *Antiquities of Warwickshire,* vol. ii, 1730 edition, 916.

29. MS. Ashm. 1136, f.69.v.

30. Josten, *Elias Ashmole,* 1700.

31. Ibid.

32. Ibid., 1701.

33. Matthew Scanlan, "The Mystery of the Acception, 1630–1723: A Fatal Flaw," paper in S. Brent Morris, ed., *Heredom, The Transactions of the Scottish Rite Research Society,* (Washington, D.C., Vol 11, 2003). Also published as a paper in *Freemasonry on both sides of the Atlantic: Essays concerning the Craft in the British Isles, Europe, the United States and Mexico,* R.William Weisberger ed. (New York: Columbia University Press, 2002).

34. John Evelyn, MS. 173, f.9, British Library.

35. *Viz: Post Boy,* No. 5245.

36. *Freemasonry Today,* issue 18, 22.

CHAPTER ELEVEN: THE MUSEUM

1. J. A. Bennett, S. A. Johnston, A. V. Simcock, *Solomon's House in Oxford: New Finds from the First Museum* (Oxford: Museum of the History of Science, 2000), 12.

2. "New Atlantis" in Arthur Johnson, ed., *Francis Bacon* (London: BT Batsford, 1965), 171–72.

3. For example, Bennett, Johnston, and Simcock, *Solomon's House in Oxford.*

4. Ibid., 13.

5. Bod. Lib. 4 Rawl. 156 *ad finem.*

6. MS. Rawl. D. 912, f.668–668.v.

7. MS. Ashm. 1136, f.39.v.

8. MS. Ashm. 1131, f.330–330.v.

9. MS. Ashm. 1136, f.51.

10. Josten, *Elias Ashmole,* 1447.

11. MS. Rawl. D. 912, f.668–668.v.

12. Bennett, Johnson, and Simcock, *Solomon's House in Oxford,* 15.

13. MS. Ashm. 1136, f.59.

14. MS. Ashm. 1136, f.101.

15. MS. Ashm. 1136, f.72.

16. MS. Ashm. 1136, f.75.

17. March 24, 1683; *The Flemings in Oxford* (Oxford, 1913), 90.

18. MS. Wood F.31, f.176.

19. MS. Wood Diaries, 27, f.26.

20. MS. Wood Diaries, 34, f.35.

21. MS. Wood Diaries, 34, 35.v.

CHAPTER TWELVE: COMING HOME

1. Elias Ashmole: *Theatrum Chemicum Britannicum*, 443
2. MS. Ashm. 1136, f.37.
3. MS. Ashm. 1459, ff. 280–82; ff.284–31.
4. MS. Ashm. 1136, f.75.
5. Josten, *Elias Ashmole*, 258.
6. MS. Ashm. 1790, art. 3, f.39.
7. MS. Ashm. 421, f.233.
8. Ibid.
9. MS. Ashm. 1406, I, ff.F1v–55v. and elsewhere in the Bodleian's Ashmole manuscript collection.
10. MS. Ashm. 1790, f.131.
11. MS. Ashm. 1136, f.47.v.
12. MS. Sloane 3188, British Museum.
13. MS. Sloane 3191.
14. Josten, *Elias Ashmole*, 1265; MS. Sloane 3188, f.2–2.v.
15. MS. Ashm. 1136, f.48.
16. MS. Sloane 3677, f.5.
17. MS. Wood F.39, f.59.
18. MS. Ashm. 1136, f.48.v.
19. Ibid.
20. Josten, *Elias Ashmole*, 1299–1300.
21. MS. Ashm. 1136, f.49.
22. MS. Ashm. 1788, f.149–149.v.
23. Josten, *Elias Ashmole*, 1299–1300.
24. MS. Ashm. 1788, f.149–149.v.
25. MS. Ashm. 1788, ff.161.v.–162.
26. MS. Ashm. 1788, ff.161.v.–162.
27. MS. Ashm. 1788, 151–52.
28. "The Twelfth Adept" in Ralph White, ed., *The Rosicrucian Enlightenment Revisited* (Great Barrington, MA: Lindisfarne Books, 1993).
29. MS. Ashm. 1136, f.66.v.
30. MS. Ashm. 421, f.115.
31. MS. Ashm. 1136, f.64.
32. Robert Burton, *The Anatomy of Melancholy* (Partition II, Sect. V, Member 1, Subsection v, *ad fine*). Oxford, 1621.
33. MS. Ashm. 1136, f.71.v.
34. MS. Ashm. 1136, f.65.

35. MS. Ashm. 1136, f.61.

36. MS. Ashm. 1136, f.74.v.

37. MS. Ashm. 1136, f.88.v.

38. Ibid.

39. MS. Wood's Diaries, 34, f.35.

40. MS. Ashm. 1816, f.89–89.v.

41. MS. Ashm. 1814, f.106–106.v. Elias Ashmole's third wife, Elizabeth, died childless at Lambeth, Surrey, in April 1701. She was buried in St. Mary's, Lambeth, on April 10 of the same year.

Bibliography

Agrippa, Heinrich Cornelius. *Three Books of Occult Philosophy.* London: G. Moule, 1651.

Anderson, Rev. James. *The Constitutions of Free-Masons, Containing the History, Charges, Regulations &c. of that Most Ancient and Worshipful Fraternity. Printed by William Hunter, for John Senex at the Globe, and John Hooke at the Flower-de-Luce, over against St. Dunstan's Church in Fleet Street. In the year of Masonry 5723, Anno Domini.* London, 1723.

———.*The New Book of Constitutions of the Ancient and Honourable Fraternity of Free and Accepted Masons.* London: Caesar Ward and Richard Chandler, 1738.

Andreae, Johann Valentin. *Chymische Hochzeit* ("Chemical Wedding"). Strasbourg: Lazarus Zetzner, 1616. English translation by Ezekiel Foxcroft (1690) reprinted in *A Christian Rosenkreutz Anthology*, compiled and edited by Paul M. Allen, Rudolf Steiner Publications. New York: Blauvelt, 1960.

———. *Christianopolis, An Ideal State of the Seventeenth Century*, trans. F. E. Held. Oxford, 1916.

Ars Quatour Coronatorum, No. 2076, Transactions of the Quatuor Coronati Lodge (*AQC*). An invaluable collection of research papers into all aspects of Freemasonry published since the inception of the lodge in 1888. The current volume and some past transactions can be obtained from QCCC Ltd, Great Queen Street, WC2B 5AZ. The Web site for correspondence circle: www. qccc.co.uk.

Ashmole, Elias. *Theatrum Chemicum Britannicum.* London: J. Grismond for Nathaniel Brooke, 1652.

———. *The Institutions, Laws, and Ceremonies of the Most Noble Order of the Garter.* London: Nathaniel Brooke, 1672.

——— as "James Hasolle" (ed.). *Fasciculus Chemicus: OR Chymical Collections . . .* [text: Dee, Arthur] *Printed by F. Flesher for Richard Mynne, at the sign of St. Paul in Little Britain,* 1650.

Bachmann, Manuel, and Hofmeier, Thomas. *Geheimnisse der Alchemie.* Basel: Schwabe, 1999.

Bacon, Sir Francis. *New Atlantis.* 1627.

Bennett, J. A., Johnston, S. A., and Simcock, A. V. *Solomon's House in Oxford: New Finds from the First Museum.* Oxford: Museum of the History of Science, 2000.

Casaubon, Meric, ed. *A True and Faithful relation of What Passed for Some Years between Dr John Dee and Some Spirits.* Ed: Meric Casaubon, 1659. (Reprint 1978, C. W. Daniel & Co.)

Churton, Tobias. *The Gnostics.* New York: Barnes and Noble, 1998.

———. *Gnostic Philosophy.* Rochester, VT: Inner Traditions, 2005.

———. *The Golden Builders, Alchemists, Rosicrucians and the first Free Masons.* York Beach, ME: Red Wheel-Weiser, 2005.

Cis van Heertum and Roelof van den Broek, *From Poimandres to Jacob Böhme: Gnosis, Hermetism and the Christian Tradition.* Collection of essays in De Pelikaan, Amsterdam, 2000.

Clayton, Howard. *Loyal and Ancient City—The Civil War in Lichfield.* Lichfield: Howard Clayton, 1987.

Clulee, Nicholas. *John Dee's Natural Philosophy.* London: Routledge and Kegan Paul, 1988.

Conder, Edward. *The Masons' Company,* paper in *AQC,* vol. 9, 1896.

Coulthurst, S. L. and Lawson, P. L. *The Lodge of Randle Holme at Chester,* paper in *AQC,* vol. 45, 1932.

Dugdale, Sir William. *The Antiquities of Warwickshire . . . Printed for John Osborn and Thomas Longman.* London, two vols., 1730 edition.

Edighoffer, Roland. *Rose Croix et Société Idéale selon Johann Valentin Andreae,* Paris: Presses Universitaires de France, two vols., 1982.

Everard, Dr. John, translator. *The Divine Pymander* of Hermes Trismegistus. G. Moule, 1650.

Eugenius Philalethes [pseud. Thomas Vaughan]. *The Fame and Confession of the Fraternity of R:C: Commonly, of the Rosie Cross.* Printed by J. M. for Giles Calvert, 1652. (Reprinted in Yates, Frances, *The Rosicrucian Enlightenment.* London: Routledge, 1986.)

Fowden, Garth. *The Egyptian Hermes.* Cambridge: Cambridge University Press, 1986.

Freemasonry Today (journal, ed. Tobias Churton and Michael Baigent). Useful articles:

Adolph, Anthony. "Henry Jermyn, Grand Master of the Freemasons?" in *Freemasonry Today* 6, p. 46.

Peter, Robert. "Freemasonry and Natural Religion" (MA thesis summary) in *Freemasonry Today* 12, p. 40.

Scanlan, Matthew. "Nicholas Stone and the Mystery of the Acception" in *Freemasonry Today*, Spring 2000.

"New Light on Sir Christopher Wren" in *Freemasonry Today*, issue 18, p. 22.

Gilly, Carlos. "Cimelia Rhodostaurotica, Die Rosenkreuzer im Speigel der zwischen 1610 und 1660 entstandenen Handschriften und Drucke." In de Pelikaan, Amsterdam, 1995.

———. "The Theophrastia Sancta—Paracelsianism in conflict with the established churches." Paper available on Bibliotheca Philosophica Hermetica Web site (see below), in de Pelikaan, Amsterdam, 1994.

Gimpel, Jean. *The Cathedral Builders*. London: Michael Russell, 1983.

Harwood, T. *The History and Antiquities of the Church and City of Lichfield*. Gloucester: Cadell and Davies, 1806.

Hirst, Desirée. *Hidden Riches*. London: Eyre & Spottiswoode, 1964.

McIntosh, Dr. Christopher. *The Rosicrucians: The History, Mythology and Rituals of an Esoteric Order*. York Beach, ME: Weiser, 1997.

———. *The Rose Cross and the Age of Reason*. Leiden: E. J. Brill, 1992.

Josten, C. H. *Elias Ashmole (1617–1692); His Autobiographical Writings and Historical Notes, His Correspondence, and Other Contemporary Sources Relating to His Life and Work*, 5 vols. Oxford: Oxford University Press, 1966.

———. "Introduction and translation to John Dee's *Monas Hieroglyphica* (The Hieroglyphic Monad)" in *Ambix*, vol. 12, 100–101, 1964.

Jung, C. G. *The Spirit in Man, Art and Literature*. London: Ark, 1984.

Khunrath, Heinrich. *Amphitheatrum Sapientiae Aeternae* (1598, reprinted in McClean, Adam, *Hermetic Sourceworks*, available through Adam McClean's Alchemy Web site: http://www.levity.com/alchemy/home.html).

Knoop, Douglas; Jones, Gwilym Peredur; and Hamer, Douglas. *Early Masonic Catechisms*. Manchester: Manchester University Press, 1963.

———. *Early Masonic Pamphlets*. Manchester: Manchester University Press, 1945.

Knoop, Douglas, and Jones, Gwilym Peredur. *The Genesis of Freemasonry: An Account of the Rise and Development of Freemasonry in Its Operative, Accepted, and Early Speculative Phases*. Manchester: Manchester University Press, 1947.

Laithwaite, Percy. *The History of the Lichfield Conduit Lands Trust*, Lichfield: Lomax's Successors, 1947.

Plot, Dr. Robert. *The Natural History of Staffordshire.* Oxford: The Theatre, 1686.

Richards, Raymond. *Old Cheshire Churches.* London: Batsford, 1948.

Roberts, John M. "Freemasonry: Possibilities of a Neglected Topic." In *English Historical Review,* 84, 323–35, 1969.

Rogers, Norman. *The Lodge of Elias Ashmole,* paper in *AQC,* vol. 65, 1952.

Sankey, Edward (copyist), British Library, Sloane MS. 3848 f.183: "A Discourse of the history and craft of Masonry."

Scanlan, Matthew. "The Mystery of the Acception, 1630–1723: A Fatal Flaw," paper in *Heredom, The Transactions of the Scottish Rite Research Society,* Ed. S. Brent Morris, Washington, DC, vol. 11, 2003. Also published as a paper in *Freemasonry on both sides of the Atlantic: Essays Concerning the Craft in the British Isles, Europe, the United States and Mexico,* ed. R. William Weisberger. New York: Columbia University Press, 2002.

———. "Operative versus Speculative," paper in *Ars Macionica,* Brussels, June 5, 2004.

Stevenson, David. *The Origins of Freemasonry—Scotland's Century 1590–1710.* Cambridge: Cambridge University Press, 1988.

———. *The First Freemasons.* Aberdeen: Aberdeen University Press, 1988.

Swallowfield Park, A Brief History. Banbury, Oxfordshire: The Country Houses Association, 2003.

Victoria County History of Staffordshire, vol. 2. Oxford: Oxford University Press, 1967.

White, Michael. *Isaac Newton, The Last Sorcerer.* London: Fourth Estate, 1997.

White, Ralph, ed. *The Rosicrucian Enlightenment Revisited.* Great Barrington, MA: Lindisfarne Books, 1993. Collection of essays, including Princk, Rafal. T., "The Twelfth Adept" on Sendivogius and Paul Bembridge, "The Rosicrucian Resurgence at the Court of Cromwell."

Williams, W. J. *The Use of the Word "Freemason" before 1717,* paper in *AQC,* vol. 48, 1935 (re Richard Ellom, "Freemason," of Lymm, Cheshire).

Yates, Frances. *Giordano Bruno and the Hermetic Tradition.* London: Routledge and Kegan Paul, 1964.

———. *The Rosicrucian Enlightenment.* London: Routledge and Kegan Paul, 1986.

Index

BOOKS OF RELATED INTEREST

The Secret History of Freemasonry
Its Origins and Connection to the Knights Templar
by Paul Naudon

The Mystery Traditions
Secret Symbols and Sacred Art
by James Wasserman

The Templars and the Assassins
The Militia of Heaven
by James Wasserman

The Knights Templar in the Golden Age of Spain
Their Hidden History on the Iberian Peninsula
by Juan García Atienza

The Templars
Knights of God
by Edward Burman

Founding Fathers, Secret Societies
Freemasons, Illuminati, Rosicrucians, and the
Decoding of the Great Seal
by Robert Hieronimus, Ph.D., with Laura Cortner

The Occult Conspiracy
Secret Societies—Their Influence and Power in World History
by Michael Howard

Montségur and the Mystery of the Cathars
by Jean Markale

INNER TRADITIONS • BEAR & COMPANY
P.O. Box 388
Rochester, VT 05767
1-800-246-8648
www.InnerTraditions.com

Or contact your local bookseller